THE
JAPANESE
EXPERIENCE

THE
JAPANESE
EXPERIENCE

A Short History of Japan

W.G. Beasley

University of California Press

BERKELEY   LOS ANGELES   LONDON

University of California Press
Berkeley and Los Angeles, California

University of California Press, Ltd.
London, England

Published by arrangement with Weidenfeld & Nicolson

First Paperback Printing 2000

ISBN 0–520–22050–1 (cloth)
ISBN 0–520–22560–0 (paperback)

Filmset by Selwood Systems, Midsomer Norton
Printed in Great Britain by
Butler & Tanner Ltd
Frome and London

9 8 7 6 5 4 3 2 1

CONTENTS

Contents

MAPS

ILLUSTRATIONS

Between pages 110 and 111

Statue of Maitreya Buddha (*Kōryūji Temple, Kyoto*)

Buddhist temple of Hōryūji (*Ronald Sautebin, Fribourg*)

A memorial statue of Ganjin (*Tōshō-daiji Temple, Nara/Shogakukan Inc., Tokyo*)

The Phoenix Pavilion of the Byōdōin at Uji (*author's photo*)

A scene from the Tale of Genji picture-scroll (*Tokugawa Museum, Nagoya*)

The Heiji incident: the emperor escapes from the palace (*Tokyo National Museum*)

Portrait of Minamoto Yoritomo (*Jingo-ji Temple, Kyoto*)

The itinerant preacher Kūya Shōnin (*Rokuharamitsu-ji Temple, Kyoto*)

Feudal lord on horseback (*Kyoto National Museum*)

A Nō mask (*Tokyo National Museum*)

A memorial statue of Toyotomi Hideyoshi (*Osaka City*)

Himeji Castle (*author's photo*)

Between pages 206 and 207

A daimyo with his escort enters the outskirts of Edo (*Historiographical Institute, Tokyo University*)

The Shogun's apartments, Nijō Castle (*Nijō Castle, Kyoto*)

Kabuki theatre (*British Museum/Bridgeman Art Library*)

Geisha writing letters (*National Gallery, Prague/Werner Forman Archive*)

Sumō wrestlers, nineteenth century (*author's collection*)

A British squadron in Nagasaki harbour, 1855 (*author's collection*)

Japanese soldiers leave for Manchuria, 1936 (*Weidenfeld Archives*)

Japanese sign the surrender agreement, 1945 (*Weidenfeld Archives*)

JAPANESE WORDS, NAMES
AND DATES

Both Chinese and Japanese words are written by means of ideographs, which can be transcribed into western alphabets in several different ways. Those chosen for use in this book are the ones most often found in works about Japanese history published in English. Macrons to indicate long vowel sounds are given in personal names and in Japanese words printed in italics, but not in place names (e.g. Tokyo is used, not Tōkyō) or Japanese words that are usually anglicised (e.g. Shogun, not Shōgun). Japanese personal names appear in the traditional order, i.e. family name, followed by given name.

Japan adopted the Chinese lunar calendar in the seventh century and used it, subject to some variation over time, until the western (Gregorian) calendar replaced it in 1873. Dates in this book are given throughout in the Gregorian form, wherever specific information exists to make this possible. Similarly, centuries are numbered in accordance with western practice, since Japan did not possess a serial chronology until modern times.

Introduction:
Patterns and Periods

The history of Japan, like that of China, has a high degree of continuity from ancient times to the twentieth century. The Japanese have always occupied part or all of the same territory, its borders defined by the sea. They have spoken and written a common language, once it had taken firm shape in about the tenth century. Their population has been largely homogenous, little touched by immigration except in very early periods. Awareness of this has given them a sense of being racially distinct. 'We Japanese', *ware-ware Nihonjin*, is a phrase that constantly recurs.

Yet Japanese society and culture have changed more through time than these statements might seem to imply. At both the beginning and the end of the story – so far as the end can yet be told – developments within Japan have been greatly influenced by ideas and institutions, art and literature, imported from elsewhere. To talk of 'Japanese civilisation', therefore, begs a question. What is it about the history of Japan that is specifically Japanese, apart from the land and the people? It is hoped that this book might suggest some answers.

When the Christian era began in Europe, the Japanese islands were a remote and little-known part of China's 'barbarian' periphery. They acquired the rudiments of an organised state quite late in time – somewhere between the fall of the Han in China

(AD 220) and the sack of Rome by the Goths (AD 410) – and long remained thereafter a fairly primitive kingdom, ruled by ancestors, or so it is claimed, of the present imperial line. It was the arrival of Buddhism from Korea in the sixth and seventh centuries, bringing with it a wider knowledge of things Chinese, that raised them to a higher level of development. Under Buddhist tutelage, Japan became substantially Chinese, not only in religion, but also in political institutions, writing system and the lifestyle of the ruling class. The experience left a mark that was to prove indelible.

Chineseness was nevertheless confined to an urban, largely aristocratic segment of the population. Outside the capital its influence was shallow; and eventually the political and social structures that supported it began to crumble. There was no such upheaval, caused by attack from outside, as prompted the transition in Europe from ancient to medieval, but the results of decay were similar, if slower. By the eleventh century, Japan was sufficiently 'ungoverned' to begin to move from a nominally centralised and aristocratic-bureacratic state towards one that was increasingly feudal. By 1450 the process was complete: Japan was a feudal monarchy, much as France and England were in the Middle Ages. There were two main differences. One was that feudal Japan was Buddhist, not Christian. The other was that the country had two rulers, both of whom held hereditary office: an emperor of ancient lineage, who possessed influence rather than power; and a feudal overlord, the Shogun, claiming kingly privilege that rested on military force.

It is at this point that parallels between Japan and China break down. Chinese emperors in and after the fourteenth century were autocrats, served by appointed ministers who acknowledged Confucian thought as the proper guide for political behaviour. Feudal Japan, by contrast, remained predominantly Buddhist and governed by the equivalent of barons. The latter, it is true, like the older court aristocracy, turned to Chinese culture for both prestige and pleasure, but it was not until society had endured another long spell of civil war that they looked to China again for political example. Even then they did so only in limited degree.

The structure that eventually emerged under the Tokugawa (1600–1868) did not closely correspond to anything found in Europe or China. The emperor remained powerless. The Shogun grew in authority, using his personal vassals as bureaucrats and exercising tighter control over feudal lords. Neo-Confucian ideology became orthodox within the ruling class, much as in China, but without detracting from the claims of vassalage and birth as determinants of status. Chinese culture enjoyed a renaissance. Alongside it, however, there was a popular culture, patronised by 'commoners', that owed more to Japanese urban taste and urban wealth than it did to China or the traditions of the country's upper class. This was a complex pattern, not quite feudal, not quite Chinese, hinting at developments that in Europe could be labelled 'early modern', but never fully satisfying any definition of it.

Such was the Japan into which an expanding, capitalist West intruded in the middle of the nineteenth century. For China the same threat came earlier and in more aggressive guise. Chinese resistance to it, which was both traditionalist and ineffective, began a period of a hundred years of Chinese weakness and political disunity, ending in a revolution that swept away the heritage of the past. Japan's response took a different path. This was in part because her ruling class was a military one, which had methods and priorities that were not the same as those of China's mandarins. It was partly, perhaps, because her society had an institutional and cultural ambiguity that made for great flexibility. Whatever the explanation, Japan's revolution came more rapidly and served different ends. The Meiji Restoration, as it is called, not only overthrew the Tokugawa, as China's revolutionaries overthrew the Manchus nearly fifty years later, but also brought to power a group of men who were dedicated to the aim of expanding the country's wealth and strength. What they meant by this was to combine government and military structures in the western manner with modern industry, traditional ideology and a minimum of social change. It proved to be a durable formula.

In the short term, the policy brought notable success. Japan became a world power, an exporter of industrial products on a considerable scale, a name to be conjured with. A bid for empire in the twentieth century proved a step too far and ended in disaster, bringing a change of course; but by then the foundation of modern skills and social cohesion had been firmly laid, with the result that the years after 1945 saw an 'economic miracle'. Japan became wealthy, both as a country and as a place to live.

So great a transformation as that which occurred after 1868 has inevitably carried with it many unintended results. In matters that might be called 'consumer choice', they have left Japan more 'western' now than it ever was Chinese. One difference, indeed, between the ancient and the modern is that what was alien in the distant past was for the few, what is alien in the present is almost universal. Only feudalism, which dominates the centuries in between, seems in retrospect – not in all respects justifiably – to be thoroughly Japanese. Perhaps that is why its influence lingers.

CHAPTER I

Origins

The Japanese islands – four major ones, plus several hundred smaller ones round their coasts – are part of a series of island chains looped down the east coast of Asia from Kamchatka in the north to the Philippines in the south. They approach the mainland closely at two points. The straits in the north, where access to the continent is through Hokkaido and Sakhalin, has not had a prominent place in Japanese history, at least until modern times. By contrast, the Tsushima Straits, which separate western Japan from the southern coast of Korea, has been the principal route, commercial, cultural and military, between Japan and the older centres of civilisation on the mainland. These straits are about 100 miles wide. Since two islands, Tsushima and Iki, serve as staging points, it was possible for even quite primitive craft to effect a crossing, but the length of the voyage, plus frequent bad weather, made the passage difficult. The Mongols discovered this to their cost when they tried to invade Japan in 1274 and 1281.

The sea was less of a barrier to foreign culture than to foreign armies. From the seventh century onwards, if not earlier, the religion and philosophy, the art and literature, the economic skills and governmental institutions of China found their way to Japan, at first via Korea and the Tsushima Straits, then more directly across the East China Sea. In much the same manner, though twelve centuries later, the ideas, institutions and technology of Europe and America began to arrive on a comparable scale, this time by the 'ocean' route. These are central themes in Japanese history.

Because cultural imports were not preceded or accompanied by political control, they established themselves in Japan by virtue of their utility or prestige. This enabled other cultural elements, themselves indigenous, to retain a significant role in Japanese life. Shinto, for example, which was the country's primitive religion, served to promote the myth of imperial divine descent at one end of the time-span and helped shape modern nationalism at the other; feudalism, much akin to Europe's, but in origin and character entirely Japanese, dominated the long middle period of Japanese history, both socially and politically; while the Japanese language, for all that it was written from earliest times in the Chinese script, survived as the preferred mode of expression for popular literature, whether poetry or prose. Japanese, not Chinese, was always the language of romance, humour, tales of war.

Myths

Some aspects of native culture go back to lifetimes well before the written record, which makes their origins difficult to disentangle or explain. Writing is said to have been introduced to Japan by a scholar from Korea in AD 405, but the first accounts of the country's earliest history and legends, compiled in Japan, were set down very much later than that. They appear in two chronicles dating from the eighth century, the *Kojiki*, completed in 712, and the *Nihon Shoki*, also known as the *Nihongi*, completed in 720. Both belong to a period when Chinese ideas were taking hold among Japan's élite; both use the Chinese script (indeed, the *Nihon Shoki* is written entirely in Chinese); and both look to Chinese models of historical writing for their methods of dating and compilation. They sometimes transpose selected incidents and speeches, plagiarised from Chinese texts, into a Japanese context. When reading them, therefore, it is hard at times to distinguish Japanese fact from Chinese style.

It is remarkable in these circumstances that what the chronicles have to say about national origins has come to be regarded as quintessentially Japanese. After all, there is evidence of Chinese concepts in the way in which the supposedly 'Japanese' heavenly deities are described; some of the legends are similar to those of other parts of Asia, notably Korea and Manchuria; and there are distortions of fact and chronology, designed to glorify Japan's imperial line for the sake of reinforcing the authority of the rulers under whom the books were written. Despite all this, the narrative, as the chronicles set it down, has in substance been an object of respect for many millions of Japanese almost ever since. It is a part of the national heritage. For this reason, a summary of it is a necessary starting-point for the discussion of Japanese history.

The *Kojiki* begins, in the words of Chamberlain's translation of 1882, 'when chaos had begun to condense, but force and form were not yet manifest'. Thereafter, as the High Plain of Heaven separated out from the mass, deities emerged, from whom were descended Izanagi and Izanami, male and female procreators of the islands of Japan. They were also the progenitors of a further generation of gods and goddesses, among whom were the sun-goddess Amaterasu, the moon-god Tsukiyomi (who plays very little part in the rest of the story) and the storm-god Susa-no-o. In the most famous version — the chronicles provide alternative 'traditions' at a number of points — we are told that Izanami, while giving birth to the fire-god, dies of her burns. Greatly distraught, Izanagi follows her to the Nether World and insists on seeing her, only to discover that she is already in a state of putrefaction. Since this makes her a source of contamination and therefore taboo, he takes to flight, seeking to purify himself by lustration; and as he bathes himself, Amaterasu is born from his left eye, Tsukiyomi from his right eye, Susa-no-o from his nose (so observing the left-right–centre order of precedence that Japan derived from China).

Of these three deities, Amaterasu is sent to rule the High Plain

3

of Heaven, assisted by Tsukiyomi, while Susa-no-o, a fierce and cruel figure, is dispatched to the Nether World. Before going, however, his visits his sister. They quarrel. Thereupon Susa-no-o engages in a number of outrageous acts, breaking down the barriers between the rice-fields, and flaying a piebald colt, which he casts into the hall where his sister is weaving. The incident, clearly an attack on the norms of 'civilisation', as transmitted to Japan from the Asian mainland, gives deep offence. Amaterasu withdraws into a cave, leaving the world in darkness. The 'eighty myriads of gods' thereupon seek to lure her back, setting out offerings of jewels (comma-shaped stones called *magatama*) and a large bronze mirror, in which she can see herself. One of them also performs a dance outside her cave. When these attractions succeed in drawing her out, the other gods restrain her from concealing herself again.

Having so nearly deprived the world of light by his behaviour, Susa-no-o is punished. He is fined, his hair is plucked out – his toenails and fingernails, too, in one version – and he is once more ordered to the Nether World. He takes his time about the journey. First he goes to southern Korea. Then he crosses to the coast of Japan again at Izumo, where he kills a man-eating serpent, in the tail of which he finds a sword, called Kusanagi, 'the grass-cutter'. He presents it to his sister, presumably as a symbol of submission and atonement. Together with the jewels and the mirror used to lure Amaterasu from the cave, it becomes one of the three imperial regalia of Japan.

In the course of these events, several children are born to Amaterasu. One of them becomes the father to a son, Ninigi, whom Amaterasu – or the boy's grandfather, if one prefers an alternative text, more in keeping with Japan's subsequent social history – decides to send down as ruler to Japan. Preceded by envoys, whose task it was to pacify or subdue the evil deities living there, including descendants of Susa-no-o, Ninigi eventually descends 'with an awful path-cleaving ... through the eightfold clouds of Heaven' to Mount Takachiho, in what was later to be the 'sun-facing' province of Hyuga in southern Kyushu. He takes with him the jewels, the mirror and the sword as evidence of the authority with which he has been invested.

Ninigi is held to be the first divine ruler of Japan. In the fullness of time his descendant, Jimmu, became the first human ruler. Setting out from Hyuga to conquer his kingdom, we are told, Jimmu chose to go by ship up the east coast of Kyushu to the north of the island, then eastward through the Inland Sea, a voyage of many months, during which he made several lengthy pauses along the way. At the end of it, his first attempt to land in central Japan was repulsed by the local inhabitants. Jimmu, therefore, recognising – belatedly, it must be said – that it was wrong for a descendant of the sun-goddess to advance against the rising sun, led his men round the coast of the Ise peninsula to launch a fresh attack from the opposite direction. This time he was successful. Fighting his way into the Yamato plain to the south of Nara, he built a palace there; and on the eleventh day of the second lunar month of the following year, which corresponds to 660 BC in the western calendar, he assumed the imperial dignity.

If such a series of events occurred at all, which is doubtful, it could not have been as early as the chronicles imply. The nature of the Japanese record itself suggests as much. The date chosen by the scribes for Jimmu's enthronement was an auspicious one by Chinese standards, but it had the disadvantage of leaving the historian with many more years to fill than he had facts to fill them with before arriving at better-authenticated periods. As a result, the next eight reigns of the dynasty, as officially recorded, contain little more than genealogical information, padded out chronologically to meet editorial needs. Jimmu's reign is said to have lasted eighty years, that of the sixth emperor over a hundred. Reigns of sixty years or more are common. This seems improbable. In fact, modern scholars tend to dismiss as legendary all emperors before the tenth, Sujin, who can be dated to the second half of the third century AD. Even he remains too shadowy a figure to be wholly convincing as the founder of a dynasty, so a case is sometimes made for starting 'history' with the fifteenth emperor, Ōjin, a little more than a century later.

Some light is thrown on these earliest periods by what is said about Japan in the Chinese dynastic histories, but since it takes the form of intermittent travellers' tales, it does not help us much in making out a chronology. The most useful Chinese account is found in the *Wei chih*, part of a history compiled sometime before AD 297. It describes the arrival in the middle years of that century of envoys from the rulers of Wo (Japanese: Wa), which is usually taken to be a state in Kyushu. The Chinese court sent a return mission to Wo in AD 240, bearing gifts of swords and mirrors, and its members came back with information about the Japanese which is duly recorded. It is entirely believable: that they cultivated grains, including rice, as well as the mulberry; that they could spin and weave, but did not keep horses, oxen or sheep; that they were fond of liquor; that they showed respect for persons of importance by squatting or kneeling at the roadside with both hands on the ground. The text also described the use by Japanese of tattoos on faces and painted designs on bodies to signify rank, an assertion borne out by archaeological findings.

On politics the Chinese record, through explicit, is less convincing. The evidence suggests that the Chinese envoys did not travel beyond the coastal fringe of northern Kyushu, which left them to rely on hearsay for what they said about other parts of Japan. Their statement that Kyushu was divided into small kingdoms under local rulers is probably to be trusted. On the other hand, they were going well beyond what they had seen in person when they reported that these states were subject in some unspecified manner to a more distant land, Yamatai, ruled by a queen. It has always been taken for granted that Chinese Yamatai equals Japanese Yamato. It does not necessarily follow, however, that the 'queen's country' was the kingdom that Jimmu is said to have founded in the Nara plain, historically known as the province of Yamato. The argument that it does is strengthened by the *Wei chih*'s reference to a great burial mound, raised over the queen's tomb when she died. Such burial mounds (*kofun*) did appear in the Nara region from about the mid third century. Against that, the instructions given in the *Wei chih* for reaching Yamatai from

Kyushu – they are specified in compass directions and days of travel – would, if obeyed exactly, bring the traveller to a point in the Pacific Ocean off the southeast coast of Kyushu. Some Japanese scholars, accepting the compass bearings, but using a lower estimate for the distance travelled in a single day, have preferred to believe that Yamatai was somewhere in Kyushu. Recent archaeological finds have hinted at a site no further away than Saga prefecture. Others, accepting longer distances, but adjusting the directions, place Yamatai in the Nara plain. The case remains unproven. We cannot be sure that such a state existed there at that time.

Archaeology

Archaeology does little to solve such problems of political chronology. The Japanese were not given to erecting monuments, bearing inscriptions that named and dated their rulers. Those inscriptions that have been found are on portable articles, like swords, usually so damaged by exposure as to be illegible, or nearly so. It is only a partial compensation that the study of objects from excavated sites, especially during the past fifty years, together with improvements in the scientific means of dating them, has enabled scholars to put together a persuasive account of the phases in the prehistoric society of Japan.

The earliest evidence of human settlement appears to date from 30,000 years ago or more. In successive ice ages, the fall in sea levels led for a time to the creation of land bridges between Japan and the Asian continent: that is, to what is now Manchuria in the north, to the Korean peninsula in the west, and down the Ryukyu chain towards central and southern China. Not very much is known about the peoples who entered by these routes, but the variety of their points of departure helps to account for the existence of several different strains of primitive culture in Japan. Starting about 10,000 BC, one of these advanced to the stage of producing a rope-pattern pottery, known as Jōmon. The people who made it used tools and weapons of stone, and lived by hunting, fishing and gathering shellfish; but in later millenniums they began to supplement their diet by the addition of plants and nuts, which some scholars believe were cultivated. There are even signs of rice culture – though not in paddy fields – by the first millennium BC, as well as the grouping of pit-dwellings into small communities.

The next major change occurred about 300 BC with the emergence in southwest Japan of what is called Yayoi culture, named after an excavation site in the Tokyo region. The feature that most distinguished it from Jōmon was wet rice cultivation, carried on at first in low-lying land, subject to natural flooding. It used a type of rice that comes from the lower Yangtse basin in China, brought to Japan, it appears, through Shantung and Korea, or perhaps via the Ryukyu islands. This indication of continental influence is supported by the Yayoi culture's use of bronze for weapons and ceremonial objects. Since copper seems not to have been discovered in Japan until the early eighth century, the ore used to make these objects there – the manufacturing techniques themselves were known, perhaps brought by immigrants – must have come from China and Korea, or been obtained by melting down imported pieces. The oldest bronze mirrors, found in Kyushu, were undoubtedly imported, but from about the beginning of the Christian era craftsmen in Japan were making similar and sometimes nearly identical ones in substantial numbers. They were also making bronze bells, spears and halberds, whose size and appearance suggest that their purpose was ritual, rather than practical. The geographical distribution of these – bronze weapons in Kyushu, bells in central Japan, meeting and to some extent overlapping in the Inland Sea – suggests the existence of two distinct, and possibly rival, centres of culture, but we do not known enough to work out the significance of this.

Iron was introduced from the mainland at very much the same time as bronze, but was put to use mainly for the making of swords and agricultural implements. One result was to make the agrarian economy more productive: it is thought to have supported a population of as many as 600,000 in the early centuries of the Christian era. Yayoi culture also spread northeastward at this stage, reaching the plain round modern Tokyo by the third century AD. Paddy fields had come into existence, fed in some cases by river water through simple irrigation systems; mortars and pestles were used for milling grain; and fragments of hempen cloth have been found in some of the settlements. The use of ritual bronzes indicates a degree of social and religious differentiation. Given such evidence of a society much less primitive than that of the Jōmon period, it is reasonable to conclude that Japan was ready for a more elaborate form of political structure.

When it came, it was characterised by the appearance of burial mounds (*kofun*). The earliest group of these in the southern part of the Nara plain can be dated to AD 250–350: that is, the first century of what is known as the Yamato kingdom. The next were located on the western slopes above the modern city of Nara, at a time when Yamato power was spreading to more distant regions, in both the west and the northeast. In the fifth century, the focus shifted more towards the eastern shores of the Inland Sea (the starting-point of the sea routes to Kyushu and Korea). The tumuli also grew larger with the passage of time, marking, no doubt, an increase in the manpower and resources available to Japanese rulers. The largest of all, said to be the tomb of the sixteenth emperor, Nintoku, who reigned early in the fifth century, had a keyhole-shaped mound nearly 500 metres in length, surrounded by three moats. It has never been excavated.

Standing in rings around the tombs were pottery cylinders, called *haniwa*, which were surmounted by models and figurines of various kinds. These tell us a good deal about the nature of the society producing them. There are models of boats, much like those which are still to be found in fishing villages along the coast of Japan; models of buildings, similar to early Shinto shrines; figures of men in Chinese-style armour; models of horses, complete with saddles, stirrups and bridles. No one point of origin would satisfactorily explain the nature, dress and decoration of all that is reproduced in these objects, though the Korean peninsula seems likely to be the route by which the horses, armour, weapons and other equipment reached Japan. The *kofun* themselves resemble the burial mounds of southern Korea. The nearest equivalents to *haniwa* the present writer has ever seen are small figures and models deriving from Inner Mongolia at the time of the Northern Wei dynasty (386–535), but it would be by no means difficult to trace points of similarity between *haniwa* and the terracotta pieces found in earlier Chinese tombs.

The grave goods found in the stone chambers within the tumuli differ in some degree according to date. In the early period they included comma-shaped jewels (*magatama*), mirrors and other Yayoi-type bronzes, but from the fifth century onwards there is a prevalence of iron weapons, armour and horse-trappings, appropriate to a horse-riding warrior class, together with an increasing number of objects imported from Korea, or made by Korean immigrants, such as gilt-bronze crowns and other personal ornaments, as well as items of pottery. One of the recently excavated (but late-dated) tombs, that at Takamatsuzuka in the south of the Nara plain, was found to have well-preserved wall paintings, executed wholly in the Korean style.

In 1948 Egami Namio put forward what has become known as the 'horse-rider' theory to account for the objects associated with the tombs. Not convinced that they were satisfactorily explained by closer diplomatic relations with Korean kingdoms, though these undoubtedly existed in the fifth and sixth centuries, he argued that there had been a conquest of Yamato by mounted invaders, coming from outside. Their ultimate place of origin, he said, was one of the semi-agricultural, semi-nomadic kingdoms established by 'barbarians' along the northern frontier of China during the Han dynasty. At the end of the third century, when that area was still in turmoil following the fall of the Han, some of its people established themselves in Korea, then spilt over into Kyushu, whence Ōjin, Nintoku's father, led them against Yamato (in a manner reminiscent of Jimmu).

Egami's theory, which offends so many national and dynastic sensibilities, has not found ready acceptance among Japanese historians. They point out a number of technical weaknesses in it, not least on the matter of dating. For the non-specialist this is slippery ground. What can be accepted without undue controversy, however, is that from the fifth century onwards the development of a more powerful Yamato monarchy was accompanied, for whatever reasons, by a significant increase in the 'Korean' component in Japanese life. The horse, whose absence the *Wei chih* remarked upon, is first mentioned in the chronicles in the reign of Nintoku. It almost certainly entered Japan from Korea. Iron-working was a skill for which Koreans were famous in East Asia. It was apparently brought to Japan, like irrigation, sericulture and weaving, by the many Korean immigrants to whom the chronicles refer. Parts of the Japanese creation myth have affinities with those of Korea, which may have had an influence on the compilers of the *Kojiki* and *Nihon Shoki*. All these things, moreover, are related directly or indirectly to the power of the imperial house.

The Yamato state

In considering the influence that Korea had on the political development of Japan after the building of burial mounds began, it is convenient to start with the fifteenth emperor, Ōjin, whose reign spanned the years on either side of AD 400. His predecessors appear to have extended the control of the Yamato kings from their base in the Nara plain, first to the neighbouring regions of Japan, then to the north and west. That is about all we know of them. Of Ōjin we know more: that his accession marks a possible break in the ruling line; that he and his successors were much involved in the affairs of Korea; and that they used this connection to strengthen their authority at home. The chronicles describe Ōjin and his son, Nintoku, in much the same clichés, both of incident and language, that Chinese historians use of founders of a dynasty.

Towards the end of his life, the fourteenth emperor, Chūai, was told by his consort, the empress Jingū, that the gods had revealed to her in a shamanistic trance their wish that he should send an expedition against Korea. Chūai dismissed the command as coming from 'lying deities' – after all, there was nothing to be seen, he said, in the quarter where Korea was supposed to lie – and insisted that he must concentrate on suppressing rebels at home. At this the gods declared, once more to Jingū, that by disobedience he had sacrificed his right to rule. Nevertheless, they promised, the child she was already bearing in her womb would be emperor if she herself obeyed their wishes. Chūai died soon after. Jingū thereupon launched and led an expedition to Korea, binding a stone in her loins to delay the birth of her child until the fighting should be over. The venture was successful; the child, Ōjin, was born on Jingū's return to Japan; in due course he succeeded as emperor.

One might be inclined to disregard this story as nothing more than the echo of a palace scandal, were it not for the references to involvement in Korea. For two centuries and more after Ōjin came to the throne, Korea was to be of the first importance to Japan, both as a scene of military adventure and as a key to cultural development. In this respect the reign of Ōjin marks a new departure.

Under the Han dynasty (202 BC–AD 220) China had established two military colonies in north Korea. It was not until the early fourth century, a hundred years after the fall of the Han in China, that these finally succumbed to local attacks, but once they did so, three Korean kingdoms came into existence and engaged in a struggle for power in the peninsula: Koguryŏ in the north, incorporating semi-sinicised peoples from southern Manchuria, who had close relations – sometimes friendly, often not – with Chinese states across the frontier; Paekche in the southwest, which developed contacts with parts of China across the Yellow Sea; and Silla in the southeast, which proved in the end to be the most powerful, despite being more remote from China. Japan became involved in the struggles between them as the result of an appeal for help from Paekche soon after the middle of the fourth century. This led to a series of occasional military expeditions, Jingū's among them, which gave Japan booty, prisoners and opportunities for learning about Chinese civilisation. According to the chronicles, there was even a Japanese enclave on the south Korean coast, known as Mimana (Kaya), though modern scholars have expressed some doubts about it. By courtesy of Paekche's maritime skills and diplomatic connections, a direct link was also made with mainland China from time to time. In 425 and 478 envoys from Yamato reached the court of the Liu Sung dynasty in what is now Nanking. Another eleven missions went to China between then and 502. Paekche, too, contributed to Japanese culture, sending visitors and immigrants with a knowledge of Chinese writing and the Buddhist faith.

The prestige attaching to Japanese involvement in Korea accrued mostly to the imperial house, though there is little to show that emperors in person did much to earn it. Missions from foreign monarchs, seeking alliance, enhanced the imperial prestige. So did Buddhism in some degree. There were also more material benefits. Military loot was a form of portable wealth; trade followed in the footsteps of diplomacy; prisoners of war were a cheap form of labour, often possessing exploitable skills. Immigrants and visitors were another by-product of the connection. Those with a knowledge of Chinese writing could help with the keeping of records and accounts, enhancing the efficiency of government and the management of imperial estates, while others brought with them an expertise in metalworking or irrigation. Enjoying the lion's share of these advantages, the throne expanded its wealth and power at a greater rate than its potential rivals in Japan. When the emperor Yūryaku sent envoys to China in 478, for example, they claimed on his behalf that his forebears had already conquered 'fifty-five countries of hairy men' to the east, 'sixty-five countries of various barbarians' to the west, and ninety-five countries 'crossing the sea to the north' (*Sung shu*).

The degree of unity within this kingdom was almost certainly not very great. The most important units in fifth-century social structure were clans, or kinship groups, called *uji*. These had originated as agricultural communities, engaged in wet rice cultivation, whose hereditary heads had a duty to propitiate the gods on behalf of the *uji*'s members as a whole. Groups of *uji* were eventually consolidated into federations, forming small 'countries' (*kuni*), such as were described in the Chinese records. Their 'kings' and 'queens' had similar functions to the heads of *uji*. Yamato's 'imperial' clan had no doubt begun as one of these, but by the time of Ōjin and Nintoku it was powerful enough to claim the leadership of what one might call a federation of federations, first in the Nara plain, then more widely. The heads of other clans became attached to it as part of the ruler's entourage, among them the Mononobe, whose role was military, and the Nakatomi, court liturgists, whose ritual functions concerned the cult of the sun-goddess Amaterasu. A later addition to the court was the Soga clan, said to be of Korean immigrant descent, which owed its influence to the part it played in managing royal estates.

Subordinate to the *uji* in some cases, merely lower in the social scale in others, were organisations called *be* and *tomo*. The words are sometimes translated into English as 'guilds', but this is misleading. It is true that they existed to perform specialist functions: fishing and the gathering of mountain products; household duties at court and the conduct of religious rituals; service as palace guards; crafts such as weaving or ironworking and the making of weapons; irrigation and the care of horses. A few consisted of immigrants, for whom this was a means of integration into Japanese society. Almost all, however, cultivated land, in order to support the specialists among their number. Fictive kinship links existed between their members. In these respects the *be* and *tomo* overlapped in some degree with *uji*.

There was no administrative machinery to bind such elements into anything like a state, at least in the early days, but after the accession of Ōjin this gap began to be filled. One step was the bestowal of hereditary titles (*kabane*) on the leaders of *uji*, *be* and *tomo.* Those most influential at court were made *omi* and *muraji*: that is, ministers. Others, lower down in the scheme of things, together with local dignitaries in the provinces, were given lesser titles. There appears to have been competition for these titles: the nineteenth emperor, Ingyō, felt the need to proclaim a series of ordeals by boiling water to identify those whose claims were valid.

The growing dominance of the imperial clan, reflected in these arrangements, enabled the twenty-fifth emperor, Muretsu, to behave in ways that showed little respect for the feelings of his subjects. He 'prepared strange diversions and gave licence to lewd voices'; he drank alcohol to excess 'in the company of the women of the palace'; he diverted himself by making men climb trees, then killing them, either by cutting down the trees, or by using the men as living targets for his arrows (*Nihon Shoki*). Compare this with the same book's account of Nintoku's behaviour less than a hundred years earlier. Seeing that the people were poor because of his demands for forced labour, Nintoku had suspended the system for three years, so ensuring that 'the wind and the rain came in due season, the five grains produced in abundance . . . [and] the people had plenty'.

If this were a Chinese history, rather than a Japanese one written in Chinese, the pattern would be recognisable: Nintoku was an emperor at the beginning of a dynasty, Muretsu one at the end. Historiographical convention required the attribution of virtue to the one, tyranny and corruption to the other. In the eyes of the scribes, in fact, the monarchy was on the eve of significant change. They were right. Muretsu died without an heir towards the end of the fifth century. His successor, an obscure and distant relative, perhaps not even that, was chosen by senior members of the court.

Primitive religion

Before turning our attention to the subsequent history of the monarchy, we should consider briefly the early religious beliefs and practices of Japan, which were of some relevance to it. Our knowledge of what is now called Shinto, the Way of the Gods (*kami*), rests heavily on the *Kojiki* and *Nihon Shoki*. Because these were compiled at a time when Japan was coming under increasing Chinese cultural influence (Chapter 3), it is difficult to be sure how far the account they give of pre-Buddhist religion is distorted by the assumptions and prejudices of the scribes, who were chosen for their work because they were 'experts' in things Chinese, or even immigrants. There are, for example, traces of Chinese influence in what is said about the creation. One or two of the *kami* identified in the texts appear to be Chinese or Korean in origin, perhaps because they were deities of immigrant communities, who called them *kami* in deference to local custom. More pervasively, some concepts and vocabulary – the veneration of swords and mirrors, words like *jingū* (shrine) and *tennō* (emperor) – are found in Chinese Taoism. This may mean nothing more than that historians, writing in Chinese, used what seemed to them to be the appropriate terms for what they had to record, but it nevertheless makes it difficult to be sure that the phenomena themselves were distinctive and indigenous, or to decide what their original nature was. For instance, there has long been controversy about whether ancestor worship, to which there is reference in the chronicles, was a custom native to Japan, or part of the mind-set of the historians.

The term *kami*, not surprisingly, poses problems of translation into languages other than Japanese. To call them 'gods and goddesses', or simply 'deities', though convenient, is potentially misleading, unless one intends to make comparison with ancient Greece and Rome. The *kami* were superior beings, to whom humans might attribute supernatural powers, but they were neither omniscient nor omnipotent. They were, moreover, diverse, as well as numerous. Some, especially those named in the story of the creation and the imperial myth, were thought of as anthropomorphic, both male and female. With these one might include the tutelary and ancestral *kami* of the most powerful clans (*uji*) existing in the Nara state at the time the chronicles were compiled: that is, their *uji-gami*. Amaterasu, after all, was not only the sun-goddess, but also the *uji-gami* of the imperial house. It was natural that tradition, as stated in the chronicles, should accord a similar character and place, if at a less elevated level, to the *uji-gami* of those clan heads who served the emperor in a senior capacity.

A second category, older than the first, comprised the *kami* of the countryside: those to whom appeal was made for fertility and good harvests, or the spirits of storm and earthquake, of lakes and rivers, of mountains and forest, even particular trees and stones, from which harm might threaten. These were not as a rule anthropomorphic, though they might be demonic, or appear occasionally in human form, or take possession of humans. Some of them had links with *uji-gami*, as deities of the locality to which an *uji* traced its origin. As pressure increased to reshape the received tradition of primitive times for the benefit of an emerging monarchy, notably in the sixth and seventh centuries, most of this group of *kami* became of secondary importance. The chronicles reflect this. Throughout history, however, they retained a much greater popularity among the rural population than they did at the emperor's court.

Shinto shrines were simple in form, as were the acts of worship performed at them. It was not until the Yamato monarchy was well established that shrine building became common, starting with those at Ise and Izumo, which had political importance. Even in the modern period, many lesser shrines are no more than roadside huts or even roped-off 'spaces'. For the most part, the worshipper was expected to do no more than bow, clap the hands and provide a small offering. Priests, who were described as officials in the more notable shrines – there was originally no clear distinction between ritual (*matsuri*) and government (*matsurigoto*), whether for the emperor or for minor functionaries – would recite prayers, usually to offer thanks for favours received, or to turn away the *kami*'s wrath. The latter was most likely to be occasioned by pollution and uncleanliness, though it might be triggered by any action that disturbed the natural order. It was not in particular a response to offences against ethics or criminal misdemeanours. Shinto subscribed to no regular code of moral behaviour. Contamination by death, the physical manifestations of sickness, menstruation and childbirth, or behaviour that threatened the crop and other sources of food, such as Susa-no-o had committed – these were the things that humans had above all to avoid.

For individuals who offended, the most common ritual response was ablution or lustration, for which water and salt were provided at shrines. Exorcists could be used to intercede with the *kami* in serious cases. Ritual abstainers ensured the purity of major observances, especially at court; diviners, interpreting the cracks in heated tortoiseshells, discovered the reasons for a *kami*'s anger and sought ways to avert it; shamans, usually women, did the same by means of dreams and trances.

What is conspicuously lacking from this list is any doctrine of transcendent faith, or universal system of values, which might have given intellectual cohesion to the whole. Japanese were to find these things in Buddhism. Indeed, it may well have been their absence from Shinto that enabled the two religions to co-exist, even to establish a symbiotic relationship, for most of Japanese history.

CHAPTER 2

The Making of a Monarchy

Unlike China, Japan, at least officially, has had only one dynasty since the beginning of time. This fact has done much to determine the monarchy's nature and political role. There is a pattern to Chinese dynasties. Each begins with a phase of state building by men of vigour and ability, who bring an infusion of new blood; next comes one of 'power and glory', as their descendants enjoy the fruits of this beginning; and finally the dynasty goes into a decline, marked by a growth of luxury and incompetence at the centre, which make the country's rulers — not only the emperor — too weak to govern effectively. At this point comes chaos and confusion, preparing the way for the cycle to start again.

The pattern does not translate exactly to Japan. In Japan, it could be said, a single dynasty has gone through a single cycle, which is by definition incomplete. The first two stages, those of state building and apogee, have been comparable with China's, but the third, that of decline, has been both long drawn out and different in character. From about the tenth century onwards, Japanese emperors lost the greater part of their temporal power, as did the later rulers of dynasties in China; but they retained their thrones, as well as a measure of influence, by virtue of a quasi-religious function, rooted in the distant past. Their claim to divine descent made them the source of all legitimate authority, still wielded in their name when they themselves lacked power. In reality, it passed, sometimes by force, sometimes by more devious means, to successive houses of hereditary office-holders, initially within the court, later outside it; and since each survived at least as long as the average Chinese dynasty, these in turn could be described in the language of rise, apogee and decline. The first of them, the Fujiwara, were regents to the emperor from 966 until the nineteenth century, though for the greater part of that time they, too, were virtually powerless.

Chinese-style government

Events on the mainland of Asia during the second half of the sixth century provided a powerful motive for changes in the nature of Japanese monarchy. Of the Korean kingdoms, Silla was strong enough by 562 to engulf the Japanese foothold on the southern coast. More ominously, the Sui dynasty, having reunited China in 589, began to show signs of restoring Chinese influence in the Korean peninsula. Koguryŏ and Paekche in the north and west were the first to feel the pressure, but it soon extended to Silla, too, with the result that by 594 all three Korean states had entered into tribute relations with China, accepting nominal Chinese suzerainty in return for a promise of security and trade. It seemed likely that Japan would soon find it wise to follow suit. In these circumstances, both Japanese and Korean rulers came to recognise the advantage of having a home base that was centralised in the Chinese manner, hence better able to defend itself. The most straightforward way of creating it was to adopt a Chinese form of monarchy and government.

Buddhism had already brought about in Japan a climate of opinion that was receptive to a decision of this kind. The religion had reached Japan – or, more precisely, the Japanese court – through a mission from Paekche in the middle of the century. It did not at first make a great deal of headway, since it was opposed by clans like the Nakatomi, which had a vested interest in the worship of the *kami*. The Soga took up its cause, however, and their victory in a civil war in 587 gave Buddhism greater influence. This in turn reinforced the political motives for a close relationship with China. The Soga's principal ally within the imperial clan, Prince Shōtoku, was a devout Buddhist. As regent to the empress Suiko, an office to which he was appointed in 593 at the age of twenty, he devoted himself for nearly thirty years to promoting the growth of Chinese thought and institutions in Japan.

In medieval and modern times Shōtoku, both as Buddhist and as siniciser, has been a cult figure. The imperial collection contains an imaginary portrait of him, dating from about 700, which shows him with his two young sons, all three very Chinese in dress and hairstyle; in the Hōryūji temple at Nara, close to the site of Shōtoku's palace, there is an illustrated biography, originally painted on sliding panels in 1069; the Kōryūji in Kyoto has a statue, attributed by reason of its style to the Kamakura period (1185–1333), showing him, supposedly at the age of sixteen, seated on a chair (a Chinese habit that he did *not* succeed in making popular in Japan). Shōtoku, in fact, is traditionally held to have lived very much in the Chinese manner.

His main political achievement – though because of the nature of the records we cannot be sure how far it was indeed a personal one – was to make a start on the task of giving Japan a framework of institutions, modelled on those of China, which would turn an association of clans under the emperor's military command into something more like a centralised state. He introduced cap ranks at court in 604, in order to relate the status of office-holders more clearly to that of the monarch and each other; he began the compilation of chronicles – an activity designed to assert the legitimacy of a dynasty, as Chinese historians saw it – though the text, if completed, has not survived; and he sent embassies to the Sui, starting in 600, partly to establish his country's place in a China-centred international system, partly to carry laymen and priests to study China's society and religion. The practice was to continue intermittently until 838.

The most important political document with which his name is linked – both its date and attribution have been questioned, but there is not much doubt that it reflects Shōtoku's own ideas – is the so-called Seventeen Article Constitution of 604, more accurately described as the Seventeen Injunctions. It begins with a quotation from the Confucian Analects, asserting that 'Harmony is to be valued'. It then enjoins reverence for 'the three treasures': that is, the Buddha, the Buddhist Law and the Buddhist priesthood. Finally, it turns to the behaviour deemed appropriate at the Japanese court, whose officials it addressed. The first of these, respect for the emperor's will, is expounded in wholly Chinese terms. 'The lord is Heaven, the vassal is Earth. Heaven overspreads and Earth upbears. When this is so the four seasons follow their due course.' At a less elevated level, officials are enjoined to make 'decorous' thought their guiding principle, dealing impartially with the suits that are brought before them. They should attend at court early in the morning and retire late. They must not seek to treat the emperor's lands or subjects as their own: 'in a country there are not two lords, the people have not two masters'.

Not very much of this was put into practice in Shōtoku's lifetime. Some of it, after all, was contrary to the interests of his Soga allies, whose power rested on their efficiency and victory in civil war, not imperial autocracy. Nevertheless, what he did was significant in two respects. He set out aspirations that eventually were to be orthodox in Japanese court politics; and by sending students to China, he made it possible for his successors to proceed on the basis of a much more thorough understanding of Chinese government. Some of the students remained in China for twenty or thirty years, so witnessing both the fall of the Sui and the succession in 618 of the T'ang, a much more prestigious dynasty. The T'ang, indeed, were to become Japan's model. The first mission was sent to their capital in 630.

By the time the last of Shōtoku's students came back to Japan at the end of that decade, opposition had developed to the power and pretensions of the Soga. They were even accused of seeking to usurp the imperial dignity for themselves. A conspiracy took shape, led by a clan head, Nakatomi no Kamatari, later to found the Fujiwara house, and Prince Naka-no-Ōe, son of the reigning empress, Kyōgoku. In 645 these men carried out a *coup d'état*. As an immediate result, the two principal leaders of the Soga were killed, the empress abdicated in favour of Naka-no-Ōe's uncle, Kōtoku, and Naka-no-Ōe became nominal head of government, much as Shōtoku had been a generation earlier. Kamatari took a senior post in the new regime. Scholars recently returned from China became its advisers.

Although this event is called a 'reform' by historians, there is no convincing evidence that the purpose of the conspirators went in the first place beyond removal of the Soga. What followed, however, was a series of steps clearly designed to transfer power from clan leaders to the throne and its immediate servants. A system of administration was set out, both at the centre and in newly defined provinces, and put under the supervision of officials appointed by the court; a revised system of ranks was introduced, modelled on that of the T'ang; heads of *uji* were deprived of lands and people said to have been improperly granted in previous reigns; and although some landholders at the district level, who were thought to be of unblemished character, were made eligible for local office, the emperor's subjects were in general warned that both land and people were the ruler's — that is, not simply under the sway of their hereditary chiefs. Registers of population were to be kept. Standardised measures were introduced for the assessment of tax on rice-land. Land surveys were carried out, making use of them. New rates of tax and labour dues were announced, payable to the court and its representatives.

A further innovation, as much symbolic as practical, was a change in the Japanese calendar. Use of the Chinese calendar was always a condition of belonging to China's tribute system. Its adoption in Japan in 645 was therefore a claim to international status. From that time on, irregularly in the seventh century, but constantly thereafter until the present day, Japanese were to designate years in the way the Chinese did, according to their place in a series of named periods of time, each of which bore an era-name (*nengō*) chosen for its auspicious meaning. The *nengō* that started the series was Taika, 'Great Reform'. The first year of Taika was AD 645 by western reckoning, the second was 646, and so on. Taika was replaced by Hakuchi in 650 – the decision was the ruler's prerogative – though there was then a gap from 655 to 672, when no such label was in use. In fact, the next one of any moment was Taihō, 'Great Law', introduced in 701, when it marked the issue of administrative codes.

As was implied by the failure to use *nengō* between 655 and 672, the reform movement lost impetus after its first few years. The setback was temporary, however, since the need for reform had by no means come to an end. Almost as soon as Naka-no-Ōe became emperor under the reign-title Tenji in 661, he was confronted with a crisis over Korea. Paekche, hard pressed by the forces of Silla and the T'ang, appealed for Japanese help, as it had done before, but the expedition sent in response to the appeal was roundly defeated. Japan was once again on the defensive. When Koguryŏ asked for assistance in 668, it was refused. The result was to leave the whole of the Korean peninsula under the domination of Silla and the T'ang. Japan for its part, conscious of continued unrest at home, set out to erect defence works in Tsushima, along the northern coast of Kyushu and in the Inland Sea. This could hardly have seemed the time to abandon the task of building a stronger monarchy.

Our knowledge of Japanese state building during the second half of the seventh century is by no means complete, though it is clear that Temmu, Tenji's successor and younger brother, played a major part in it. New administrative codes, said to have been drafted under both Tenji and Temmu, have not survived. Nor is there an extant text of the Taihō Code of 701, which was to serve as the basis of Japanese government for the next 200 years. An account of political institutions in the Nara period (710–84) must therefore rest on what is known as the Yōrō Code, drawn up in 718, but not put into force until 757. It embodied the so-called *ritsuryō* system – *ritsu* is penal law, *ryō* are administrative statutes – laying it down that emperors ruled through a central bureaucracy, the structure and functions of which were described in detail. The very concept was novel, as the highly personal nature of earlier Japanese government implies.

The highest decision-making body under the *ritsuryō* system was the Daijōkan, or Council of State, founded in 689. The Council was small: three ministers, the Daijō-daijin (Great Minister of State, or Chancellor), Sadaijin (Minister of the Left) and Udaijin (Minister of the Right); four senior councillors; a few junior ones; a small secretariat. The office of Daijō-daijin was rarely filled, perhaps because its extensive powers made it a threat to the throne. On both occasions when appointments were made during the eighth century, the incumbents were subsequently dismissed for seeking to usurp the emperor's authority. This left the overall supervision of government for the most part to the Council's other senior members, amounting to half a dozen men. On major questions they made recommendations to the emperor, who was expected to approve or disapprove, but not revise them. On lesser ones they acted on their own.

Under the control of the Daijōkan there were eight executive ministries. One, the Imperial Household Ministry (Kunaishō), responsible for the management of the emperor's household and the revenue from imperial estates, stood a little apart from the rest. The others included Finance, which dealt mostly with tax receipts; People's Affairs (land and population registers); and Military Affairs (administering conscription). Three more were required to manage the huge amount of paperwork that the bureaucracy produced: drafts of laws and decrees; lists of rituals and ceremonials; records of rank, genealogy and succession among the nobility, and of appointments and promotions for officials; the texts of recommendations and petitions, together with the decisions taken about them. There was no Ministry of Foreign Affairs. A Justice Ministry presided over the legal aspects of government business. There was no system of courts, since all officials were required to administer the law in their different spheres, conducting investigations in response to complaints and petitions. They possessed no detailed list of offences that might warrant punishment, except for the 'eight outrages' of crimes against the public interest. These included treason and rebellion, serious cases of murder (those involving assault within the family, killing by dismemberment, or witchcraft) and violations of Confucian morality.

Apart from the ministries, there were several subordinate or semi-independent bureaux, one of which investigated cases of official misconduct and maintained order in the capital. Others were concerned with the imperial library, calendars, divination, court music and ceremonial dancing. Outside the capital there was a governor-general at Dazaifu in northern Kyushu, whose high rank – he was often a imperial prince – marked the importance of relations with China and Korea. The province of Settsu, which guarded the sea approaches to the capital, was also under an official of more than ordinary rank. Elsewhere there were governors in each province, appointed on rotation by the court from among the central cohort of officials, and responsible for all matters of civil and military government in their area (though they did not always go there in person). Each had a small staff, including specialists in medicine and Chinese studies. A detachment of conscripts was put under the governor's command. At the next level down were district officials, chosen from local notables and appointed for life.

While the provincial administration looks remarkably simple for what were in theory very wide-ranging duties, that of the capital seems to have been overmanned. It has been estimated that in 718 it employed about 330 officials in its upper levels, another 6,000 in lesser posts. This seems excessive for a country with a total population of perhaps 5 million. What is more, the members of this bureaucracy were enmeshed in a maze of regulations, setting out their responsibilities and their office-hours, the precedents to be followed (Chinese as well as Japanese), and the arrangements for appointment and promotion. As early as 678 Temmu had ordered that officers of both central and provincial government should report each year on the abilities of their subordinates, in order that they might be considered for

advancement. In 701 the emperor Mommu instructed those of
the fifth rank and above to record each month the number of
days on which they had been present at their place of duty.

By the time the legal commentary *Ryō no Gige* was issued in
834, these requirements had become an elaborate reporting
system, applicable to officials of almost every grade. It was based
on two criteria. A man acquired 'merit' for his diligence and
probity in office. He was credited with 'excellence' in accordance
with his success in meeting the demands it made upon him.
These demands were defined in a fairly rudimentary way. A lesser
councillor had to act in strict conformity with the instructions
he received; a guards officer must maintain rigid discipline; a
chamberlain had to be in constant attendance at court; and so on
down a long list, covering official historians, court musicians,
diviners and even barrier guards in similar manner. The combination of 'merit' and 'excellence' made it possible to allocate all
these people to one of nine classes, ranging from Superior, First
Class, for the very best to Inferior, Third Class, for those who
were said to flatter and lie, or showed themselves avaricious and
dishonest.

That this structure as a whole was more appropriate to a
country of the size and complexity of China than it was to one
as 'backward' as Japan is obvious enough. Yet it was not just a
blind copy of the T'ang model. Apart from a number of technical
differences, which need not detain us here, the *ritsuryō* system
departed from Chinese practice in two major respects, which are
important to an understanding of the Japanese monarchy. One
concerns the role of inherited rank. The other was a product of
the theory underlying the emperor's own authority.

Eighth-century Japan was not a meritocracy, however much its
reports on officials might make it seem so. Parallel to the hierarchy
of office, and at least equally significant, was a scale of numbered
ranks, subdivided into sections. Only those who held ranks one
to three could be chosen as minister in the Council of State.
Ranks four and five gave entry to other senior posts, filled by
direct imperial appointment, while ranks six to eight were for

more humdrum members of officialdom. Below those again were unnumbered ranks for minor functionaries. Such ranks were a qualification for office, not a reward for filling it successfully. What is more, at the very highest levels they were reserved in practice for descendants of former clan heads and other senior members of the court aristocracy, together with offshoots of the imperial house. The children and even grandchildren of such persons could enter the structure as of right at one of its higher points.

As a result, posts that carried the greatest influence became the preserve of a circle of families, which mere bureaucratic efficiency did not enable others to penetrate. For example, between 701 and 764 the offices of Minister of the Left and Minister of the Right were shared by men from only five of these. Nor did the narrowing of opportunity end there. Of the eleven senior officials of the Council of State in 772, no fewer than eight were from the Fujiwara house, founded by Nakatomi no Kamatari; two more were relatives of the Fujiwara; and the other was descended from the Mononobe. In other words, those branches of the old clan aristocracy that had committed themselves to the new Chinese-style governmental institutions had found in 'careers' a substitute for the private control of land and people on which their ancestors had relied. Those in the Council of State possessed real power, for the emperor could take no executive action without them. In addition, they enjoyed valuable emoluments, as did many of their associates. Men of the eighth rank and above were exempt from labour service and regular state taxes on land. Both rank and office carried financial advantages, either in the form of allocations of revenue from stated groups of tax-paying households, or as periodical grants of tax goods from the treasury. These benefits, which were substantial for those of the fifth rank and above, had a tendency to become customary, even though they were in theory official emoluments. One is bound to conclude that emperors like Tenji and Temmu had succeeded in their aim of breaking down the independence of the clans only by converting one segment of the clan leadership into privileged, hereditary members of what on the face of it was an appointive bureaucracy. In the long run, this was to undermine the power of the monarchy itself.

Despite this institutional weakness, Japanese emperors had a theoretical source of authority that made them in principle more secure in their position than those of China were. In China the emperor, as Son of Heaven, ruled as mediator between Heaven and Earth. His tenure was sanctioned by Heaven's will, expressed in what was called the Mandate of Heaven (*t'ien-ming*); but it was widely believed that this could be withdrawn if he failed to provide just and stable government, or behave in accordance with the Confucian ethic. Were he so to fail, the divine displeasure would be revealed for all to witness in heavenly portents, or natural calamities, or popular unrest. All these were signals that the emperor had lost the right to rule. There was no such doctrine in Japan. An emperor who reigned by virtue of divine descent could not be subject to a conditional mandate of this kind, even though his relationship to the sun-goddess, Amaterasu, could be likened in some ways to the Chinese emperor's claim to be Son of Heaven.

Japanese emperors had no objection to preaching from a Chinese text when it suited their purpose. In 683 Temmu issued a decree stating that 'auspicious signs' had been observed, confirming that government was 'in harmony with the laws of Heaven' (*Nihon Shoki*). Yet in the same document he described himself as 'a God Incarnate'. The second of these concepts, moreover, seems to have had a practical impact on his policy. He reinstated the practice of installing an imperial princess at the Ise shrines to worship Amaterasu on the emperor's behalf. When he ordered the compilation of the *Kojiki*, he required it to show that the bonds between the emperor and the *kami* were 'the foundations of imperial rule'. The *ritsuryō* system, of which he was one of the architects, placed the ceremonies of enthronement and succession, conceived within the tradition of imperial divine descent, under the supervision of the Jingikan. This was a body responsible for matters concerning the worship of *kami*, which technically outranked the Council of State. In a court where other forms of protocol and ritual were overwhelmingly Chinese, these exceptions mattered.

Capital cities

Rulers whose court was in so many respects Chinese aspired to have a palace and a capital that were equally so. During much of the sixth and seventh centuries, the two concepts of palace and capital had been almost synonymous. They moved for each new reign, because death caused ritual pollution. Still, from the time the Soga came to power in 587, the moves were small enough to make the Asuka district in the south of the Nara plain the dynasty's political heartland, giving its name to a century's history. It was there that the earliest Buddhist temples were established. It was also there that Japan's first real capital city was built. This was Fujiwara, conceived by the emperor Temmu, but completed by his widow and successor, who moved the court to the new site in 694. Modelled on Loyang, which was then China's capital, the city measured some 3 kilometres by 2 in size; had a Chinese-style grid of streets, divided into eastern and western halves by a central north–south avenue; and included a large palace enclosure, placed at the northern end.

Fujiwara was destroyed by fire in 711, one year after the court had left it for a city known historically as Nara, though more accurately called Heijō (the name given to China's prototype for the great T'ang capital, Ch'ang-an). Heijō had a river route to the Inland Sea, which may be why the place was chosen, but in other respects it was similar to Fujiwara, if a good deal larger (5 kilometres by 4). Unlike Chinese cities it had no walls, but it had two gates, Suzakumon in the north and Rashōmon in the south, a pattern that was to be repeated more famously in the next capital, called Heian.

There was a great deal of open space within the city, despite its

urban ground-plan: wide avenues; two large enclosures forming
the palace precinct, its buildings surrounded by open corridors;
extensive grounds for temples and aristocratic mansions. The
palace itself comprised buildings of two different kinds. The
ceremonial ones were recognisably Chinese in style. Though a
little modified by later rebuilding, an example of them – a long,
low wooden structure with white plaster walls and a curved roof
of tiles, set on a raised stone plinth – can still be seen in modern
Nara at the Tōshōdaiji, a Buddhist temple to which it was transferred as a lecture hall. Other buildings within the precinct,
used mainly for living accommodation, were more 'Japanese' in
appearance, as were those of the aristocracy, who were allotted
plots in the city in accordance with their rank. Lacking the stone
plinth, the plaster walls and the tiled roof, these usually had
planked floors, supported on pillars set directly in the ground,
and were roofed in thatch or shingles. A report by the Council of
State in 724 complained that too many of the city's dwellings
lacked dignity. Nobles of the fifth rank and above were urged to
build more impressive ones, painted in red and white, and give
them roofs of tiles: that is, to adopt the Chinese style.

Not even temple buildings always passed this test: the Tōdaiji's
great treasure house, the Shōsōin, which still survives, has something of the look of an oversized log cabin. This serves to remind
us that Japan did not at this early date adopt the Chinese practice
of building in stone or brick, whether because of the lack of
appropriate materials and skills, or because of the risk from earthquakes. One result was a high degree of impermanence. Fire was
a constant hazard. In fact, our knowledge of the architecture of
the period owes less to surviving examples in the ordinary sense
than it does to replicas, created by centuries of rebuilding, which
disaster or decay occasioned from time to time. Rebuilding, no
matter how carefully carried out, may not always have been exact.
Nor can we be completely sure about original locations. Buildings
like these were remarkably easy to move, given sufficient manpower. When we read that the Yakushiji was removed from Asuka
to Nara, this is likely to be the literal truth.

Though we have no contemporary pictures of it, eighth-century Nara almost certainly lacked visual grandeur, despite the desire to impress that was evident in its planning. It was not until they built castles in the sixteenth century that Japanese architects created buildings with as great an impact on the observer as that produced by Europe's classical monuments or medieval churches. With the exception of pagodas – constructed in wood they look strangely un-Chinese – even palaces and temples were mostly single-storey, their roof spans restricted by lack of engineering knowledge. Wooden walls, left unpainted, helped to render them unobtrusive, while dispersal over level, often wooded sites denied them a dominating presence. Restraint in this sense was to be a lasting feature of Japanese art, but it meant that Nara, unlike Ch'ang-an, impressed more by its acreage than its splendour.

The city comprised people, as well as buildings, of course, and these were much more colourful, at least if they were members of the aristocracy. Costume, also Chinese in manner, was much less sober than it was later to become. Leaving aside the princes of the imperial house, there were over a hundred nobles of the fifth rank and above, wearing, at least on formal occasions, robes of some opulence. Hundreds more held lesser ranks. A surprisingly large proportion of these persons were immigrants. A list of noble families compiled in 815 (by which time the total had risen slightly from its Nara levels) showed that about one family in three of those included in it came originally from China or Korea: more than 170 out of nearly 1,200 came from China, some 240 from different parts of Korea. To the nobility one must add several thousand non-noble government servants, plus a considerable number of priests and other residents of religious establishments, comprising a substantial upper class. Then there were the artisans and craftsmen. Many of these, too, were immigrants, engaged in silk weaving, metalworking or one of the other kinds of technical expertise needed, for example, to build and decorate palaces, shrines and temples. In addition, there was a large floating population of temporary inhabitants, including militia on duty in the capital, and men and women performing labour service there. Estimates of the total have varied widely, but Nara may well have contained 100,000 persons in the early eighth century, rising to as many as 200,000 by the time the court departed in 784. Thereafter it declined rapidly in size and population as Heian took its place as the centre of government.

The transfer to Heian took place in two stages. Early in Kammu's reign (781–806) the decision was taken to move north again, this time to Nagaoka on the Yodo river. The step was taken in 784; but in the next year or two a high-profile assassination there, followed by natural calamities, which were blamed on malignant spirits, brought second thoughts. Another site was chosen, farther north still, in a mountain bowl between the rivers Kamogawa and Katsuragawa. In 794 it was made the capital and named Heian, the city of Peace and Tranquillity (no doubt in the hope that this is what it would prove to be).

To students of history the event is momentous. Heian is not just a place but also a label, marking the apogee of classical, aristocratic culture in Japan. Contemporaries, lacking foresight, presumably found the occasion more routine, the latest in a series of such decisions. It was not even thought to warrant the introduction of a new era-name (*nengō*). Enryaku, the name chosen when Kammu came to the throne in 781, remained in force until he died in 806.

The new city was a little larger than Nara, but in other respects the two were very similar: a grid of avenues and streets, divided into eastern and western quarters by a central avenue, which linked the northern palace precinct to the southern gate; no walls, except those which separated districts; a population largely employed in government. Both were modelled on Ch'ang-an, the capital of the T'ang, though on a smaller scale. Heian's buildings showed the same contrast between those in the Chinese style for the conduct of public business, their roofs green-tiled and supported on crimson pillars, and those for residential purposes, built of unpainted wood, thatched, or roofed in cryptomeria bark. There was a pleasure park south of the palace for the exclusive use of the court. Aristocratic residences, repeating the motif, had landscape gardens to the south of their open courtyards. Indeed, the most striking difference between the old and the new was the ban on Buddhist temples in Heian's centre, designed to reduce the religion's influence at court. It seems difficult to believe, if one looks at the city now.

Heian was to remain the emperor's home for over a thousand years. During that time many things changed. A number of 'detached' palaces were added, as refuges from fire and ritual pollution, or for the use of abdicated monarchs. Large commercial quarters developed, as artisans and tradesmen multiplied. Settlement spilt eastward across the initial boundaries along the banks of the Kamogawa, distorting the pattern of the grid. Even the name changed: long known informally as Kyoto, 'the capital city', this became its regular description from the eleventh century. All the same, for the first hundred years and more of its existence, Heian provided a familiar setting for the forms of government and culture that Japan had evolved in Nara. It was not until the tenth century, when the connection with China weakened, that they were seriously undermined.

The Fujiwara regents

During the first part of the Heian period (894–1185), power at court fell more and more into the hands of the Fujiwara house. The foundation of its political fortunes had been laid by Nakatomi no Kamatari. The part he played in the *coup d'état* that overthrew the Soga in 645, then in the reforms designed to strengthen the throne in the next two decades, ensured for his descendants the rank and imperial patronage that gave them access to high office. His son, Fubito, was the first to bear the name of Fujiwara. Fubito's sons, in turn, founded the family's four main branches, of which the northern house was to prove the most powerful. Fubito also married a daughter to the emperor Mommu. This both reinforced his own prestige and began a custom that was to last for centuries. Generation after generation of Fujiwara daughters were married into the imperial line, until a young emperor or heir to the throne was more likely than not to have one Fujiwara as father-in-law, another as maternal grandfather. While the court was still in Nara, the Fujiwara had begun to exploit these advantages to build up a network of 'clients' at various levels in the bureaucracy, making use of their access to the emperor through marriage ties to influence appointments. In addition, they established for themselves a strong position in the Council of State, through which they were able on most occasions to dominate the central government machine.

After the move to Heian, the emphasis changed. Early in the ninth century, the emperor Saga set up a private office within the palace to handle paperwork under his own supervision, following the example of several great noble houses, including the Fujiwara, who had developed such a machinery to deal with the complex affairs of their estates. A substantial amount of government business, concerning land rights and taxation, was diverted to these offices and thereby removed in part from the jurisdiction of the regular ministries. The Fujiwara were in a better position to profit from the device than either the emperor or the rest of the nobility. The emperor's actions were severely circumscribed by protocol. The Fujiwara, on the other hand, were not only the greatest of the noble houses, wealthier and more influential than their peers in rank, but also had 'family' standing in the affairs of the palace. Their position was formalised in 866, when Fujiwara Yoshifusa was made regent (Sesshō) to his grandson, the emperor Seiwa. This was the first time the post had been filled by someone not of royal blood. In 887 Yoshifusa's nephew and adopted son, Mototsune, completed this structure of familial control by creating a new office, that of Kampaku, to extend the powers of the regent into an emperor's adult life. Mototsune himself, having been Sesshō until then, became Kampaku. His descendants monopolised both posts until the Kamakura period (1185–1333), when they passed to other branches of the Fujiwara house.

Because they bypassed formal government institutions in this way, the Fujiwara had no need to replace the monarchy. Their example was later followed by feudal rulers, using different offices. Yet the regents did not rely exclusively on matrimonial influence and their undoubted skill in bureaucratic manipulation. They were ruthless, both in removing stubborn opponents – including emperors, if need be – and in persuading Fujiwara daughters into suitable marriages. They were ready to use force to gain their ends, though usually through bands of armed retainers, rather than private armies. It would be misleading, therefore, to treat them as no more than subtle and successful courtiers.

The most magnificent of them was Fujiwara Michinaga (966–1028), the story of whose life and times is told in an eleventh-century chronicle entitled *Eiga monogatari*, or The Tale of Splendour. Michinaga had luck: several senior nobles who might have challenged him for office died in an epidemic in 995, leaving him regent at the age of thirty. He also had four daughters, three of whom he married to emperors, one to a crown prince. At the zenith of his career, just after he took Buddhist holy orders in 1019, the retired emperor was his son-in-law, the reigning emperor was his grandson, the crown prince was both son-in-law and grandson. One of his Fujiwara sons succeeded him, first as Sesshō, then as Kampaku. Yet there is little in the chronicle about what he did with the power this eminence gave him, other than build a Buddhist monastery. Its dedication was a famous spectacle, recorded in detail. There was a performance of the lion dance and a procession of carefully chosen monks; spectators attended from the court in a veritable traffic jam of ox-drawn carriages; commoners, afraid of not getting near enough to see, went in even greater numbers on the day of rehearsal.

It was not to be expected that dignities of this kind could be won without opposition. Some of it stemmed from rivalries between branches of the Fujiwara house itself. Some – intermittently – marked attempts by the imperial family to resume a measure of control. One of these came under the emperors Uda and Daigo, following the death of Fujiwara Mototsune in 991. It centred on Sugawara Michizane, one of the few outstanding scholar-statesmen to emerge from Heian's education system, a man whose immediate ancestors, starting with only modest rank, had risen to a place of some distinction by dint of scholarly reputation and ability in office. So, at first, did Michizane himself. He held several minor posts after graduation from the university, all requiring a superior knowledge of Chinese; became professor of Chinese literature in 877; and was made governor of a province in 886. This was a bureaucratic career pattern, very Chinese in character, more than an aristocratic one. What changed it was that on his return to the capital he was chosen by the emperor Uda as a suitable recruit – able, and from a background likely to guarantee his loyalty to the throne – to take part in a move against the Fujiwara. Promoted well beyond his expectations, he was made Minister of the Right in 899, hence a member of the Council of State, an advancement almost unheard of for one of his birth. Yet it was not enough to make sure of victory over the Fujiwara. After Uda abdicated in 897, Michizane lost the certainty of royal support. In 901 he was accused of plotting against the new emperor, was stripped of office, and was sent to a post in Kyushu. This was tantamount to exile. Fujiwara pre-eminence was restored.

Michizane himself died in Kyushu in 903, an event followed by storms and earthquakes in the capital, which were blamed on his angry ghost. To appease it he was posthumously pardoned and advanced in rank. Forty years later a Shinto shrine was erected in his honour at Kitano in Kyoto. This most Confucian of senior ministers was therefore transformed into a *kami*, in which capacity he is now the patron to whom examination candidates appeal.

Later efforts to counter the influence of the Fujiwara were to carry greater weight, because they involved the emperor and his family more directly. The emperor was still central to the political system, after all, since it was in his name that government was carried on. Even the Fujiwara recognised the need to treat him with due ceremony and respect, at least in public. They found it convenient nevertheless to ensure that reigns were short, for once a ruler reached years of discretion he might well become less biddable. Abdication at an early age became the rule. Ten emperors had reigns that spanned the years from 858 to 986. Their average age when their reigns came to an end, whether by death or abdication, was a little less than thirty years. Their average age at death was forty-seven years. The interval between the two, where it occurred, was spent as a rule in Buddhist monasteries. Not all the abdications were voluntary. Some, indeed, are mysterious. The emperor Kazan, according to one account, simply disappeared from the palace one night in 986, to be discovered next day in a monastery (though a different version claims that he went there under Fujiwara escort).

Abdication was nevertheless a double-edged weapon for the regents, since it provided ex-emperors, if they had a mind to do so, with an opportunity to exploit the filial piety of their sons and successors. The first to make a significant move in that direction was Go-Sanjō* (r.1068–73), a rare non-Fujiwara monarch, who had reached the throne because of a lack of suitable Fujiwara candidates. As emperor, he began by taking steps to amass 'private' land rights for the imperial house itself, seeking to make it more independent of state revenue. He then abdicated, leaving his son, Shirakawa, to continue the process under his own supervision. Shirakawa abdicated in his turn in 1087 and lived until 1129. Both men remained politically active after abdication, building up a private administrative structure, known as the In-no-Chō, which was much like the house organs of the Fujiwara and other great families. It ran the family estates, handled the paperwork of land rights and tax exemption in consultation with the state bureaucracy, and created a body of officials of its own, some of whom also held posts in the formal government structure. In other words, the emperor's father, through the device of abdication, acquired a power base of much the same kind as the Fujiwara already possessed.

---

* The prefix Go- in Japanese reign-titles means 'the later'; thus Go-Sanjō is 'the later Sanjō'. Sanjō II would be the western equivalent. The same applies to some other famous emperors, such Go-Toba and Go-Daigo (Chapter 5).

There were thus two networks of 'private' authority in the capital during the later Heian years, one headed by an ex-emperor, the other by a Fujiwara regent or Kampaku. Both were backed by other elements within the aristocracy, both were engaged in constant rivalries, centring on the succession, or land rights, or appointments to office. Force was sometimes involved, used even against the emperor's person. In 1160, for example, in the course of the so-called Heiji disturbance, which became the subject of a well-known picture scroll, both the ex-emperor Go-Shirakawa and the emperor Nijō were seized by armed insurgents, acting for rival contestants, who were trying to bring about changes in senior appointments.

It is difficult to judge how far these political developments affected the capital's ruling class as a whole. Perhaps it was not a great deal. The lives of most of its members, after all, revolved around the regular bureaucracy. They were concerned with administration, not with policy or high politics; and since the established structure of government had been only bypassed under the Fujiwara, not abolished, there were still things for them to do. This was in any case a society in which 'place' counted for more than function. Both in and out of the workplace, human relations were wrapped in a web of etiquette, based on rigid distinctions of rank. A man's reputation, if one can trust the picture drawn by contemporary literature, depended less on competence in office than on the composition of graceful poetry, or skill in music and dancing. Poetry contests were taken very seriously. So were other polite accomplishments, like board games (*go* is one which has retained its popularity) and incense guessing. Outdoor pursuits – not for women, who were rarely expected to venture out of doors, except to visit temples and festivals – included highly ritualised forms of sport, like *kemari* (a kind of handball played with the feet) and mounted archery (*yabusame*). *Sumō* wrestling was a popular spectator sport, as it still is.

These have the appearance of occupations for a wealthy, leisured élite whose members had little by way of demanding duties to perform. The judgement may be a little harsh – the most vivid descriptions of Heian life were written by ladies of the court, who may well have ignored those parts of their menfolk's daily round from which they were themselves excluded – but one is certainly left with the impression of a world that was frivolous as well as status-bound. The capital had some of the characteristics of an aristocratic village: a limited human and geographical base, which made people and places familiar to almost everyone; strict codes of acceptable behaviour; a wealth of shared superstitions. Over it all presided an emperor, who was usually young, surrounded by respectful courtiers, but much overborne in matters of politics by both his father and his father-in-law. The atmosphere was exceedingly metropolitan. Provincial offices carried a rank one degree lower than their equivalents in central government. Being sent to one of them, even as governor, was to be sentenced to the wilderness. Indeed, to most of its inhabitants the very outskirts of Heian itself seemed distant and forbidding.

CHAPTER 3

Buddhism and Chinese Culture

Buddhism – as it evolved in India, before moving north and east – offered its believers in its simplest form a prospect of personal salvation: that is, an escape from the cycle of birth and rebirth in a world of suffering, to be achieved through prayer, scriptures and meditation. The immediate purpose was to free the individual from preoccupation with the self. This could most easily be pursued by abandoning the life of everyday temptation, in order to follow a better one in poverty, asceticism and monastic calm.

By the time the religion reached Japan from China, it had become a good deal more elaborate than this. Sects had developed, each emphasising particular forms of devotion, or certain parts of the Buddhist scriptures (sutras), or both. It had incorporated into its pantheon a multiplicity of figures, varied in type and origins: several manifestations of the Buddha, both historical and conceptual, which were credited with a range of different powers and qualities; bodhisattvas, who had reached the brink of Buddhahood themselves, but refrained from entering it in order to bring salvation to others; guardian devas and attendant demons, sometimes recruited from other religions. The motives for adopting it had also changed, at least for China's northern neighbours. To them, Buddhism had become a part of Chinese culture. It was therefore a symbol of civilisation and a passport to membership of an international élite of which China was the acknowledged focus. Beyond that, it was a powerful supernatural force – more so than gods of local origin – which could be called on to protect both rulers and their subjects from foreign attack, pestilence or natural disasters.

Buddhism and Shinto

In 552, or possibly 538, depending on which set of records one believes, the ruler of Paekche sent a Buddhist monk to Japan, bearing an image of Buddha and copies of sutras, to urge that the religion be adopted there. The proposal, when put to senior members of the court, precipitated conflict. The immigrant Soga clan, persuaded that the introduction of a Chinese religion would serve to gain favour with both China and its deities, urged acceptance, pointing out that Buddha was everywhere worshipped in the 'frontier lands', save only Japan. The Mononobe and Nakatomi, as spokesmen for the traditional religious values of Japan's agricultural community, objected that such action would offend the *kami*. The emperor, too, inclined to this view, since his own position as priest-king depended on the indigenous beliefs. He therefore ruled that the Soga be allowed to worship Buddha by way of trial, but only privately. The decision produced a battle of omens. A pestilence gave the Mononobe and Nakatomi grounds for having the Soga temple destroyed; a fire at the palace cast immediate doubt on the wisdom of this step; an epidemic swung the pendulum back again; imperial illness brought further consideration. The contest finally became involved in a succession dispute in 587, in which the Soga were victorious. Putting their own candidate on the throne, they were able thereafter to ensure that Buddhism had the patronage of the court.

Under Prince Shōtoku (Chapter 2) the spread of Buddhism was coupled with Chinese-style reforms of political institutions, designed to strengthen the central authority. There was much building of Buddhist temples and monasteries, employing Korean architects, Korean artists, and Korean and Chinese priests. Most of these establishments were placed close to the centres of power, and much official favour was shown to them. All this contributed to the monarchy's prestige. The Soga duly profited. Apparently aware of this advantage, the conspirators of 645, although they overthrew the Soga, did not attack the religion they had favoured. The emperor Kōtoku (r.645–54) was said in the chronicles to have 'honoured the religion of Buddha and despised the way of the *kami*' (*Nihon Shoki*). In 651 Buddhist ceremonies were held in his palace. In 652 lectures on Buddhism began there. Government supervision over priests, nuns, and their lands and buildings, instituted in 623, was scrupulously maintained. In the following century, the Yōrō Code made clerics subject to the civil law, not only for lay offences – bribery, drunkenness, brawling – but also for religious ones, such as the propagation of false doctrines. The only evident concession to their otherworldly status was that the penalties they suffered when convicted were less severe than those imposed on laymen.

By 741, when orders were given that at each provincial capital there must be a Buddhist temple, able to offer up prayers for the country's safety, Buddhism had the standing of a state religion in Japan, though it still shared that role with Shinto. One stated motive for the 741 decree was to give thanks for the protection that Buddha had afforded during a smallpox epidemic. In 743 the emperor gave further evidence of his gratitude in another decree, announcing that a great bronze statue of the Buddha Vairocana was to be built and installed at Nara. In 749, accompanied by ministers and senior court officials, he attended a ceremony at the newly completed Tōdaiji there, which was to house it, in order to celebrate the discovery of gold deposits in northern Japan, which were enough for the statue's gilding. The emperor expressed humility, describing himself as Buddha's 'servant', even his 'slave'; but almost immediately afterwards he addressed a rescript to the court, announcing rewards and honours to mark the event, in which he attributed Japan's good fortune with respect to gold, not only to Buddha, but also to 'the guidance and grace of the gods that dwell in Heaven and the gods that dwell on Earth': that is, to the two principal categories of *kami*. His own function as priest-king, it appears, could not be held to rely exclusively on an alien religion.

Buddhism, after all, remained essentially Chinese. Most of its senior figures, both men and women, had come to Japan from China or Korea. Its scriptures were written in Chinese. Its priests, if they were to be given proper ordination, had to receive it from these new arrivals, or go to China to the centres of their faith. The sects established in Japan were all Chinese in origin. The Hossō sect, which possessed two of Nara's most famous temples, the Kōfukuji, endowed in honour of Nakatomi Kamatari, and the Hōryūji, founded by Prince Shōtoku, had been introduced from China by a Japanese monk who had studied there in the seventh century. The Ritsu sect had invited a well-known Chinese monk, Ganjin (Chien-chen), to come to Japan to establish a seat of ordination in 753. It was many years and many adventures before he got there – he arrived in Kyushu at his sixth attempt – but he eventually practised ordination in Nara at Tōdaiji, before transferring to Tōshōdaiji, where his Chinese disciples succeeded him as abbots.

Tōdaiji was the headquarters of the Kegon sect, so named after the Kegon Sutra, the basic tenet of which is that the historical Buddha (Sakyamuni, known in Japanese as Shaka) is a manifestation of the supreme and universal Buddha, Vairocana, and is himself manifested in lesser Buddhas in a myriad worlds. The concept is represented visually in many statues and paintings, showing Vairocana seated on a lotus flower with a thousand petals, each petal a universe, on each petal a Buddha. Perhaps because one could see in this imagery a parallel with the temporal power, Kegon received special favour from the Japanese court. The great bronze Buddha at Tōdaiji, known throughout Japan as the Nara Daibutsu, became one of the country's principal Buddhist monuments.

All the sects established at Nara were courtly and scholastic, doing little to attract those members of the population who lacked Chinese linguistic skills. With the move to Heian, from which these sects were largely excluded, something of broader appeal began to emerge. In 804 the monk Saichō (767–822) was given permission to travel to China with one of Japan's official missions, in order to complete his studies of the Tendai (T'ien-t'ai) sect and secure accreditation from it. He returned in 805 to found a sect of that name in Japan. Its senior temple, Enryakuji, was built on Mount Hiei, dominating Heian's northern outskirts. From there it could protect the capital from evil spirits (and intervene on occasions in the city's politics, as later events were to show). Tendai doctrines were based on the Lotus Sutra (*Hokke-kyō*), which taught the central importance of a single universal Buddha; but it also recognised the need for faith in the bodhisattva, Kannon, and endorsed the practice of meditation, as well as giving heed to various forms of esoteric Buddhism. As a result, Tendai became an eclectic core from which other major sects were eventually to break away.

No less influential was Saichō's contemporary, Kūkai (774–835). He, too, went to China in 804, but he stayed until 806, studying the Shingon (True Word) teachings, which had been recently introduced into China from southern India. They focused on the universal Buddha, Mahavairocana (Dainichi in Japanese), rather than on Sakyamuni; but the sect's most notable characteristic was its concern with magic and esoteric rituals, using mantras (secret verbal formulae) and mandalas (diagrams setting out concepts of the Buddhist world) for purposes of worship and exposition. On his return to Japan, Kūkai established himself and his followers on Mount Koya to the south of the Nara plain. From there he exercised a distant but significant influence on the court. This was partly because courtiers had already acquired a taste for ritual and magic in other contexts, but it was not unrelated, perhaps, to the fact that they looked on Kūkai as one of themselves. He was of aristocratic birth, wealthy enough to have given a feast for 500 monks when ordained in China. He was also a scholar and poet of some reputation. Among his writings there is a wide-ranging survey of Chinese and Indian religious thought, as well as a detailed and systematic account of the rules for composing Chinese verse.

It is clear, therefore, that China exercised as much of an influence on Japanese religion as it did on the country's political institutions. For many centuries, in fact, the *kami* were reduced in the national context to secondary standing. Buddhism had had ample experience of coming to terms with the worship of local gods in the course of its passage through Central and Southeast Asia. *Kami*, which were multifarious but inchoate, posed no new problem; and since the two religions were concerned for the most part with different areas of religious and human experience, a form of co-existence was soon established between them. Within the palace, emperors had a Buddhist chapel for their personal use, but took part in Shinto ceremonials at their enthronement and on other suitable occasions, such as rice planting and harvest. Both kinds of priest were expected to invoke the help of their respective gods in times of trouble.

The first public sign of a more far-reaching relationship came with the inauguration of the Nara Tōdaiji in 749. In 747 the court had appealed for intercession with the *kami* on behalf of the work being carried out there. The priests of the Usa shrine in northern Kyushu, which was dedicated to Hachiman, a *kami* linked by tradition with the emperor Ōjin, not only responded promptly to this appeal, but also carried the symbolic presence of their deity in procession to Nara, in order that he might become the temple's guardian when it was complete. The practice was extended in later years to many other temples and monasteries, which received *kami* to protect their precincts and *torii* (shrine gates) to mark their entrances. More immediately, it brought material benefits to the Usa Hachimangu. The shrine was raised to high court rank, a device used previously to bestow state subsidy and tax advantages on certain Buddhist houses. Hachiman himself was later recognised as a bodhisattva.

These initiatives opened the way for Buddhist priests to take part in Shinto rites, a practice that was given official approval in

759. From this it was only a short step to asserting that the *kami* were manifestations of Buddhas or bodhisattvas, a claim of the kind that had been advanced in China to link Confucius with Vairocana. The first such reference to *kami* was made in general terms in a document of 859. In 937 the doctrine was applied for the first time to a specific *kami* (Hachiman). By the Middle Ages there are references to Hachiman as an avatar of Amida (Amitabha) and to Amaterasu as an avatar of Dainichi (Mahavairocana, whose Sanskrit name means Great Sun).

The relationship between Buddhism and Shinto outside the metropolitan area developed differently. As Buddhism slowly penetrated the countryside, the belief spread that *kami*, like humans, were unenlightened beings, condemned to their present state because of their actions in other lives: that is, by karma. They sought enlightenment in the Buddhist manner, but their sufferings and frustrations on the path towards it were given vent meanwhile in malevolent uses of miraculous powers – in earthquakes, floods, pestilence and crop failures – to the evident discomfort of their human neighbours. Instead, therefore, of setting the shrines of *kami* as guardians at the gates of Buddhist houses, it was better to establish Buddhist temples at or near Shinto shrines, so as to help both the *kami* and the local inhabitants in this situation. The Hachimangu at Usa was one of the first to benefit from this arrangement, but eventually such *jingū-ji*, or 'shrine-temples', as they were called, numbered many thousands.

In this way, Buddhism emerged as the senior partner in something like a symbiosis between the two religions. In the legal codes (*ritsuryō*) each had a separate section, but in less formal contexts the distinction between them was anything but clear. Like Shinto, Buddhism acquired shamans, healers and diviners, despite some official disapproval. Shinto for its part contributed a range of rites and gestures to ward off evil or misfortune that seem to have been common to both. Ennin, a distinguished Buddhist monk, who was later to be abbot of Tendai's Enryakuji, when seeking to ensure a safe voyage home from China in 839, engaged the services of a Shinto diviner and himself made offerings to two

47

kami, the god of Sumiyoshi, who was the patron of seafarers, and the Dragon King of the Sea. If even learned clerics behaved like this, treating Buddhas, bodhisattvas and *kami* as members of a single pantheon, it is easy to see why others made little distinction between them.

Tribute missions and Chinese learning

The urge to acquire a greater knowledge of both Buddhism and Chinese political institutions was a principal motive for the missions that Japan sent to China between 607 and 838–9. There were nineteen of these, an average of one every twelve years, though the intervals were in fact irregular. They were of considerable size: two ships carrying 250 men in the early years, rising to twice that many in the eighth century. Activity on this scale shows how highly they were valued by the state. So does the fact that the voyages were carried on despite considerable dangers. Japanese ships, flat-bottomed and depending largely on oars, were not entirely suitable for long and often stormy passages across the East China Sea (the route that had to be followed once the coast of Korea was made politically inhospitable by the rise of Silla). Nor were their commanders well informed about the conditions they would encounter. Many ships were wrecked; others had to turn back; nearly a third of the travellers who set out from Japan in the Nara period seem never to have returned. In 752 the senior envoy, having reached China, chose not to face the voyage home. In 838 several senior members of the mission, having twice tried without success to reach the China coast, pleaded illness to avoid another attempt. They were punished.

The majority of those who made up the members of one of these expeditions were seamen, guards and attendants, who were not in a position to contribute greatly to Japan's knowledge of the Chinese world. They were not permitted as a rule to go beyond their port of arrival. At the other end of the social scale were the envoy and his deputy, men of high rank, chosen for their literary reputation, who were accompanied by several other senior officials as councillors, plus interpreters in Chinese and Korean, diviners, doctors, a painter and scribes. A troupe of musicians completed the party, no doubt to add to its dignity. The ambassador and his entourage were entertained at China's expense once they reached the Yangtse region, travelling to the capital, Ch'ang-an, where they were housed in the state lodgings set aside for foreign envoys. While there they presented formal greetings from their emperor, together with suitable 'tribute' gifts; took part in various ceremonies at the court; then set out for home bearing Chinese gifts – more valuable than those they had brought – together with the books, paintings, images and other objects they had been able to collect.

These elements of the mission can be described as diplomatic relations, rather than personal study, though some of the envoys pursued what enquiries they could into the procedures of the Chinese court or the nature of Buddhist and Confucian doctrine. More detailed investigations were left to their staff. The painter was expected to copy pictures and sketch images. The doctor took the opportunity to enhance his understanding of Chinese medicine. One member of the mission of 838–9 paid what appears to have been a staggering amount (in gold) for lessons in the playing of the lute (*biwa*) from a famous Chinese teacher.

There were also Japanese students and student-priests, who were not part of the envoy's diplomatic entourage, but whose studies had official sponsorship. Their numbers were fairly small, but as they often stayed in China for a number of years, receiving a stipend from the Chinese government if what they proposed to do had its approval, they added much greater depth to their country's knowledge of China and its culture. Their careers, too, were likely to benefit, more so, as far as one can judge, than those of the officials. Two such students who went with the mission of 608, one layman and one priest, having remained in China for thirty years, returned to become advisers on reform to those who carried out the *coup d'état* of 645. Another, Kibi no

Mabiki, who went in 717, stayed for seventeen years; became head of Nara university and lecturer to the court on the Chinese classics; went to China again as vice-ambassador in 752; and ended by becoming a senior minister. Among the clerics, we have already had occasion to mention Saichō and Kūkai, who came back to Japan to found two major Buddhist sects in the early ninth century. All these are exceptional cases, of course, which is why they are well known, but there are many more who became technical experts or respected scholars at a rather more modest level of achievement.

A smaller contribution to Japanese knowledge was made by Chinese and other foreign missions coming to Kyushu, or even to Nara and Heian. The Chinese ones were a formal recognition of tribute status, valued for the gifts they brought, but not particularly educational. Those from Korea and other nearby states, described in the Japanese chronicles as bringing tribute from their rulers, were chiefly an excuse for trade. Trade, in fact, once established, was to continue in the hands of Chinese and Korean merchants long after the tribute missions came to an end. It was principally in goods for which the missions had created a demand: medicines, perfumes, silks, damasks and brocades from China, plus some books and paintings; metalwork, cosmetics, honey and ginseng from Korea; skins, including those of bears and a kind of tiger, from Parhae, a kingdom on the Manchurian border. The returns were silk floss and the simpler textiles: that is, the same items that were sent by Japan as 'tribute' to China.

The impact of these relationships on Japan was very varied. A report by a returning ambassador in 719 prompted a revision of Japanese court dress in the most recent Chinese style; another a century later led to reforms in protocol. Since many of the imports were luxury goods, the first choice of which went to the imperial house and members of its court, they served to make the atmosphere of the capital more Chinese and contribute to a more 'civilised' way of life. In 756 the empress Kōmyō donated to the Tōdaiji the treasures collected by her late husband, the emperor Shōmu. They became the nucleus of a famous collection, housed in the Shōsōin. Among them were a Chinese New Year card, an ivory foot-rule, several mirrors, musical instruments, medicines and medicine jars, weapons, personal ornaments, combs, a Korean ink-stick, a glass bowl and cup, carpets, clothing, Chinese shoes, trays, spoons, even an iron ceremonial plough. All were of mainland origin, demonstrating, it has been said, that Japan was by this time the Silk Road's eastern terminal.

For Japanese who stayed at home, an understanding of China and its institutions rested more on the books the envoys brought home than on the kind of objects to be found in the Shōsōin. A catalogue of Chinese texts available in Japan in 891 lists over 1,700 titles, their subject-matter ranging from the Confucian classics, legal codes, ceremonial and protocol to medicine, divination and calendars, history and poetry. With the help of explanations from officials, doctors, priests and scholars who had been to China, plus Koreans and Chinese settled in Japan, these were to be the basis for a massive adoption of Chinese culture.

Not all of it was directly related to Buddhism and the power of the state, though these were central to it. Buddhist monks, like western missionaries of a later era, brought with them much more than the tenets of their faith. As scholars they expounded Confucian philosophy. When Japan's first state university was established in 647, it was a Korean priest who was made head of it. As men of education, priests also had some understanding of mathematics (for temple building and land measurement), of irrigation (for the management of estates) and of medicine. They painted pictures and wrote poems. Their religion itself was highly literate, so teaching Chinese was almost a pastoral duty.

It is difficult to be sure how widely Confucianism spread in Japan in these early centuries, but there can be little doubt that conformity with its ethical code, at least outwardly, was expected of officials in Nara and Heian, as it was in Ch'ang-an. Confucian doctrine held that human society mirrored the relationship between Heaven and Earth; that right behaviour was required to ensure a proper balance between the two; and that behaviour in turn was a product of self-cultivation, disciplined by education.

The sons of Japanese officials were trained in these ideas, together with some relevant skills, at the Nara university. After preliminary study of the Chinese language, they were expected to acquire a thorough knowledge of the Confucian classics and an acquaintance with the kind of practical mathematics that they might have to use in keeping tax records or supervising public works. In 728 the syllabus was expanded to include Chinese literature and law, which quickly became the most popular of its courses.

Students from families holding the fifth court rank and above, who qualified for admittance to the university at the age of thirteen, were guaranteed entry to an official career without the need to pass examinations. Those below that rank needed permission to enrol, followed by success in one of the four grades of examination, in order to obtain a post in the bureaucracy. We have some idea of what these tests required, since one of the imperial anthologies of Chinese poetry, published in 827, includes, rather surprisingly, a number of specimen examination papers, together with typical answers. The questions were philosophical, calling for essays comparing Buddhism and Confucianism, or commenting on the relative weight that should be attached to the virtues of loyalty and filial piety, if the two conflicted (a standard Confucian dilemma). The answers, equally abstract, were stereotyped statements of Confucian truths, exhibiting rhetoric more than logic. A Chinese examiner would have found them wholly familiar.

By the tenth century, the influence of the university was on the wane. Undermined by the creation of private academies for the sons of the high-born, its reputation declined still further as its professorships became hereditary and its graduates found their way into nothing more than routine posts. The Chinese ideal, in fact, was proving weaker than Japan's devotion to the privileges of birth.

Problems also arose in another field of state-supported learning, that of calendrical astronomy. In China, because the idea was accepted that heavenly portents were an indication of the monarch's virtue, and hence his right to rule, the study of calendars and the movements of the heavenly bodies was entrusted to a well-staffed and highly regarded department of officialdom. In Japan a supposedly similar body was established in the *ritsuryō* structure, but its achievements were not strictly comparable. In the first place, its name, the Yin–Yang Bureau, implied that astrology and fortune telling were an important part of its duties. In addition, its staff seem never to have acquired a sufficient grasp of the necessary mathematics to be able to make their own corrections to the lunar calendar, especially its adjustment to solar time. The Chinese calendars that had come into use during the Nara and early Heian periods continued in force without amendment once official relations with China came to an end after 839, becoming more and more inaccurate with the passage of time; the headship of the bureau, like similar posts in the university, became hereditary; and the bureau's principal task in its later years was the preparation of an annual almanac, setting out such information as the dates of spring and autumn equinoxes, summer and winter solstices, and solar and lunar eclipses, together with the times of sunrise and sunset. All these had ritual or magical importance. To them were added personal fortune telling for each day, plus notes about lucky and unlucky directions and taboos, drawn variously from Buddhist, Taoist and Yin–Yang sources. This was something less dignified than the office in Ch'ang-an would have thought appropriate.

Another institute in the *ritsuryō* system dealt with the teaching and practice of Chinese medicine, primarily for the benefit of the court. Both treatment and pharmacopoeia were based on knowledge first brought to Japan by Korean and Chinese doctors, who were invited there in and after the mid-sixth century, but this was later supplemented by the studies of two Japanese Buddhist priests, who went to China with the mission of 608, as well as by what the doctors attached to subsequent missions learnt. Acupuncture, moxibustion (cauterisation of the skin), massage and exorcism all found their way into Japanese medical treatment in this way, as did various forms of tantric magic. Drugs were imported from both China and Korea, though substitutes for some of them were eventually found in Japan and listed in Japanese publications on *materia medica*. By contrast, Japanese doctors do not seem to have acquired a full understanding of Chinese pathological theory until much later in history.

There is a parallel here with the failure to grasp the underlying principles of astronomy and mathematics for use in calendar making, which suggests a greater concern with the practical aspects of Chinese science and technology than with its fundamentals. One is reminded of the attitude of a group of Japanese students, sent to London in 1867, who complained at being given a general western-style education, when what they had come for was a technical training. They wanted to master 'particular arts and sciences', they said, not 'to be called an educated man'. For them, as, perhaps, for Japanese going to China earlier, more 'useful' and less time-consuming studies had advantages.

Literature, art, music

Japan's adoption of the Chinese script as a means of writing texts in Japanese, which happened at a very early date, greatly complicated the language. Japanese is polysyllabic and highly inflected. Chinese is monosyllabic and tonal. To combine the two was inherently clumsy. By the tenth century, the situation had been a little improved by the development in Japan of a phonetic syllabary (*kana*) from the cursive forms of certain Chinese ideographs, which could be used instead of ideographs to indicate such things as tenses or the positive and negative forms of verbs; but even so, Chinese loan-words and phrases remained embedded here and there in Japanese sentences, pronounced either in an approximation to that of the Chinese original, or as if they were the Japanese polysyllabic words of similar meaning. As many generations of students can testify, the result is not a language of the utmost clarity. Perhaps for that reason it has been most successfully employed in producing poetry, religious exhortations or popular literature. Other kinds of written statement – laws, histories, scriptures, commentaries, land records – have until modern times been made for preference in Chinese, still the country's classical language. There were, for example, six 'national histories' in Chinese, starting with the *Nihon Shoki*, all organised as chronicles in the Chinese manner and providing a continuous record down to 887. Japanese also showed a taste for massive documentary collections in Chinese, covering a range of subjects from history, law and politics to Buddhist exegesis. The tradition has continued, though not always in Chinese.

As men of culture, Japan's government officials for many centuries followed the example of their Chinese counterparts in writing poetry in Chinese. Po Chü-i became their favourite model, once a knowledge of his works was brought back by the mission of 838–9, but as early as 751, the date of a volume entitled *Kaifūsō*, the court began to publish anthologies of Chinese poems, written chiefly by its members. Most of the contributions were formal, sometimes elegant, comments on 'serious' themes like Buddhism and philosophy, or occasional poems for banquets and other such celebrations. They were not highly regarded by those Chinese who came to know of them. A collection made by a Chinese merchant in Japan at the beginning of the eleventh century, taken back to China and presented at an imperial audience, was described, according to the *Sung shu*, as polished, but 'shallow and of no merit'.

In the ninth century, the writing of Chinese verse seems for a time to have stifled an earlier and more vigorous tradition of poetry in Japanese. Ballads and folk-songs are to be found scattered throughout the *Kojiki* and similar texts, written down in the Chinese script, but otherwise entirely Japanese in language. They set the pattern for two enduring habits. One was that of inserting verse into prose narratives, both historical and fictional. The other was the writing of poems in a 'pure' form of Japanese, rarely using Chinese loan-words.

The habit of writing court poetry in Japanese is best represented in the first and most famous of Japanese anthologies, *Manyōshū*, a collection deriving mostly from the seventh and early eighth centuries, which contained more than 4,500 poems. The great majority of these were 'short' poems (*tanka*) of thirty-one syllables, arranged in lines of 5–7–5–7–7, a format which became so universally popular as to be called *waka*, 'Japanese poems'. There were also a number of longer compositions (*chōka*), as well as some in Chinese. *Tanka* were already by this date a highly developed poetic tradition, graceful, perceptive, focused on human relationships, though too brief to sustain extended themes. The imagery is sharp, often brilliantly evocative. The subject-matter, unlike that of most contemporary Chinese verse in Japan, dwelt much on personal experience, ranging from sexual love to the pains of parting and separation and death. A modern scholar has pointed out that of 145 poems written by Japanese envoys sent to Silla, two-thirds are devoted to thoughts of home and the families they left behind.

There is a freshness about the poems in the *Manyōshū* that one does not always find in later compilations. In the latter, emotion is not infrequently reduced to sentimentality, or else appears as a mannered melancholia. Long poems, too, became rare, reducing the variety and diluting the emotion. The *chōka* in *Manyōshū* – there is one on poverty and another on the death of a child which particularly come to mind – conveyed a much greater depth of feeling than is commonly found in *tanka*.

The sharp distinction between a Chinese and a Japanese style that is manifest in poetry does not occur in visual art at this early date. Shinto, though the simplicity of line and colour that characterised its shrines had a lasting effect on Japanese architecture, did not favour at first the representation of gods and priests, whether in paintings or statues. As a result, depiction of the human figure was overwhelmingly Buddhist, or else Chinese and derivative. It had a degree of variety, because there were a number of Buddhist styles of different geographical origin, but since orthodoxy claimed the right to make rules for the visual image as well as religious faith, there was little room for something distinctively Japanese.

Much of the earliest Buddhist art, especially statuary, was the work of immigrants or their immediate descendants. This makes it difficult at times to distinguish between pieces made in Japan and those that came from abroad, except by reference to their materials. Many of the bronzes made by the new arrivals show clear Korean influence, as one would expect; but since Korea owed much to China, as China did in turn to other parts of Asia, even indirectly to Greece, what entered Japan was already diverse in origin. It also required a mastery of the technology of casting, which was not easily won. By 749 it had been sufficiently acquired to make possible the casting – after several unsuccessful attempts – of the Tōdaiji's Buddha, 16 metres high and using 400 tons of bronze, but on a smaller scale artists often worked in wood and dry lacquer. This was not only cheaper, but also more likely to produce a graceful line. The pieces they produced, especially those in which lacquer was applied over a frame of hollow wood or cloth, then sometimes coloured, were much more naturalistic than the early bronzes. They were also more 'contemporary' by the standards of the T'ang, whose artists had largely abandoned the archaic styles that Japan had first derived from the mainland. Many of those now working in Japan, after all, came directly from China. The Tōshōdaiji has both wood and lacquer statues of Buddhas and their guardians, made by Chinese disciples of the founder, Ganjin (Chien-chen). There is also a notable one of Ganjin himself, said to date from 763.

Once the capital moved to Heian, the Nara artists had to rely more on the patronage of Buddhist houses than of the imperial court. This encouraged them to produce statues in wood in the manner of the Tōshōdaiji studio, rather than the more expensive (and pretentious) bronze. Much of their work consisted of standing figures, carved from single tree trunks, hollowed at the back to prevent the material from splitting, and touched with paint to colour the eyes, lips and hair. An innovation was the occasional appearance of statues of *kami*, perhaps reflecting the growing assimilation of Japan's two main religions. For example, in the guardian shrine attached to the Yakushiji there is a figure of

Hachiman, dressed as a Buddhist monk and accompanied by a very matronly empress Jingū.

The paintings of these centuries have proved less durable than the statues, but enough survives to show that they, too, were very continental in manner and inspiration. The Hōryūji temple complex provides some of the best examples. After its main hall was burnt down in 670, it was rebuilt and decorated with murals, apparently by artists of Korean or Chinese origin, using imported pigments. These murals were themselves destroyed by fire in 1949, except for a small section that had been removed for repair, but by that time the paintings had been well enough recorded and reproduced for it still to be possible to study them. They consisted of four main panels, depicting the paradises associated, respectively, with the Buddhas Shaka, Amida, Miroku and Yakushi, plus portraits of bodhisattvas and heavenly guardians. The Hōryūji also has a portable shrine, dating from the middle of the seventh century, on which Buddhist scenes in several Chinese styles are painted in oils on lacquered cypress panels.

Another Buddhist theme, stimulated by the paintings that Kūkai brought back from China in 806, was the mandala. Typically, this depicted the Buddhist pantheon, in an arrangement showing the Buddha Dainichi at the centre, surrounded by other Buddhas and bodhisattvas in concentric circles or ordered rows. The design was intended to emphasise Dainichi's centrality to the faith; and because the preparation of such a painting was conceived to be a religious act – the imagery was held to embody the deities themselves – it was carried out by monks trained in painting, not by the lay craftsmen employed by religious houses for other kinds of work. An outstanding example is the interior decoration of the five-storey pagoda of the Shingon sect's Daigoji, erected in 952 on the southwest outskirts of Heian.

There must have been a great deal of painting in Nara of which we now have no record at all. Apart from what was being done in temples and monasteries, there was a Painters' Bureau, established by the state in 728 to supervise and execute the decoration of public buildings, which had a staff of four master painters and sixty assistants, plus others who were recruited to carry out particular commissions. Each man seems to have pursued his own task, either working on outline or filling in colour; but as the buildings on which these skills were exercised have since been rebuilt or destroyed, we have no identifiable examples by which to judge the method's effectiveness. Indeed, what pictures we do have from this period we owe almost entirely to their preservation by the great religious establishments. The inventory of items in Tōdaiji's Shōsōin, for example, includes twenty-one screens, showing landscapes and scenes of palace life, or depicting birds and plants, all in the Chinese manner. Only one is now extant, a painting of a group of Chinese ladies. Yakushiji has a picture of a Buddhist goddess, dating from 771–2, which from its appearance could easily be the portrait of a T'ang court lady, while four parts survive of an eighth-century picture scroll (*e-maki*) of the Sutra of Causes and Effects (*E-ingakyō*). This is a Japanese copy of a Chinese original, telling the life of the historical Buddha, Sak-yamuni (Shaka). Landscape, buildings and costume are all very Chinese, but there are traces of Japaneseness in the faces and attitudes of the human figures in part of one scroll.

Music, which was closely linked to dance, was equally Chinese. Musicians are recorded as having arrived in Japan from the mainland as early as the fifth century, bringing with them a variety of instruments, but we know little of what they performed. In the seventh century a type of dance-drama, called *gigaku*, said to have originated in southern China, was introduced into Japan from Paekche. The dancers wore masks, some of which, preserved in the Hōryūji and Shōsōin, are thought to represent non-Chinese Asians as seen by the Chinese: they have long noses and the kind of facial expressions given to Buddhist demons in statues and paintings. Their dancing was accompanied by flute, cymbal and drums, but as there have been no performances of *gigaku* since the seventeenth century, not enough is known of either the dance or the music to reconstruct them with confidence.

Fortunately, this is not true of *gagaku*, the music that accompanies another kind of dance, *bugaku*. Both are still performed by court musicians and dancers in the imperial palace and at certain festivals. There are two styles, one associated with Korea, the other with China and Southeast Asia, as well as some elements attributed to Shinto ritual music of very early date. The corpus, which was assembled by the state's Office of Music in the Heian period, is therefore eclectic, like so much else in the ancient culture of Japan. The dancers are men, wearing rich costumes, predominantly in red (China) and green (Korea); the orchestra includes a wider range of percussion, wind and string instruments than are used in *gigaku* (it includes the *biwa*, thought to be of Persian origin); and the tempo is slow, though it may well have been faster in Nara and early Heian.

Enough has been said in this chapter to show how extensive was the influence of China and Korea on Japanese art and culture in the seventh, eighth and ninth centuries. Together they created the country's 'classical' tradition, which proved to be both pervasive and enduring. Even so, as contacts with China became unofficial and less frequent in and after the tenth century, so Chinese ideas and Chinese styles became less powerful in Japan, making room for others, notionally 'Japanese', to take their place beside them. It was in this phase that the country developed a distinctive Sino-Japanese culture of its own.

CHAPTER 4

The Ebbing of the Chinese Tide

The T'ang dynasty was overthrown in 907. For the next fifty years China was divided into several competing states, which were not brought together under a single ruler until the first Sung emperor came to power in 960. That event was the start of a new phase in Chinese history. The capital was moved to Kaifeng. Thereafter, government came to rely much less on landowning aristocrats than in the past, its principal officials recruited from less affluent – and less independent – 'gentry'. Commerce grew rapidly, towns became larger and more wealthy. Against that background there developed an age of cultural brilliance, in which the importance of Buddhism declined, but philosophy, painting and the making of porcelain flourished.

The tenth century was also a turning-point for Japan, though for the most part in a contrary direction. The spectacle of China in disarray did nothing to reinforce the country's Chinese-style monarchy and political institutions, faced by an aristocratic challenge from the Fujiwara and their allies (Chapter 2). In addition, the Nara land allocation system, designed to bolster the imperial authority, fell more and more into decay. Public land gave way to private land, greatly to the advantage of the nobility and the main religious houses, a process carried out chiefly through the creation of a number of large, amorphous private estates (*shōen*). At the local level these sustained a class of landed warriors, who in time were to pose a threat, not only to the monarchy, but also to the civilian aristocracy of the court.

As the influence of China grew weaker in political life, so it did in culture. The end of tribute missions to the mainland in the closing years of the T'ang, itself a symptom of changing circumstance, reduced the flow of knowledge to Japan (Chapter 3). Though trade continued, and Buddhism itself stayed strong, Japanese literature and art no longer looked to China with the same deference as before. The loosening of the bond, in turn, enabled cultural skills and preferences of indigenous origin to emerge, or in some cases re-emerge, with the result that by the twelfth century there was, if not a reaction against things Chinese, at least a detectable change of direction in cultural development. What had once been overwhelmingly Chinese was becoming Sino-Japanese, a hybrid.

Public land, private land

Under the Nara codes, all land belonged in theory to the emperor, to be distributed and taxed by officials acting in his name. Some was granted to the state's own servants in the ruling class in accordance with their rank and office. Some was earmarked for the support of shrines and temples. All other irrigated rice-land was allotted to the cultivators on the basis of household size, men receiving more than women, free persons more than slaves. These allocations were to be reviewed every six years, that is, two years after each population census; and in the interval between revisions the fields, known as *kubunden*, could not be transferred by sale or inheritance. They were subject to tax. So was all rank-land, as well as the office-land of local officials, though the office-land of provincial and central officials remained tax-free. Shrines and temples were not required to pay tax on their holdings.

Land tax, amounting to about 3 or 4 per cent of the crop, was not in itself a very heavy burden, but cultivators also faced other imposts. They were required when called upon to serve as conscripts (one man per household), equipped at their household's expense. They had to provide labour for public works on sixty days a year. In periods of distress they qualified for loans of seed-rice from the authorities, but as these were repayable at harvest time at rates of interest between 30 and 50 per cent, they were not an unmixed blessing. The poorest, in fact, especially in the provinces closest to the capital, where official supervision was more strict, were tempted in times of hardship to abandon their holdings and seek alternative means of livelihood, either by farming in remoter regions or as hired labourers in the capital. This was held to be against the interests of the state. A decree of 893 ordered the capture and return of peasants escaping to the northern provinces, but measures such as this did not prevent a shortage of labour on many of the labour-intensive irrigated fields. It was made worse from time to time by epidemics of measles and smallpox – a by-product, it appears, of relations with the mainland – which produced sharp fluctuations of population in affected areas.

In an attempt to maintain the country's tax base, the Council of State sought inducements to keep farmers on the land. In 723 it ruled that land reclaimed by restoring an abandoned irrigation system could be held without reallocation for a single generation, while land brought under cultivation for the first time could be kept for three generations. By this provision farmers were offered some hope of gain from efforts to improve their land. It was not enough, however. Another decree in 743 provided that newly reclaimed land could be held in perpetuity: that is, could be passed to the developer's heirs. This in effect created a right of private property in land.

The principle of public ownership was also being undermined in other ways. The majority of households, being of fairly stable size and composition, were entitled to much the same amount of land at each reallocation. This being so, officials found it simpler to let them have the same fields, which eventually came to be considered theirs by custom. Moreover, as the bureaucracy struggled with the system's manifold complexities, reallocation was often carried out late, or took place at more extended intervals, possibly not at all. After about 800 the redistribution of land required by the law became infrequent and irregular. At the same time, tax officials were becoming lax about forwarding revenue to the central government.

It was in these circumstances that there emerged private landed estates. The regulations under which it was permitted to bring new land into production, then retain it outside the *kubunden*, favoured developers who had status and resources: religious houses, both national and regional; members of the nobility, usually acting through agents; and men of substance in the locality, who might themselves be minor officials. After all, it was necessary first to acquire land for development, often by purchase. This done, the land had to be cleared and an irrigation system built, a task requiring a substantial labour force (usually recruited by hiring peasants from nearby areas, who might become cultivators on the new estate when the operation was completed). The final step was to register the land as privately held. This involved lodging documents with the relevant local and central offices – a task, like the rest, which would not be easy for smallholders, acting alone.

It is usual to translate the word *shōen*, the name given to these estates, as 'manor', but this suggests a greater unity of landholding and ownership than was in fact the case. The nature of *shōen* depended a good deal on local conditions, but there was usually some kind of tax-free nucleus, deriving either from the status of the nominal developer (a senior court official, a shrine or temple, perhaps) or from a specific permit issued by the government. To obtain the latter would in any case require the intervention of a powerful court family or religious order as a rule. The nucleus was likely then to be expanded by commendation: other local landholders, in the hope of sharing the tax-free privilege, or of receiving comparable benefits, such as office within the *shōen*, would join their own parcels of land to the estate, though not all these would be made tax-free. In this way, a number of different people came to have a variety of interlocking rights in the land. These were known as *shiki*, which usually comprised a percentage of the crop. The cultivator had a customary share, which his descendants could inherit. So did the first developer of the new land, usually called the proprietor (*ryōke*), who might not be resident, if he had other holdings of any size. Further shares went to estate officials, often agents of the proprietor, or men of some standing who had commended their land to him. Finally there was a 'patron' (*honke*): that is, a noble or religious house with influence in the capital, whose function it was to provide political protection. The patron, too, was entitled to a share.

By the end of the Heian period, a *shōen* typically had at its centre a house and land held personally by the senior estate official. Its cultivators owed him both dues and labour. The rest of the land, larger in area, was that of the proprietor. The cultivators resident on it were divided into the relatively well-to-do, part of whose land was worked for them by others, possibly transients, and the smallholders, dependent on family labour. The more affluent households were likely to include a number of menials (*genin*), who were virtually slaves.

The rice paddies, which were the most highly prized part of the complex, depended on natural water supplies – possibly enhanced by storage ponds – distributed through a system of irrigation channels. Most of this irrigated land was held by the proprietor, estate officials or the better-provided local inhabitants, who would furnish seeds for the crop, perhaps also oxen for ploughing. The poor peasants had to make do with dry fields, or non-irrigated rice plots, created by burning off the ground cover. They could not afford to eat rice, which they grew to pay as tax and dues, living instead on millet, supplemented by roots and wild grasses, plus the fish, birds or animals they could catch. Their clothing was made mostly from hempen cloth, hemp being a dry-field crop. So were most of the cereals they ate – barley and millet – as well as soya beans, vegetables and mulberry (for silk), which went to their social superiors. An estate, both for its residents and its absentee proprietors, was therefore largely self-sufficient. Only items like salt, iron agricultural tools and pottery had to be provided from outside.

As *shōen* increased in size and number, the financial effects became far-reaching. Aristocrats like the Fujiwara, who were powerful enough to be patrons many times over, grew wealthier by virtue of their income from land, and hence relied less on the emoluments of office. State revenue, by contrast – and it was this that sustained the emperor's own expenditure, as well as the government machine – became less dependable. In the ninth and tenth centuries, an attempt was made to overcome the problem by requiring tax payments to central government to be made in the form of fixed quotas, which provincial and local officials had a duty to meet (though they were allowed to retain any surplus they collected). In the eleventh century, the court turned also to the scrutiny of land rights, especially those of *shōen*. The results were fiscally disappointing. From the time of Go-Sanjō a different approach was tried: land confiscated after an investigation of title found its way, not back into the pool of *kubunden*, but into new *shōen*, registered in the name of ex-emperors, or imperial ladies, or one of the religious houses under imperial patronage. In other words, the emperor set out to solve his own financial problems by recognising in principle the legitimacy of *shōen*. By the end of the Heian period, the imperial house had acquired rights in something like a thousand such estates, spread through sixty provinces, more than any other family or institution in Japan. By doing so it increased its wealth, but further undermined the finances and the authority of the central government that acted in its name.

The rise of a warrior class after 800

Further evidence of the decay of Nara institutions had come in 792, when the conscript system was abandoned. Provincial officials relied thereafter on forces recruited locally, usually from members of leading families in the countryside, who could afford to mount and arm themselves. At times the units so formed had police powers entrusted to them by the court, thereby becoming semi-official. Other men of similar background entered the service of local proprietors (*ryōke*) who had developed private estates. More found employment in the capital, perhaps as imperial guards, enjoying minor court rank, or in the entourage of Heian nobles. In other words, there was now a profession of arms, which could be followed in either the public or the private context.

After the middle years of Heian, warriors of this kind were to be found in all parts of Japan, but it was in the Kanto plain, Japan's largest single area of arable, bounded by the sea on one side, by the mountains from Hakone to Nikko on the other, that they were at their most numerous. The Kanto was the main supply base and recruiting ground for armies sent against the Emishi, the primitive tribes in the north. Because of the experience that the campaigns gave them, Kanto fighting men were better versed in the skills of warfare than the rest. They also took the lead in developing a warrior code, distinct from the rules of behaviour that bound the aristocracy. It emphasised courage in battle, as one would expect, but also personal loyalty to those who were deemed to be lords. In this were the seeds of vassalage. There was also a fierce pride in status and reputation. It became common for a man, when a skirmish or a battle was about to begin, to ride out in front of his fellows to announce his name and lineage, together with his previous feats of bravery, in order to find an opponent worthy of his steel, one who would meet him in single combat. To support such boasts, prowess in battle had to be proved, preferably by the taking of heads.

These warriors were becoming known as samurai, armed 'retainers', though not yet in the sense of an ordered status that the term acquired in the Edo period. Some Heian samurai might hold high rank, if they served the emperor or a Fujiwara lord. Others were little more than bodyguards, or provincials with modest land rights of their own. These found men to whom to pledge their loyalty among provincials of higher social standing than themselves. Although the high-born of the capital were reluctant to take provincial posts, because they carried lower rank and less prestige than those at court, they were well aware that service in distant regions promised private gain. A provincial governor, like his subordinates, could manipulate tax collection to his own advantage. He could also use his office as a means of acquiring land rights in his own name. Some who profited in this way thought so highly of the benefits that they chose to stay in the province when their appointment came to an end, enlarging their landed interests, establishing family and supporters in nearby holdings, forming marriage ties with influential neighbours. By the tenth century there had come into existence in this way an upper layer of provincial society, whose members still had links with the court, but no longer wholly depended on it for favour. They acquired a following among local warriors; and with their support they undertook military adventures, sometimes against provincial rivals, sometimes against 'rebels' in the emperor's name, sometimes against the Emishi in the north. Out of the shared experience there grew a relationship that had the character of vassalage.

Two families, the Taira and the Minamoto – one might better call them clans, for they had many branches – stood out from the rest. Both were of imperial descent. Both acquired extensive land rights in the Kanto in the tenth and eleventh centuries, becoming in the process what the court had reason to consider 'overmighty subjects'. In 940 one of them, Taira Masakado, seeking to extend his influence in the provinces where he had estates, went so far as to give himself the title of 'New Emperor' and nominate provincial governors of his own. It took an alliance of regional magnates like himself, acting for the emperor in Heian, to bring him to heel. Fifty years later, Minamoto Yoshiie (1041–1108) acquired so great a reputation by victorious campaigns in the north that men flocked to declare their allegiance and commend their lands to him. This so alarmed the court that a decree was issued, prohibiting the practice. Yoshiie submitted. He remained none the less a figure of importance in the capital.

Taira and Minamoto were not mere provincials, after all. From the time of Fujiwara Michinaga (966–1028), the Minamoto had acted as the military arm of Fujiwara power, winning senior court office for their pains and a reputation as the regents' 'running dogs'. Yoshiie returned to Heian after 1091 to contribute to this role. Meanwhile the Taira, led by the Ise branch of the house, were pushing their lands into central and western Japan, becoming in the process patrons of the famous shrine at Miyajima on the shores of the Inland Sea. Once established in that region, they, too, took up a career in Kyoto, serving the retired emperors in their contests with the Fujiwara. In this way they set the stage for a struggle for power between the two great warrior clans, the outcome of which was Japan's first feudal government (Chapter 5).

Heian culture

The move away from Chinese models in Heian culture did not become evident until the middle of the period. During the first hundred years of Heian, Chinese learning was still the norm among the members of the aristocracy and officialdom. The court continued to publish collections of their Chinese verse (three of which were arranged in accordance with the rank of the contributors). Most of the poems themselves were serious in theme and no more than graceful in achievement, like those produced in Nara. They were also overwhelmingly masculine in authorship, since Chinese studies were not believed to be a proper accomplishment for women. With the passage of time, however, the prestige of things Chinese declined. Even Sugawara Michizane, who was a better Chinese poet than most, contributed to the change: his refusal to go to China as envoy in 894 marked the end of Japanese missions to Ch'ang-an. Thereafter, although Chinese remained the country's classical language, giving access to Chinese culture through books, there was no longer the stimulus of occasional personal contact with the artistic and intellectual world of the Chinese capital.

Buddhism, too, though still indebted to China in matters of doctrine, adjusted to its Japanese surroundings in other respects. Buddhist houses, whose highest ranks were filled from the aristocracy, gave a lead in the development of private estates (*shōen*). Some acquired their own military force, composed of lay mercenaries or priests bearing arms. The most powerful increased their wealth and influence through branch temples, becoming larger in the process. By late Heian the Enryakuji, headquarters of the Tendai sect, supervised something approaching 400 branches and had over 3,000 buildings in its complex on Mount Hiei.

From the tenth century, however, there came a change of religious mood, as Heian society became more and more a prey to melancholy and disillusion. Men and women, faced by weak emperors, extravagant (and notoriously immoral) nobles, luxury-loving clergy and poverty-stricken peasants, began to seek a more satisfying religious experience than was afforded by the scholastic, scripture-based Buddhism of the past. They found it, as often as not, in the cult of Amida. Japan was approaching, it was said, the long-predicted onset of the Latter Days of the Law (*mappō*), when the faith would enter a phase of decline, in which it would be hard for believers to secure salvation by their own unaided efforts. They would need the help of those with greater spiritual standing than themselves – that is, of bodhisattvas – if they were to escape the sufferings of this mortal life. Amida (Amitabha) was the one to whom they chiefly turned.

In 985 the Tendai monk Genshin wrote a book that set out the argument for this in powerful terms. It began with a graphic description of the Buddhist hells, to which those who failed would be consigned. He contrasted this with an account of the Pure Land of the Western paradise, entry to which could be secured by those who sincerely invoked the name of Amida. The book was enormously popular, partly, perhaps, because so much of it was gruesome. Unlike some of his predecessors, however, Genshin did not use his popularity to found a new sect. Instead, his ideas spread widely within both Tendai and Shingon. They also contributed to a similar movement focused on Jizō (Ksitigarbha), a bodhisattva whose powers were thought to be more efficacious in saving men from hell than in leading them to paradise.

The new religious attitudes had an important impact on Japanese literature and art in the second half of the Heian period, when the preoccupations of both became more human and this-worldly, their context more recognisable as Japanese. Their idioms of expression were also more Japanese, exemplified in prose tales (*monogatari*) and narrative picture-scrolls (*e-maki*). One step in this direction was a resumption of the publication of court collections of poetry in Japanese, a practice abandoned for many years. The first to appear, early in the tenth century, was entitled *Kokinshū*. Compared with the eighth-century *Manyōshū*, it contains hardly any long poems, a good many anonymous ones, more by women, fewer by the highest-ranking members of society. Sentiments are more refined – one is tempted to use the word pejoratively – and love poems less carnal. There are many references to the seasons, conveyed in detailed observations of birds and flowers, of wind and snow and rain. It is not difficult to believe that poems such as this were a part of aristocratic social intercourse, contributions to poetry contests on set themes. Slight, mannered, yet sharp in their imagery, they were to lay down the standards for Japanese verse for hundreds of years.

One of the contributors to *Kokinshū* was Ki no Tsurayuki, a noble who served as governor of Tosa, a province in Shikoku, between 931 and 934. After his tour of duty he travelled back to the capital, gratefully, one suspects, and mostly by sea, a 55-day journey that seemed full of peril and discomfort to a lifelong resident of Heian. He wrote an account of the voyage (in Japanese, not Chinese), which is known as *Tosa Nikki*. It contains many poems, interwoven with the prose by way of greetings and fare-wells, or as comments on the scenery. This gives his writing something of the air of a literary exercise. It is nevertheless about real people doing real things, hence a forerunner of later works that go by the name of history. There is a touch of the everyday about it, missing from much of Japan's early writing: the pilot who interrupts a farewell party because wind and tide are right for departure, only to be dubbed 'a man of no sensibility' for his pains; alarms about the risk of storms or attack by pirates, bringing urgent appeals for help to both Buddha and the *kami*; the discovery, when the travellers reach Heian, that the governor's house and garden have suffered from neglect, despite being entrusted to the care of a neighbour.

The *Tosa Nikki* has a quite different range of subject-matter from that of other diaries in the middle years of the period. Most of these, written by court ladies, were accounts of personal experience within the narrow social circle of the palace and aristocracy: problems of marriage, the behaviour of lovers, visits to temples and festivals (ostensibly, at least, for the purpose of writing poems), the choice of clothes for such occasions, comments on the people encountered in the daily round. It is all very charming and delicately expressed, sometimes witty, occasionally acid-tongued, but contains hardly a hint of how life is lived in the capital at large, let alone the rest of Japan.

Much the same is true of Japan's first major novel, The Tale of Genji (*Genji monogatari*), written early in the eleventh century. The author was in all probability Murasaki Shikibu, a court lady whose diary was also published. Her novel, however, is a much more considerable piece of work. It tells the story of the life and loves of Prince Genji, son of an emperor, but not in the line of succession, whose birth and social graces make him well-nigh irresistible to the ladies he encounters (starting with one whom the emperor married after Genji's mother died). The plot is diffuse, its broader themes, where they exist, only lightly sketched, its characterisation subtle. This makes for a closely observed but unexciting narrative, appropriate to the way of life that it describes. There is some reference to intrigues for office and their great importance to the aristocracy, but not in other respects very much about the practice of politics and government. Genji's brief and voluntary exile, when he is out of favour, is a gentlemanly affair, taking him to the coast a mere 50 miles away, where he has estates to support him. Later, we are told, he rises to a position of considerable influence, but this, too, impinges very little on the story. The book, in fact, is much more about its women than its men, despite Genji's central place in it.

All these works were written by aristocrats and read by aristocrats, accessible to many because they were in Japanese, popular in the world that they described. They were not regarded as 'serious' literature, which by Chinese standards excluded fiction in any case. Other tales had even less claim to dignity. Among the earliest was The Tales of Ise (*Ise monogatari*), a collection of stories, mostly about the amatory adventures of a single character, which may have been the inspiration for parts of *Genji*. Each story provided the theme for a poem. By contrast, The Bamboo-cutter's Tale (*Taketori monogatari*), which also dates, like *Ise*, from the early tenth century, is a folk-story. It tells how a tiny girl, found by the bamboo-cutter in a bamboo plant, quickly grows into a beautiful princess. Many men court her; each is set a test, which he fails; and in the end she is claimed again by her own people, the Moon-people, who had imprisoned her in the bamboo by way of punishment.

Tales of a Time Now Past (*Konjaku monogatari*) was a book on an altogether larger scale. It brought together more than a thousand stories, most of them very short, some from India and China, others from Japan, telling of men and women who are described as being real people, identified as to period, rank, office, village or temple, as the case may be. Many of the tales are about popular Buddhism, especially the doctrine of karma, setting out the influence, good and bad, which human actions can have on one's fate, either in this life or in a future one. Others take up ethical themes, such as filial piety. At the opposite end of the spectrum are tales which are sexual, even pornographic. In general, the contents are grouped by theme, whether religious or secular: daring, skill and ingenuity, the prowess and ideals of warriors, malevolent and supernatural creatures. One of the best known is the story of the Dōjōji bell and the widow who becomes a snake to secure revenge on a faithless lover-monk. This was later a famous play. Another is

'Rashōmon', of which Akutagawa Ryūnosuke wrote a twentieth-century version, made into a film by Kurosawa Akira. It describes how a man goes into the forests round Kyoto with his wife. They meet a robber, who first persuades the man to exchange his bow for a sword, then uses the bow to force him to submit. Tying the man to a tree, the robber rapes his wife. (The film version, it should be said, is less straightforward than this.)

The enormous variety of material to be found in the prose fiction of late Heian, set against backgrounds that range from the court to village life, was the beginning of a literary tradition lasting well into the nineteenth century. The main addition to it during the middle ages was a category of war tales (*gunki monogatari*), appropriate to the tastes of a warrior ruling class. The Edo era (1600–1867) added novels of urban life. In both periods there also existed a new kind of historical writing, the 'historical' tales (*rekishi monogatari*), written in Japanese, which also had their forerunners in Heian. To one of these, The Tale of Splendour (*Eiga monogatari*), we have already referred when discussing the rise of the Fujiwara. It was compiled at various dates during the eleventh century, probably by women, though this has not been established with any certainty; and it took up the narrative of Japanese history from the point at which the official chronicles in Chinese had come to an end (the year 887). The last date recorded in it is 1028. Another such work, The Great Mirror (*Ōkagami*), dating from the late eleventh or early twelfth century, covers much the same period (*c.* 850–1025). Both works are anonymous.

These histories are in one respect traditional in format, being chronicles centred on the affairs of the court, especially its politics. In *Eiga monogatari*, anecdotes are interpolated into the chronological framework: items about the family history of the Fujiwara and the imperial house, together with descriptions of ceremonial occasions. They provide more colour and human detail than were ever to be found in the official histories. *Ōkagami* does more. It elaborates the format, first, by adding separate sections of biographical and other supplementary information in the manner of China's dynastic histories, and second, by setting out its text as if it were an exchange of reminiscence and opinion between two very old men, who had lived through the events that were being described. This contrives a place for incidents – not always disinterested, one suspects – to illustrate the kind of self-seeking, pettiness and drunken violence that were often part of the struggles for power at court. There is a tone of criticism about it that is absent from the very much blander pages of *Eiga monogatari*. There is even an attempt to identify causation in a rudimentary way, mostly in the form of references to karma.

If Heian histories were about the court, Buddhism long remained the chosen subject of art. During the ninth and tenth centuries, statuary continued to be religious, hence Chinese or Indian in appearance, though some of the later examples became more Japanese in dress and features. Painting, also religious in subject, grew more elaborate as it tried to express ideas about Amida and Jizō: that is, to depict bodhisattvas and some of the more ferocious deities. In the Phoenix Hall of the Byōdōin near Uji, commissioned in 1053, door panels and murals show several versions of Amida's descent, escorted by a large retinue of saints and guardians, to welcome the soul of a dying believer into paradise. There is a similar work on hanging scrolls at Mount Koya, the headquarters of Shingon. In both cases the main figures are traditionally Buddhist in style, but they are set in a clearly Japanese landscape.

This kind of work marks the emergence of what are called 'Japanese' paintings (Yamato-e), to distinguish them from those in the Chinese style (Kara-e). Subjects became more obviously Japanese and not necessarily Buddhist. There are murals in the Hōryūji, dating from 1069, which tell the life of Prince Shōtoku. By the twelfth century, Japan had a portrait painter, Fujiwara Takanobu, recording contemporary personalities at the court. His subjects, supposedly sketched from life, astonished his contemporaries by their fidelity to the originals, while his style was to become the norm in portraits of the great in the Kamakura, Muromachi and Edo periods.

The process of moving away from Chinese models can be

seen most clearly in the history of picture-scrolls (*e-maki*). These originated in China, where they were produced in very large numbers before and during the T'ang. The earliest recorded in Japan – hardly any are extant – were imports, copies or imitations in typically Chinese format. That is to say, the scroll was divided into panels from right to left, the top half of each panel being an illustration, the bottom half the text. There are literary references to later scrolls of this kind in the ninth century, though none survive. Nor do those from the tenth and eleventh centuries, when there is evidence that the technique was frequently in use, either to illustrate the diaries and *monogatari* of the period, or to keep a record of ceremonies and festivals. Scrolls, like poetry, had a place in courtly parlour games.

It was not until the twelfth century that the picture-scroll became established as a major art form in Japan. There are four outstanding examples from that time. The first, belonging to the early part of the century, comprised a series of scenes from the novel *Genji monogatari*, each scene taking up the full height of a panel (21.8 cm) and preceded by the relevant section of the novel's text. Paper and calligraphy are both part of the design. Colours are rich and thickly applied; the viewpoint is obliquely from above; roofs are omitted to afford a view of interiors; and faces are represented conventionally (a hook for the nose, two slits for the eyes, a red dot for the lips). Most of these conventions are to be found in subsequent Japanese art, especially Edo prints and book illustrations.

A quite different kind of work, produced some decades later, was the *Shigisan-engi*. Its subject is a folk-tale about a miracle involving a Buddhist priest and a flying ricebowl. Nearly all the scenes are set out of doors, unlike *Genji*, and include large numbers of peasants, assembled in crowds and depicted in lightly coloured line drawings of dramatic movement. Facial expressions, individually drawn, are lively, almost caricatures, having a strong resemblance to those to be found in some nineteenth-century Hiroshige prints. The scroll itself is a continuous whole, not broken up into separate panels. This was a new technique, which was to be the norm in later *e-maki*.

Ban Dainagon e-kotoba, unlike the first two works, describes a real event, taken from the ninth century: a fire at one of the Heian palace gates, started in the course of a dispute between two courtiers. Here both types of treatment are combined. Interiors are in the manner of *Genji*, except that the faces of the nobles are given more expression; exteriors are more like *Shigisan*, especially where there are crowd scenes of guards and firefighters. The colour is often vivid, the details of dress and weaponry are drawn with care.

The fourth of this group, *Chōjū-giga*, is not at all like any of the rest. It is the work of painter-monks, not court artists; it has no written text; and it consists of black line drawings without any colouring. The first (and most famous) of its four scrolls shows animals engaged in human–type activities: swimming, wrestling, archery, conducting Buddhist ceremonial. It is often taken to be social satire. The second scroll consists of realistic drawings of animals, real and legendary. Both these are attributed to a Buddhist monk called Kakuyu, painting in the mid twelfth century. The remaining two scrolls are by a different hand, probably in the following century. One shows monks and laymen at play, the other, which is sometimes distinctly heavy-handed in its humour, various animals in parodies of human action.

The new trends in literature and art that belong to the second half of the Heian period, principally its final hundred years, manifest, one must suppose, the effect of upper-class patronage and prevailing human attitudes on the work of writers and artists. In other words, they reflect changes in society. At the same time, both *e-maki* and *monogatari* established criteria in subject-matter and style that are now taken to be inherently 'Japanese'. They were to last until Edo, or even beyond. Culturally, therefore, the later part of Heian was not only a break with the past, helping to confirm the influence of Chinese civilisation in Japan as an aspect of the 'classical', but also a bridge to the next – predominantly feudal – phase of Japanese history.

CHAPTER 5

Japanese Feudalism

The terrain has not made Japan easy to govern as a single unit. Sea passage between the four main islands depends on weather conditions. Interiors are mountainous. In Honshu and Kyushu, which have been the heartland of history, a mountain spine, high and rugged in places, runs from northeast to southwest, dividing the Pacific and Japan Sea coasts. From it spurs lead down to narrow coastal plains, enclosing steep valleys, which are the principal means of access to the interior. Rivers are short, fast running after summer rains, dwindling in the drier winter. They cannot be used for transport, except near the sea and in the small number of more extensive plains surrounding the modern cities of Sendai, Tokyo, Nagoya, Kyoto-Osaka and Fukuoka.

The geographical obstacles to centralised rule were overcome in early centuries, if at all, by virtue of the emperor's prestige, reinforced by claims of divine descent and the adoption of an imported culture in the capital. In modern times, better transport and communications have served the same end. Between the two, Japan had a more loose-knit political structure, akin to that of feudalism in medieval Europe. It was slow to develop. One essential ingredient, vassalage, by which vertical relationships within a landholding military class were governed, was already present to some degree in the eleventh century (Chapter 4). Another, serfdom, defining the peasant's subordination to lord, did not exist in Japan in its European form, because the two land systems differed; but the fact of subordination was never in doubt, while the institutions that embodied it became more like those of Europe in and after the fifteenth century.

It must also be said that samurai were not in all respects equivalent to European knights, if only because the nature of warfare was not the same. In a land of steep, terraced hillsides and flat valley floors, laid out in flooded rice-fields and crossed by irrigation channels, one cannot easily picture heavily armoured knights, lances levelled, charging on horseback against their enemies. For most of history, samurai had lighter and more flexible armour than their European counterparts. Their chosen weapons were the bow-and-arrow when mounted, the sword for hand-to-hand fighting on foot. They were therefore cheaper to arm. Samurai needed smaller fiefs than knights, which made them more numerous, if less affluent.

Warriors, vassalage and landholding were first brought together in what might be called a feudal state as the result of Minamoto victory over the Taira between 1180 and 1185. By choosing to exercise his power thereafter from Kamakura, not Heian, Minamoto Yoritomo made a clear distinction between himself and previous 'advisers' to the emperor. He also provided historians with the first of a series of non-imperial labels for Japanese history. These were the places from which Shogun, or feudal overlords, ruled – Kamakura (1185–1333), Muromachi (1336–1573), Edo (1603–1868) – or the family names of lines of Shogun (Ashikaga, Tokugawa). The periods these identify were not equally 'feudal'. During Kamakura there was still a balance of sorts between the court, representing the vestiges of imperial rule, and the Bakufu, through which the Shogun exercised his power. In Muromachi, despite the fact that emperor and Shogun shared a capital city, Japan moved much closer to a truly feudal type of government and society. In Edo the transition to a modern state began, though vassalage remained the key to status and authority. All three stages were preceded by periods of civil war.

The Kamakura Bakufu (1185–1333)

In the twelfth-century struggles between the Taira and the Minamoto (see Chapter 4), the Taira were at first the more successful
of the two. Eventually, victory in a series of clashes between 1156
and 1160 enabled them to expel the Minamoto leaders from the
capital, leaving it under their own control. Taira Kiyomori (c.
1118–81) promptly took a leaf from the Fujiwara book. He had
himself appointed Daijō-daijin (Great Minister of State); put Taira
kinsmen into a range of other key posts in central government;
and married a daughter into the imperial line. In 1190 the emperor
Takakura was forced to abdicate, making way for his half-Taira
heir, Antoku, who was Kiyomori's grandson.

The headship of the Minamoto house had meanwhile passed
to Minamoto Yoritomo (1147–99), sent into exile in Izu province
at the edge of the Kanto plain. The years he spent there laid the
foundations for a Minamoto revival. In 1177, by marrying the
daughter of Hōjō Tokimasa, a local official of Taira descent, he
acquired Tokimasa as ally, then as vassal. He also became aware of
how important land rights were to the Kanto's fighting men, a
lesson he never forgot. When the opportunity came to seek
another trial of strength with the Taira leadership, he accordingly
offered all who would follow him written guarantees of title to
their land, whatever their lineage. This won local Taira warriors
to his cause, as well as Minamoto.

In the summer of 1180, having had indications of support
from members of the imperial family, who were jealous of Taira
Kiyomori's pretensions, Yoritomo raised the standard of revolt.
His first moves ended in defeat. From a refuge in the Hakone
mountains he then put together another force and tried again,
this time with success. By the end of the year, his opponents
were in retreat towards the capital, while Yoritomo settled down
to consolidate his hold on the Kanto plain from a base established
at Kamakura.

In 1183 Yoritomo's cousin, Yoshinaka, led a Minamoto advance on Kyoto. He soon captured the city, but the victory was less than complete, since the Taira fled, seeking safety in their lands to the west and taking with them the child-emperor, Antoku, together with the symbols of his authority. At this point Yoritomo sent his young half-brother, Yoshitsune – a hot-head, in the estimation of his fellow commanders – to conduct the rest of the campaign. In the spring of 1184 his forces won a resounding victory at Ichinotani, near modern Kobe, a battle, as the chronicles tell the tale, in which the turning-point came when Yoshitsune himself led a headlong mounted charge down a steep escarpment to fall on the Taira flank and rear. His bravado made him a legend.

The final confrontation came in a naval battle – or, more precisely, an engagement fought by samurai in ships – at Dannoura in the Shimonoseki Straits. This was in April of the following year. Despite the greater maritime experience of those who fought for the Taira, the weakness of their leadership – Kiyomori was dead, his surviving sons lacked resolution – plus the fighting qualities of battle-hardened Minamoto troops, once more gave Yoshitsune the advantage. When all seemed lost, a Taira court lady seized the boy-emperor and jumped with him into the sea. Both drowned. So, too, did Kiyomori's widow. With them went the sword from the imperial regalia, never to be recovered (though it was eventually replaced). Many Taira warriors committed suicide, preferring to drown rather than face capture. Local tradition says that their ghosts still haunt the scene.

These events not only confirmed Yoritomo's power, they furnished an abundant crop of war tales for Japanese literature. Some of them are true (as far as one can tell). Others are the product of fertile imaginations, not always well informed. There is, for example, a fog of uncertainty about Yoshitsune's fate after Dannoura. It seems clear that Yoritomo came to think of him as a potential rival; that he nevertheless contrived to escape to a refuge in the north; and that he was betrayed and killed there, his head sent to Kamakura. Yet the details of the story have been so embroidered over time as to become more fiction than fact, its hero, at least in Edo drama, was Yoshitsune's loyal retainer, Benkei.

One nineteenth-century version even claims that Yoshitsune survived and made his way to the Asian mainland, where he emerged
again as the Mongol leader, Genghis Khan.

More soberly, the campaigns and the stories they engendered
had a vital place in shaping the warrior code. Courage and loyalty
remained its central themes, as they had always been. Taking part
in set-piece battles, however, instead of local skirmishes or urban
quarrels, provided a wider audience for the incidents in which
these qualities were displayed. In such a situation, warriors became
more aware of the good opinion of their fellows. Loyalty, a manly
sentiment, began to take precedence over other, less urgent ties,
like duty to wives and family. Indeed, those who took part in
these events acquired a greater sense of being an élite, marked out
from lesser men, not only by pride in bearing arms, but also by
the dignity of vassalage. They began to see themselves collectively
as potential rulers, no longer simply as 'retainers'. Minamoto
Yoritomo was able to make use of them.

The Taira had chosen to control Japan by controlling the court,
as the Fujiwara had done. Yoritomo took a different view. Content
to impose his will on Kyoto from outside, he concerned himself
with the day-to-day management of the sources of his strength,
the land and warriors of the Kanto, creating what was to become
the Bakufu. The first steps were taken during the civil war. To
muster an army, Yoritomo had won over warrior-landholders to
his cause by promises to guarantee their land rights. In return he
required pledges of fealty and service, enrolling samurai of Taira
as well as Minamoto blood to his vassals, or 'house-men' (gokenin).
After 1183, when the fighting moved to the west, their numbers
were increased by recruitment from the provinces through which
the Minamoto armies passed, producing a total of over 2,000
men by the time hostilities ended. Many of these were men of
substance, leading warrior bands of their own.

To regulate his dealings with this large following, Yoritomo
had founded the Retainers' Office (Samurai-dokoro) in 1180,
named after a Fujiwara house-organ of similar function. As his
power grew, however, so did the needs of his administration.

Towards the end of 1184, two further offices were added: a General Office, later called the Mandokoro – another Fujiwara label – to handle Yoritomo's 'governmental' functions and the record keeping they required; and a feudal court, the Monchūjo, to adjudicate on disputes over land rights, boundaries and questions of vassalage. Although the latter's jurisdiction was in theory only over *gokenin*, it inevitably had to deal as well with complaints that were brought against them by non-vassals. This brought the greater part of the landed class within its purview.

There was little chance that a concentration of power as great as this could exist without reference to imperial authority. Late in 1183, when his troops were in occupation of Kyoto, Yoritomo's actions in the Kanto were given the emperor's blessing. A few months later the court gave its approval for an advance against the Taira in the west. Even so, it was December 1190 before Yoritomo himself set foot in the capital again; and although in 1192 he accepted the title of Sei-i-tai-Shōgun (abbreviated as a rule to Shogun), there is little indication that he saw this step as needed to confer legality on what he had achieved. The title made him nominally commander-in-chief in the north, giving a welcome measure of authority over samurai who were not his vassals, but beyond that he does not appear to have valued it unduly. He relinquished it before he died. In practice, indeed, it was his thirteenth-century successors who made the Shogun into *de facto* ruler of Japan. Yoritomo himself was content to rely on preponderant force, together with the co-operation of a Fujiwara ally at court, Kujō Kanezane, who became regent in 1186.

In devising the institutions through which to exercise his power, Yoritomo had as adviser another court noble, a bureaucrat named Ōe Hiromoto, who was invited to Kamakura in 1184. In 1185, when the civil war came to an end, Ōe recommended the extension to regions previously held by the Taira of two wartime offices, that of *shugo* (the military governor of a province) and *jitō* (a steward attached to a private estate, or *shōen*, representing Kamakura's tax-related interests). Both were to be chosen from Kamakura vassals. One object was to increase the Minamoto's reach, of course. Another was to reward the *gokenin* for their services. The outcome was the creation in many parts of Japan of a network of officials, owing their first loyalty to Kamakura, who existed side by side with those appointed by Kyoto. The military governor was responsible for peacekeeping in his province. Stewards were to supervise the payment of dues from the estates on which they served, separating the part that was payable as tax from that which was owed to the various holders of land rights (*shiki*). Since these were issues about which disputes frequently arose, the *jitō*, like the *shugo*, was part of a general system of law and order. Thus Minamoto *gokenin* were spread widely through Japan, able to enrich themselves at no cost to their lord, either from tax revenue – a well-established practice among local officials of all kinds – or by the receipt of *shiki* of their own in the relevant estates. Their income, in other words, derived not from the Shogun, but either from the local population, or from the religious institutions and civil dignitaries who already held rights in *shōen*. As events were to show, this was not a formula for lasting peace in the countryside.

After Yoritomo's death in 1199, there were disturbances at the highest levels in Kamakura. His eldest son, Yoriie, was stripped of power in 1203, murdered in 1204; the next head of the house, Sanetomo, Yoriie's younger brother, was murdered in 1219. Sanetomo proved to be the last of Yoritomo's line. This left power in the hands of the most influential of the Minamoto vassals. Hōjō Tokimasa, Yoritomo's father-in-law, had been appointed regent (Shikken) to Yoriie in 1203 and had arranged Yoriie's murder in 1204. His son, Yoshitoki, replaced his father in 1205. Together they made the Hōjō regency a permanent feature of the Kamakura Bakufu.

Encouraged by what he believed to be the resulting weakness in Kamakura, the ex-emperor Go-Toba set out to restore the authority of the court. He rallied support among the warriors of central and west Japan, then sent an army against the Kanto in 1221, only to see it soundly defeated by Hōjō Yoshitoki. The victory was a signal for increasing Hōjō control of the Bakufu. The Minamoto were succeeded as Shogun by Hōjō nominees, at first Fujiwara nobles, later princes of the royal blood. All were chosen as boys, then sent back to Kyoto on reaching manhood. In this way the Shogun, like the emperor, became a figurehead, subject to the same constraints – except the marital ones – that the Fujiwara had for centuries used to control the imperial line. There was also a new level of Bakufu dominance in Kyoto. Many of the ex-emperor's own *shōen* were confiscated, some soon to be restored under the supervision of *gokenin* as stewards, others to be distributed to the Hōjō and their allies. The powers and emoluments of *jitō* were more clearly spelt out, an implicit threat to the revenues of both emperor and courtiers. Yoshitoki's heir, Yasutoki, was installed in Kyoto as resident governor with the title of Rokuhara Tandai. Go-Toba was sent into exile, the reigning emperor replaced by another of Kamakura's choice.

The Hōjō remained effectively rulers of Japan under these arrangements until 1333. In 1232 they introduced a legal code of their own: a 'house law', defining the duties of *shugo* and *jitō*, setting out the penalties to be imposed on vassals who offended against the rules of discipline and behaviour, and laying down the principles on which disputes over landholding and succession were to be resolved. Their courts, although feudal, in the sense that they claimed jurisdiction only over *gokenin*, soon acquired an enviable reputation for evenhandedness in cases that court nobles, religious establishments and others aggrieved over land rights brought before them. Documents were carefully scrutinised, witnesses examined both in person and in writing, great efforts made to ensure that the court and its friends were not unjustly treated. All this bolstered the Bakufu's authority.

The judicial policy was part of a sharing of power between two separate political systems. Despite the military force at his disposal and the wide powers exercised on his behalf by *shugo* and *jitō*, the Shogun was not in a position to be despotic. Nor were the Hōjō. Formally, the latter, as a fourteenth-century court historian described them, were mere 'rear vassals': that is, a vassal's vassals. The Shogun himself was not a feudal overlord in the usual sense. He was a symbolic figure, recruited from Kyoto, not even a warrior. The bonds of loyalty to him were inevitably weak. At the same time, the emperor, though his claims to absolute power were clearly unrealistic, was not devoid of political function. He continued to preside, at least in name, over a Chinese-style bureaucracy; issued laws that were binding on all but the Shogun's *gokenin*; named civil governors to provinces; received the taxes they collected. He had the means, moreover, to muster a sufficient body of armed support to challenge Kamakura in the field. This had happened in 1221, and was to happen again in 1333.

Nor can the lower levels of Japanese society be described as wholly feudal at this time. Small cultivators, living in earth-floored two-room huts, still suffered from a heavy burden of imperial taxes if they were on 'public' land. Immediately above them a mixed stratum of more substantial local residents included farmers with larger holdings, part of which was likely to be taxable by the state; local government officials appointed by the court, who also held land; officials of private estates (*shōen*); and Kamakura vassals, serving as *jitō*. More affluent, these had houses with wooden floors, outbuildings for their servants and cattle, perhaps a surrounding earth embankment to protect them against casual violence. They might all possess rights (*shiki*) in one or more of the district's *shōen*, but this did not guarantee unity of allegiances. Local officials were part of a structure stretching upwards to Kyoto's ministries. *Jitō*, as *gokenin*, had obligations to the Shogun's council. Estate officials acted on behalf of absentee patrons and proprietors, most of whom would be court nobles, or nominees of the imperial family, or the heads of religious institutions, though some might belong to powerful warrior houses. It is hard to disentangle the feudal from the non-feudal in such a situation.

The pattern was not a stable one, moreover. Despite Kamakura's efforts to restrain them, *jitō* did not remain content with the modest share of the crop – 11 per cent at best – that they were allotted as recompense for their services. There were many devices by which they could enlarge it. In particular, since their duties placed them between the cultivators and the estate officials on the one side, and the patrons and proprietors on the other, it was easy for them to hinder, or even block, the distribution of dues from the former to the latter. They could therefore set a price for their co-operation. One 'compromise' that emerged quite frequently was for percentage dues to be made fixed annual payments, leaving the *jitō* to pocket any excess he might be able to collect. Another was division of the land itself, part of it handed to the *jitō* in private title, in return for a promise that dues on the rest would be delivered without fail.

Given that *jitō* were the Shogun's vassals, who were assumed to enjoy official favour, many patrons and proprietors accepted such terms, or even offered them. Those who did not, especially if they were confident of their own political backing, sought justice in the Bakufu's courts. By doing so, they presented Kamakura with a difficult choice. To support the *gokenin* would offend influential plaintiffs, most of them linked with the court or with major shrines and temples. This would run counter to partnership with Kyoto, which the Bakufu still valued. To find against the vassals, on the other hand, would risk undermining their loyalty. It is not surprising that an attempt was therefore made to hold a middle line. Inevitably, it satisfied neither party.

Refusal to support their more extreme demands with respect to land aroused a sense of grievance among *gokenin*. It was made more severe by the results of Mongol attacks on Japan in the second half of the thirteenth century. When Khubilai Khan became emperor of China in 1260, he set about restoring that country's international dignity, as expressed in the tribute system. Japan in Chinese eyes had in the past been part of it. He therefore sent a letter to the 'king' of Japan, demanding that envoys be sent to pay him proper homage. Though not exactly threatening – neither side, it said, 'would wish to appeal to arms to settle this question' – the messengers from Korea by whom it was delivered to the Shogun in 1268 were clear that it should be taken seriously. Hōjō Tokimune, then regent in Kamakura, ignored it. Khubilai's response took time to materialise, because he wished first to be sure of his position on the mainland, but in November 1274 a fleet carrying 40,000 troops appeared off Hakata in northern

Kyushu. Landings were made; but although the Mongols proved better organised for fighting than the Japanese, they failed to establish a satisfactory bridgehead. Facing problems of supply, they finally withdrew. Storms scattered their ships as they made for home.

There followed an uneasy interval of preparation for another trial of strength. Fresh Mongol envoys arrived in Japan in 1275 and 1279, demanding submission. They were executed. The *gokenin* in Kyushu were ordered to make ready for a new attack; reinforcements were mustered; a defensive wall was built along the north Kyushu coast. Then in June 1281 the expected enemy appeared: two fleets this time, one from Korea, one from south China, bringing no fewer than 140,000 men. For several weeks fierce fighting raged along the Kyushu beaches, neither side gaining the upper hand, but in August the weather intervened in the shape of a typhoon, dispersing the Mongol ships with heavy losses. To many Japanese, notably Buddhist and Shinto priests, it was the 'divine wind' (*kamikaze*), sent by the gods in answer to their prayers.

The Shogun's vassals, especially those in west Japan, saw things differently. They had stood for several years awaiting the second attack; were to remain on military alert, expecting more (this situation lasted until Khubilai's death in 1294); and despite having borne much of the cost of the conflict, had almost nothing to show for it, whether by way of booty or additional land grants. Where rewards were made to those who had excelled, they involved, as often as not, confiscation from those who had failed. Both blamed the Bakufu for ingratitude. Yet there was less now that they could do to make their discontents felt. The Hōjō had responded to the foreign threat by tightening their hold on the conduct of affairs: more family appointments made to Kamakura offices; many extra posts – lucrative ones – acquired throughout the country. By 1333, when at last they were overthrown, members of the Hōjō house were military governors (*shugo*) in more than half Japan's provinces, stewards (*jitō*) in an enormous number of estates.

What proved to be the catalyst in bringing about their fall was a crisis in relations with the court. Ever since 1221 Kamakura had intervened actively in Kyoto, choosing emperors, insisting on the appointment of particular officials. It assumed still more authority because of the Mongol wars. In 1275, when a fresh succession dispute arose, involving rival claims on behalf of two sons of the emperor Go-Saga, who had failed to choose between them before he died, the Bakufu stepped in to arbitrate. They and their successors, it ruled, were to constitute two imperial lines, reigning alternately. The result was to involve the Hōjō in much recrimination. Eventually, in 1326 Go-Daigo, emperor of what was called the junior line, refused to accede to a Hōjō request to abdicate in favour of a candidate from the senior one. After a further five years of acrimonious dispute, he was threatened with armed attack unless he complied. Go-Daigo fled from the capital. Captured and formally banished in 1332, he escaped in 1333. Once again troops were sent against him, led on this occasion by Ashikaga Takauji, a man who could claim descent from Minamoto Yoritomo. Go-Daigo won him over with lavish promises of reward. With Ashikaga help, an 'imperial' army, consisting mostly of disaffected samurai, was sent against Kamakura. In July the city was captured and burnt, and the last of the Hōjō committed suicide.

Feudalism in the Muromachi period (1336–1460)

Go-Daigo proved to be better at intrigue than government. His object, it soon appeared, was to restore the kind of institutions that had existed before the emperors lost their power, ignoring the changes that had taken place meanwhile. To this end, he chose court nobles as his principal officers, serving in Nara-style posts; refused to appoint a Fujiwara as Kampaku; refused – much more dangerously – to make Ashikaga Takauji Shogun. A programme was launched to restore to the aristocracy the land rights that had fallen into warrior hands. Since the only effective military force at his disposal was composed of samurai, this, too, was folly.

For his part, Ashikaga Takauji appears in later histories as Japan's traitor *par excellence*. When he transferred his allegiance to Go-Daigo in 1333, he had abandoned his wife and sons in Kamakura, where they were likely to be held, he knew, as hostages for his loyalty. His wife, he argued, being a Hōjō, would come to no harm, his sons could be smuggled out by the guards he left behind for that purpose. In any case, 'in great undertakings one does not consider trivial things'. Following this principle, in 1335 he turned his coat again. Capturing what was left of Kamakura, he led his army against the emperor's capital, which he seized in 1336. Go-Daigo fled again, taking with him the imperial regalia, without which, he claimed, no ruler was legitimate. Disregarding this tradition, Takauji installed his own chosen candidate as emperor. The new man promptly made him Shogun.

Once Japan had acquired a warrior class, there were two avenues of power that were open to a prospective overlord. One was control of the court, which offered the prospect of legitimate authority and an opportunity to exploit the imperial prestige. The other was to depend more openly on the loyalty of warriors, secured, as it had to be, by confirmation of their lands. The Taira had opted for the first. The Minamoto, followed by the Hōjō, chose the second. Ashikaga Takauji, backed already by an army in the field, but faced – unusually – by a hostile emperor, or ex-emperor, ready to resort to force, decided that Kyoto was more critical to his success. He established himself in Muromachi, a district of the capital. To it he transferred the Bakufu's central institutions, inherited from Kamakura.

The decision proved to be a mistake. Although members of the Ashikaga house were to hold the office of Shogun until 1573, for a century and a half of the time the country was engaged in intermittent civil war. The first phase of it, known as the war between the northern and southern courts (Namboku-chō), was so named because the two sides declared allegiance to rival imperial lines, one ruling in Kyoto, protected by the Ashikaga,

the other, headed by Go-Daigo and his heirs, in exile in the
Yoshino mountains to the south of the Nara plain. The latter had
no army of any size, but attracted to their cause some notable
'loyalist' warriors – the most famous was Kusunoki Masashige –
who kept their hopes of success alive in a series of guerrilla
skirmishes. To this contest in the central provinces were added a
number of smaller quarrels throughout the country, prompted by
greed for land or family ambition, but carried on in the name of
the northern and southern courts. As a result, all Japan was
kept in ferment until 1392, when the third Ashikaga Shogun,
Yoshimitsu, abandoning his former protégés, persuaded the
southern line to come back to Kyoto.

Disorder, it proved, was fertile soil for the growth of warrior
landed interests. The Ashikaga, unlike the Hōjō, were unwilling
to act against their provincial followers, who were therefore left
to seek compensation for the costs of war wherever they could
find it. Inevitably, most did so at the expense of the proprietors
and patrons of *shōen*. This led in time to a widespread reallocation,
not only of land rights (*shiki*), but also of the land itself. In 1368
Muromachi announced that, where disputes arose, the division
of land between claimants would be the norm in reaching a
settlement, except where the land in question had as its patron
the imperial house, or one of the branches of the Fujiwara
qualified to fill the office of Regent, or a religious establishment.
The exceptions were large, but the decision meant that *shōen* were
now more likely to be broken up into smaller parcels, each under
single ownership. Japan was moving towards a pattern that can be
compared with the European fief.

Associated with the change was a degree of territorial con-
solidation. In troubled times, land could be more easily defended
than rights, the support of distant kin was less esteemed than that
of well-armed neighbours. Men therefore tried to bring together
scattered holdings and abandon those too distant to protect. There
was also some modification of kinship structures. Family heads,
reluctant to divide their holdings among several heirs, chose to
name one or two to inherit the bulk of the estate, while laying

down instructions for keeping it together. Women's rights of inheritance necessarily suffered in this situation, because they were thought less likely, whether because of marriage or otherwise, to be able to hold what they were given. So did those of cultivators, who had to deal more often now with a single resident lord, able to put them under greater pressure. By the time the process was complete – and that was not until Japan's next long spell of civil war in many areas, starting late in the fifteenth century – the country was divided for the most part into estates of modest size, each more compact than those of the past and subject to unified control.

Those who benefited most from the years of turbulence in the fourteenth century were the military governors (*shugo*) appointed by the Ashikaga. In order to prosecute the civil war, they were given new powers: the collection of supplementary taxes for the Shogun's war chest, which were described as temporary, but had a way of becoming regular; and a measure of authority over local samurai, for the purpose of raising a force in case of need. With this as leverage, they were able to offer protection to their neighbours and build a private following. They also acquired fresh lands of their own. By the end of the century, the *shugo* was likely to be the largest landholder in the province to which he had been appointed. There would probably be a few others of substance, too, men much like themselves, but holding lands and office elsewhere. A high proportion of the local landholders of lower status were either vassals of these greater men, or acknowledged their influence in some less formal way. The *shugo*'s position, therefore, relied much less than it had before on Muromachi's favour.

Modern historians describe these men as *shugo-daimyō*, a hybrid term that places them at an intermediate stage between appointed military governors, as known in the Kamakura period, and the quasi-independent regional lords (daimyo) of the sixteenth century. The nature of their power implies at least the rudiments of subinfeudation. Under Kamakura, *shugo* and *jitō*, though different in function, had been equals in status, in so far as both were direct vassals (*gokenin*) of the Shogun. Under the Ashikaga, the *shugo* were given an authority which put that equality in question; and as they acquired provincial vassals of their own, not all of whom owed a duty to the *shugo*'s overlord, they assumed a median place in the scale of vassalage. In this respect, too, Japan's feudalism was becoming more like Europe's.

Among the most powerful *shugo-daimyō* were several who were family members or senior vassals of the Ashikaga. The Hosokawa, for example, an Ashikaga branch house, holding office as deputy Shogun, were made *shugo* of no fewer than seven provinces, mostly in central Japan. By contrast, in west Japan the two outstanding names were those of Shimazu and Ōuchi, houses that rose to prominence without the help of Ashikaga connections. The Shimazu of southern Kyushu were descended from a Minamoto *gokenin* appointed as steward (*jitō*) to a former Taira estate, Shimazu-shō, from which the family subsequently took its name. In 1336 they declared allegiance to Ashikaga Takauji, who made them *shugo*. By the end of the fourteenth century their struggles against the *shōen*'s patrons, the Konoe family, had made them lords – not stewards – of an estate which included half the arable land in the three southern Kyushu provinces. The most important of these was Satsuma.

The Ōuchi had their base in the provinces of Nagato and Suō (later known in combination as Chōshū) at the western end of the Inland Sea. They were local officials in the area, recruited as *gokenin* to Minamoto Yoritomo during the wars against the Taira, then made *jitō* to a local *shōen*. In this capacity they accumulated land rights. When the Hōjō fell, they supported the Ashikaga, who made them *shugo* of Suō, an office in which they exploited their judicial and administrative powers to build up a following, both there and in neighbouring Nagato. At their peak they were dominant in the whole of the region west of Hiroshima: *shugo* of six provinces and possessors of a 'capital' at Yamaguchi, which won such fame as a centre of culture that it was known as 'the western Kyoto'.

One of the principal losers by these developments, apart from the patrons of *shōen*, was the Shogun. By choosing to establish his base in Muromachi, Ashikaga Takauji had separated himself by some 300 miles from his lands in the Kanto, which had previously been his source of revenue and fighting men. True, he put the Kanto in the hands of a branch family, its head serving as his deputy (Kanrei) in the region; but in the long run, kinship was to prove no guarantee of loyalty, whether in the Kanto or elsewhere. His successors, therefore, could not rely on the Kanto's military force as a means of keeping overmighty lords in order. Other means of bolstering their authority had to be found.

One obvious device was to take court office, which still carried weight in the eyes of provincial lords, even those of considerable standing. In 1394, having settled the quarrel between the northern and southern dynasties, at least superficially, Yoshimitsu was made Daijō-daijin, head of the emperor's council. It was a post reserved to nobles of the very highest rank. Thereafter he took an ostentatious part in the social and ceremonial life of the capital.

More controversially, he re-opened relations with China in 1401 on the tribute basis from which Kamakura had held aloof. Describing himself in a letter to the Ming emperor Yung Lo as 'Your subject, the King of Japan' – Japanese patriots have condemned him for it ever since – he was given leave to send two ships to Ningpo every two years. The practice was to continue (with some irregularities) until China withdrew the privilege in 1549. This, too, was a step designed to give the Shogun a higher profile in his dealings with feudal lords, but there were also economic benefits. Japan had once more gained entry to the China trade on privileged terms. The ships that were sent there carried, in addition to envoys bound for the Chinese capital with tribute gifts, as many as two or three hundred merchants, who paid for their passage and the transport of their merchandise. Such payment was made to the sponsor of the voyage. This was sometimes the Shogun; but in later years the privilege might be granted (for an appropriate consideration) to a Buddhist house, a Shinto shrine or one of a handful of powerful lords. They in turn might pass the work of setting on foot the voyage to the merchants of a favoured city, organised in guilds. At each level there were profits to be made.

Return gifts from the Ming, among which copper coins and silkstuffs were most highly prized, were of greater value than those Japan sent, as they had been at the time of the T'ang (Chapter 3), but it was now the Shogun who received them, not the emperor. In addition, the merchants brought back cargoes purchased on the Chinese open market. These included, as they had always done, silk and drugs, together with books, paintings and ceramics, all of which sold at high prices in Japan. A percentage went to the Bakufu, making up in part for the loss of income from the Shogun's Kanto lands, which were no longer fully under his control. The rest played a part in stimulating the growth of a commercial economy in Japan.

Not all was gain, however. The price Japan had to pay for China's consent to these arrangements, apart from the formalities of political subservience such as had to be observed by Japanese envoys, was co-operation in a drive against piracy. Pirates from the seas to the west and north of Japan, often based in the territories of lords like Shimazu and Ōuchi, had made large-scale attacks on the China coast in the fourteenth century. Yoshimitsu sent consignments of supposedly pirate heads to the Ming as an earnest of his readiness to suppress them. Yet it was always doubtful whether he had the means to do so. His writ did not run in Kyushu and western Honshu much of the time. His successors had even less power to intervene there, once civil war broke out again after 1467. The lords of that region usually gave the pirates a measure of protection. They also sought to trade with Ningpo on their own account, sometimes intercepting the official tribute ships and seizing the tallies (*kangō*), provided by the Ming, which showed a mission to be legitimate. The result was a level of turbulence in the trade – it was not unknown for rival Japanese missions to come to blows in Ningpo harbour – with which Ming officials at last lost patience. By the same token, the incidents bred a measure of resentment among the powerful lords of west Japan, directed against the Ashikaga.

The revenue that the Ashikaga were able to draw from the China trade was supplemented by yields from domestic commerce. Throughout the Kamakura and early Muromachi periods, agricultural production had been steadily increasing in Japan because of the introduction of double-cropping, new strains of seed, better irrigation, and more widespread use of fertilizer and farm animals. This made surpluses available, offered to purchasers in local markets and – on a more important scale – in Kyoto and other towns and cities, especially those that developed along the shores of the Inland Sea. Merchants who engaged in the manufacture of rice-wine (sake) in those centres, or in money-lending, often became rich, like those in the China trade. Coins, imported from China, were becoming more widely used.

The Bakufu found ways to tap this wealth. City merchants were brought under official patronage, their associations required to pay fees for the advantages this gave them. So were those religious houses that took part in trade and financial operations. Urban housing in the capital was taxed. The result was to make the Bakufu's finances less dependent on land and to provide a more flexible source of funds, which could be used to finance a less 'feudal' type of central administration.

Part of the money raised helped to pay for a local core of more or less full-time Bakufu officers. The regime had taken over from Kamakura a body of middle-ranking vassal-bureaucrats, men who handled most of the work of government and regarded the Shogun as their lord. In case of need, they could call on a permanent force of 2,000 or 3,000 mounted samurai, enfeoffed with lands in the neighbourhood of Kyoto, to keep order in and around the capital. This was particularly important because a number of leading shugo-daimyō, who were members of the councils responsible for the work of the Mandokoro and Samurai-dokoro, were required to live in the city under the Shogun's eye. It was hoped to limit their independence in this way, by separating them for much of the time from their lands. It also, however, provided opportunities for conspiracy. One Shogun, Ashikaga Yoshinori, tried in the fifteenth century to make use of his loyal officials and personal guard to support a more autocratic form of rule in Kyoto, which would enable him to overrule his *shugo* advisers in the Bakufu councils. But the effort failed. In 1441 he was murdered by one of those whose influence he sought to undermine.

What seemed at this stage to be emerging at the centre in Japan was something like an Italian city state of late medieval Europe: a regime based on Kyoto and the nearby provinces, only partly feudal in its revenue and officialdom, and exercising little power in the remoter hinterland. By contrast, the rest of Japan was moving towards a more fully feudal pattern of lordship, fief and vassalage. The first result of this contradiction was a renewal of civil war. After 1460 succession disputes within the Ashikaga house, fanned by the ambitions of leading *shugo* lords, led to fighting in the capital, which grew in scale and scope until it embraced the whole of Japan. It eventually opened the way to a new political order, in which feudal lords acquired greater power within their lands, but became in other respects more subject to the Shogun's authority. So far-reaching was the change that it is more convenient to treat it separately (Chapter 7).

CHAPTER 6

Medieval Culture

1200–1450

The rise of feudalism eventually caused a decisive break with
Chinese political institutions in Japan. It brought no such clearcut
change in the nature of Japanese culture, though it contributed
to a shift of emphasis. Where Chinese civilisation had struck deep
roots, as it had in art and religion, it continued to flourish; and
when Japan's links with China were renewed in the thirteenth,
fourteenth and fifteenth centuries by the travels of Zen monks, it
was given fresh impetus by the influence of Sung and Ming. In
literature, by contrast, the trend that had begun at the very end
of Heian, that of prose writing in Japanese for an audience
wider than the court nobility, strengthened in Kamakura and
Muromachi.

When court aristocrats lost their place as the country's most
powerful patrons, first to the Shogun and his immediate vassals,
then more and more to provincial lords, it was warrior preferences
and tastes that came to determine the work of artists and authors.
Samurai were to be for several hundreds of years the men who
commissioned major buildings, who endowed monasteries, who
were commemorated in portraits, who bought pictures, who gave
employment to writers. Yet it does not follow from this that war
tales became the only product of literature, or pictures of war the
universal form of art. Senior samurai, following the example of

China's bureaucrats, thought themselves rulers as well as soldiers. Logically, they had to have the civil skills (*bun*), in addition to the military ones (*bu*), which the tasks of government required. For the sake of their prestige, they needed cultivated minds. This implied at least a passing acquaintance with classical literature and art.

Pre-feudal culture did not therefore wither on the bough because of neglect by an uncouth soldiery. Minamoto Yoritomo employed a Kyoto bureaucrat, Ōe Hiromoto, as adviser on civil institutions; the Hōjō wrote poetry; Ashikaga Shogun, especially Yoshimitsu and Yoshimasa, promoted a taste for Chinese painting, of which they were enthusiastic collectors. Court nobles of lower rank found in this situation a fresh source of income, to make good part of what they no longer received from land or official emoluments: they became teachers and advisers about the artistic traditions of Nara and Heian to aspirants from the military class. In this way, a knowledge of classical culture was given feudal sanction, extending its life into modern times.

Under feudal rule a certain refinement of taste, not only in terms of what had been valued by the aristocracy in the past, but applying also to novelties like Nō drama, the tea ceremony (*cha-no-yu*), flower arrangement (*ikebana*) and the cultivation of miniature trees (*bonsai*), spread more widely, if more thinly, through Japanese society. The change was of a piece with the dispersal of wealth and status that characterised the age politically. Arbiters of taste no longer belonged only at the emperor's court. Some also gathered at Kamakura. At Muromachi the Ashikaga held court in their own right. A number of provincial lords, like the Ōuchi in Yamaguchi, had highly regarded 'capitals'. In many other parts of the country were less important centres, where story-tellers could find an audience and priests convey the rudiments of art, while an expansion of farm production and domestic commerce produced, certainly by the fifteenth century, a proportion of wealthy commoners, aspiring to the style of life that samurai had chosen. They were the forerunners of the 'people's culture' of the Edo period.

Buddhism

Buddhism, though still Chinese in doctrine, became less scholastic during the feudal period, hence easier for the less educated members of society to comprehend. Two new sects, focusing on Amida as the path to human salvation, were the principal instruments in this change. One was Pure Land (Jōdo), which derived from China via the teachings of the priest Hōnen (1133–1212). A critic of the formalism and monastic preferences of the Buddhist establishment of his day, he argued that sincere invocation of Amida's name (*nembutsu*) was all that was needed to secure rebirth in the Western Paradise. A generation later, Shinran (1173–1262), who had briefly been a disciple of Hōnen, took the argument one step farther. Once there had been a single act of invocation, he proclaimed, provided it were heartfelt, salvation was assured. This belief became the distinguishing feature of True Pure Land (Jōdo Shinshū, usually known as Shinshū), which remains Japan's largest sect.

Neither man, it appears, began with the intention of founding a separate religious organisation. Shinran, indeed, went so far as to abandon his priestly vows, taking a wife and having children. Their successors, however, faced by both temporal and ecclesiastical persecution, found that they had in the end to organise in self-defence. By the Muromachi period they had created a structure of authority, locally and nationally, and could command a fighting force of substantial size. It was to be politically significant after 1460, playing a part in Japan's civil wars.

By making salvation depend on the simple invocation, 'Namu Amida Butsu' (Praise to Amida Buddha), Hōnen and Shinran made it easier to welcome into the faith many who could not read the scriptures, had no time or taste for the monastic rule, and were unwilling to commit themselves to a complex pattern of ethical rules in their daily lives. In the process, some other elements of the older religions also disappeared, including the comfort to be drawn from participation in elaborate rituals, which reinforced belief in one's own salvation, and ways of coming to terms with the supernatural; but with the passing of time, means were found to make these deficiencies more bearable. Hōnen and Shinran became charismatic figures, even saints, who had handed down a 'doctrine'. Amida was held to be a miracle worker, invocation something like a magic formula. Ippen, a thirteenth-century Jōdo monk, went so far as to encourage chanting and dancing in his efforts to convert, issuing amulets – a quarter of a million, it is said – which were held to be a protection from disasters in this life and a promise of salvation in the next. The result of such ameliorations of the code was to make religious practice less austere than the founders might have hoped, but it won over many adherents.

Both Jōdo and Shinshū retained a strong communal base, which was an enormous advantage in troubled times. The cohesion and security it gave to villagers and urban residents in the civil wars of the fourteenth and later fifteenth centuries left Jōdo with a huge following in and around Kyoto, Shinshū equally in the Kanto and northeast. Yet it would be wrong to conclude on this account that the more traditional and outwardly 'Chinese' schools had been driven from centre-stage. By reason of their landed wealth and close relations with the court, Nara houses like the Tōdaiji and Kōfukuji long retained a provincial standing equal to that of many feudal lords, while Tendai's Enryakuji continued to intervene in Kyoto politics. Even when their temporal power began to erode, these sects remained the champions of the ortho-dox, whom the state could not readily ignore. Jōdo and Shinshū were by comparison outsiders, owing much of their success to the growing instability in the body politic.

Another strand in the religious history of the Kamakura period, Zen Buddhism (Ch'an in Chinese, meaning meditation), was more directly linked to samurai. There had been traces of Zen in Japan from very early times, but it was not until it won support among the Shogun's vassals in the thirteenth century – the war-riors esteemed its self-discipline and disregard of book learning, their superiors welcomed Zen's detachment from the court – that it became a factor of consequence. There were two Zen schools, Rinzai and Sōtō, both Chinese in origin, which had in common a belief that enlightenment was best achieved by contemplation under the guidance of a master. Rinzai put its emphasis on *kōan*, the study of a problem not open to logical solution (most famously, 'what is the sound of the clapping of one hand?'). Sōtō favoured *zazen*, meditation on the meaning of life while seated in the lotus posture. Both practices had by tradition been introduced to China in the early sixth century by the Indian monk Bodhidharma, known in Japan as Daruma. He, it was claimed, had sat for nine years in meditation facing a wall. As a result, the story goes, he lost the use of his arms and legs; and from the sixteenth century onwards, Japanese made dolls to commemorate this feat of endurance and concentration, small and pear-shaped figures as a rule, designed to return to the upright position when pushed over. They were believed to be amulets, giving protection against smallpox, and lucky charms, bringing the fulfilment of a wish, whether for better harvests or some more personal ambition.

The Tendai monk Eisai (1141–1215), who brought Rinzai to Japan, was attracted to it during visits to China made in 1168, then again in 1187–91. On his return, finding that his seniors at Enryakuji were reluctant to give it the standing he thought to be its due, he decamped to Kamakura in search of a warmer welcome. Sōtō's founder, Dōgen (1200–53), a court noble by birth, was in China from 1223 to 1227. He, too, was impressed by Zen's high reputation there, but preferred Sōtō to Rinzai because it was 'purer': that is, more monastic in outlook and less secular in its affiliations. He therefore refused invitations to Kamakura on his return, deciding to strike out on his own and settle in the province of Echizen (modern Fukui). So while Rinzai became the school of Zen that found greatest official favour, first in Kamakura, then in Muromachi, Sōtō recruited adherents from less politically influential regions.

Because Zen attached prime importance to the role of the teacher in preparing a disciple for enlightenment, it was much concerned with Japan's relations with China, where the most distinguished teachers were to be found. A fifth of the Zen monks whose lives are recorded in one biographical work are said to have visited China. Musō Soseki (1275–1351), abbot of the Zen house of Nanzenji in Kyoto, is thought to have persuaded Ashikaga Takauji to seek to resume relations after the breach that the Mongol invasions caused. In the thirteenth century, Zen masters from China had been invited to Japan, or came as refugees from the Mongol conquests. Kenchōji, the leading Rinzai monastery in Kamakura, had no fewer than three Chinese abbots after 1246. Under the influence of men like this, Japan moved gradually towards the Chinese practice of giving some Zen houses, designated by the state as *gozan* ('the five mountains'), authority to regulate those of lesser standing. In Kamakura the selected institutions included the Kenchōji and Engakuji. Kyoto's Nanzenji was added at the end of the century. During the Muromachi period, the Tenryūji at Arashiyama, on the outskirts of the capital, was also named as one of them. By the middle of the fifteenth century, there were as many as 300 Rinzai establishments under the direction of the *gozan*, some of which were given a secondary supervisory role in their own provinces.

Because of their close connection with Chinese masters, Zen monks developed an expertise in Chinese studies that qualified them as intermediaries in the introduction of new strands of Chinese culture to Japan. Some monasteries were directly involved in the China trade itself. Once tribute missions were resumed under Ashikaga Yoshimitsu, their monks, as men of learning, much better versed in the Chinese language than their fellow-countrymen, went with them as interpreters, or even envoys. Back in Japan again, they became teachers of the tea ceremony, calligraphy and ink-painting (*sumi-e*), all deriving from their Chinese experience; made the poets Li Po and Tu Fu widely known; gave expositions of Sung Neo-Confucianism; laid out landscape gardens in the Chinese manner; and introduced Japan's artists and collectors to the painting and ceramics of the Sung. In short, they took over the task of cultural education that had been neglected in the capital since the eleventh century.

Before leaving the subject of Buddhism, a little needs to be said about one other sect, Nichiren. It was founded in the middle of the thirteenth century by a Tendai monk, after whom it is named (an unusual circumstance). He rejected what he conceived to be the doctrinal laxity of the Pure Land sects, insisting instead on the primacy of the classic Lotus Sutra (*Hokke-kyō*); and while he grudgingly accepted the new-fangled practice of invocation, he required that it be directed towards the Lotus Sutra, not towards Amida. There were several concomitants of this traditionalist attitude. One was an ethic comprising Shinto and Confucian elements, such as had already found a place in Tendai eclecticism. Another was belief in an emperor-centred polity. The latter proved offensive to feudal rulers; and since Nichiren argued his case for it in a highly combative manner, he came into conflict with Kamakura on a number of occasions. One of these led to a spell of exile on the island of Sado. Nevertheless, in later times his reputation for patriotic ardour, stemming not only from his loyalty to the emperor, but also from his efforts to rally Japan against the Mongol attacks, gave his successors a role in the development of Japanese nationalism.

Prose literature and drama

Before the seventeenth century, Japanese literature contains little that could be called political philosophy, apart from occasional passages in the histories. The early chronicles, taking their lead from China, were always careful to make a case for the reigning dynasty, though they did so by the use of arguments that would not have been acceptable in China itself – those of the emperor's divine descent – and they avoided direct discussion of the issues that this raised. This was politics, but not philosophy. Indeed, imperial rule was not challenged, whether by historians or by events, until the Heian period. Nor was the challenge then an open one, since the Fujiwara chose to wrap their power in imperial authority.

Minamoto Yoritomo broke the pattern. By steadfastly refusing to live at court, while issuing orders from 300 miles away, he made it idle to pretend that he was a member of the Kyoto 'system', speaking for a ruler whose will he interpreted. Once he was dead, the measures that the Hōjō took to make the Kamakura Bakufu a separate organ of government, having a writ that ran through all Japan, made the situation more obvious still; and the Ashikaga, for all that they took up residence in part of the emperor's capital, continued this tradition of separateness. Historians of the period had therefore to decide how to accommodate their narrative to the fact that Japan had two rival centres of power, each claiming to be legitimate.

The first person to confront the problem was a Buddhist priest, Jien, who wrote a history entitled *Gukanshō* (Notes on Foolish Views) just before Go-Toba's attack on the Hōjō in 1221. Jien was brother to Kujō Kanezane, the senior court official (Sesshō) who worked closely with Yoritomo. He had himself served as chief abbot of the Tendai sect on several occasions. He was therefore a member of the Fujiwara élite, closely connected with that section of it which had recognised the need to come to terms with samurai power. His book reflected this. Its narrative was in chronicle form, set in the framework of imperial reigns, but passages of comment inserted here and there – some of them very jejune – revealed an underlying belief in cycles of historical change, shaped by the Buddhist concept of inevitable decline. This belief was softened by a recognition that decline could be checked, if no more than temporarily, by the will of Amaterasu, working through the imperial line and the Fujiwara house. The most recent example was what had been done by the Kujō, when faced by Minamoto victories.

To justify this somewhat self-seeking argument, Jien put forward his own view of imperial authority, couched in historical terms. Given the imperatives of lineage, he wrote, some emperors would necessarily prove to be incompetent or unprincipled. It was for this reason that Amaterasu had from the beginning laid it down that good government required a sharing of power between ruler and minister (a Confucian choice of terminology). The Fujiwara had been the first to be advanced to the place of leading minister in accordance with this formula. When they had lost their grip on affairs, ex-emperors had come to take part of the responsibility, followed in turn by Taira and Minamoto. The nature and legitimacy of a regime, in other words, did not depend exclusively on the lineage of the ruler. It took account also of his capacity to govern. If he could not keep order, others must do so, in accordance with the will of Amaterasu.

A refutation of this modified version of the doctrine of the Mandate of Heaven (*t'ien-ming*) came a little over a century later from the pen of Kitabatake Chikafusa. He, too, was a court noble, though of the Murakami Genji house. A supporter of Go-Daigo in his contest with the Ashikaga, he went into exile with him to the Yoshino mountains, where he achieved some reputation as a soldier in the fighting that followed the events of 1336. He also wrote a book that gave him lasting fame: *Jinnō Shōtōki* (A Record of the True Descent of the Divine Sovereigns), completed between 1339 and 1343. Its immediate purpose was to set out the claims of Go-Daigo to be the legitimate ruler of Japan. To this end it stressed the importance of the imperial regalia (mirror, sword and jewels) that Go-Daigo had carried away from Kyoto; described Japan as uniquely 'the land of the gods' (*kami*), contrasting it with China, where frequent changes of dynasty had produced 'a country of notorious disorders'; and insisted that the imperial succession was ordained immutably by Amaterasu, never to be set aside by human action, or varied in the light of an emperor's virtues and defects. In this Kitabatake was speaking for a 'loyalist' view, directly opposed to the pragmatism of Jien. It has recurred again and again in later writing, notably after 1800.

When he turned to the events of his own day – they were, after all, his reason for writing – Kitabatake was forced to admit that Go-Daigo had failed in his dealings with Ashikaga Takauji. This might well have implications for the succession in the short term, he conceded, since there was now a war between northern and southern courts, but these aberrations were secondary. In the last analysis, the precept that the succession rested on descent, not competence, was not to be denied.

The debate about the respective roles of emperor and Shogun, which was to be resumed under the Tokugawa, was an innovation in historical writing in Japan. No longer a simple record of ceremony and intrigue in an almost static set of institutions, the *Gukanshō* and *Jinnō Shōtōki* recognised the fact of revolutionary change, sought to explain it in a rudimentary way, and expressed controversial opinions about it. This was history with a political purpose extending far beyond the validation of authority. Other medieval works in the field did not so readily enter on this dangerous ground. Official histories continued to be produced. They were much the same in manner and technique as the so-called national histories of Nara and Heian, even to being written in Chinese, but were compiled by servants of the Bakufu, not the court, and embodied the changes of attitude that this made prudent. There were also less formal works, called 'historical tales' (*rekishi-monogatari*) and 'war tales' (*gunki-monogatari*), arranged in chronicle form, but designed for entertainment rather than instruction.

These, too, reflected changing times. They had narratives full of warlike action and deeds of valour or betrayal; were tinged with a mood of Buddhist melancholy, equating 'change' with 'decline'; and dwelt above all on human action or supernatural influence as the fountain-head of events. They were, in other words, more human and dramatic than what had earlier passed for history. Nor were they only meant to be read in the silence of the study. Most were modified over time to make them suitable for recitation to a less sophisticated audience than court romances such as *Genji* had enjoyed, perhaps even an illiterate one. Recitation was often accompanied by the playing of a lute (*biwa*), in order to set the mood, or illustrated by scenes from picture-scrolls (*e-maki*). The reciters, usually blind, were numerous enough by the fourteenth century to have formed a guild in Kyoto.

Three of these tales, compiled in the Kamakura period, dealt with incidents in the late-twelfth-century struggle between the Taira and the Minamoto. The most famous was *Heike monogatari* (Tale of the Taira House), which devoted the greater part of its space to the lives of Taira Kiyomori and Shigemori, plus Minamoto Yoshinaka and Yoshitsune: that is, the men who could be presented as tragic and heroic. Minamoto Yoritomo, less romantic, because he was above all the builder of a political order, was left in the shadows. On a not dissimilar theme, a later work, the inappropriately named *Taiheiki* (Record of Great Peace), tells of Go-Daigo and his efforts to overthrow the Kamakura Bakufu. The text, spanning the years from 1318 to 1367, is more narrative than chronicle; includes descriptions of fighting, poems, sentimental anecdotes and Buddhist moralising; and was often recited in later years, though not, it seems, to music. The author or authors are unknown. The fact that several variants exist makes it difficult to claim that a consistent political line was taken – this may be caution on the part of the various editors – but Ashikaga Takauji emerges as an unsympathetic character, while the loyalist, Kusunoki, is an object of admiration and respect. This suggests a leaning towards the southern court, the more romantic cause.

Subject-matter of this kind, accompanied as it was by a wealth of vivid detail, has made these books a treasure trove for later writers and dramatists in Japan. The reciters, who helped to make them popular, also drew upon collections of prose fiction in the manner of *Konjaku monogatari* (Chapter 4), which were still being put together. The choice implied a reaching out towards a different section of the population (and a source of income that did not depend on aristocratic patronage), but the result was to create a world of folk-heroes, both real and imaginary, known for the first time to a substantial part of the Japanese people. It became an element in the national heritage, familiar to those of every age group to the present day.

Drama also began to seek a wider than aristocratic audience, specifically in what became known as Nō and Kyōgen. Both derived originally from performances at Shinto shrines and festivals, Nō being a kind of dance, Kyōgen a display of acrobatic clowning. By the end of Heian, they had developed into public entertainment, but it was not until much later, when it found a patron in Ashikaga Yoshimitsu, that Nō acquired a more serious reputation. Thereafter it changed rapidly in style and complexity. By the seventeenth century, it was being performed by highly trained players, wearing masks and accompanied by chorus, flute and drums, very much as it is today. There were written texts (closely followed by *aficionados* in a modern theatre, as opera is in the West), marked with a notation designed to indicate the chant.

The men most responsible for this transformation were Kanami (1334–84) and his son Zeami (1363–1443). Kanami was above all a performer. Zeami was both dramatist and author of theoretical treatises on his art, laying stress on the need for elegance and restraint in a player's movements. The language he used was literary, not colloquial. His plots drew heavily on *Heike monogatari* and other such works, placing their action – if such it can properly be called, since physical movement is slow and stylised – in the upper reaches of society, both warrior and noble. Ghosts and wandering monks were introduced to provide explanatory comment or exchanges, and Japanese poems (*waka*) appeared in the dialogue here and there.

Nō as Zeami reshaped it was a far cry from Kyōgen, though the two were regularly staged together. Kyōgen had a good deal about it of the vaudeville sketch: a script that was little more than a synopsis, to be elaborated by the players; no masks or chorus; much mimicry and horseplay. Its plots might be described as social satire, making fun not of the very highest in the land, since that could well be dangerous, but of the samurai, monks, thieves, artisans, peasants and their various womenfolk encountered in everyday life. Favourite themes were the unimaginative dealings of a stupid master with his streetwise servant, or haggling between man and wife.

Bringing Nō and Kyōgen together in a single play-bill ensured that both the high-born and the commoners in the audience found something to their taste. The actors were men of low status, their sponsors drawn from the Shogun's rather than the emperor's court, their customers very varied. This social mix set the drama at some remove from the aristocratic traditions of Heian, when music, dancing and the recitation of poetry had been skills for courtiers to demonstrate to each other. The theatre was becoming professional.

Chinese influence on the arts

In literature, the medieval period saw an increasing devotion to Japanese themes and style, accompanied by a modest degree of popularisation. Development in the visual arts took a different course. During Kamakura, at least, there was a great deal of continuity with late Heian. The replacement of members of the imperial court as patrons by feudal rulers and their warrior supporters certainly had an effect on choice of subject-matter, but it did not immediately bring about changes in style: members of the feudal class, seeking a reputation as men of culture, rightly entrusted with civil power, did so within the accepted canons of taste. In architecture, for example, the rebuilding of Nara's Kōfu-kuji and Tōdaiji, destroyed in the wars between Taira and Min-amoto, was carried out by the latter with a minimum of innovation, except, perhaps, in statuary, the new versions of which showed greater strength and realism than the old. The same was true of portraiture, both in sculpture and in painting. Much of it now was of lay figures, especially heads of samurai houses, com-memorated in pictures that were commissioned by their vassals or descendants. This was, no doubt, an attempt to assert a claim to dignity on behalf of rulers, many of whom lacked distinguished lineage, but the manner of it in many cases – especially pictures of Shogun – was unmistakably that of the school of Fujiwara Takanobu (Chapter 4). Most such subjects were shown in court dress, though in later years some were in armour or on horseback, as befitted men whose claim to fame was prowess in battle.

1 *(previous page)* Statue of
Maitreya (Miroku) Buddha, Kōryūji,
Kyoto. Said to be a gift from Prince
Shōtoku, it dates from the early
seventh century, when the Kōryūji
was founded by a wealthy
immigrant family (Korean or
Chinese). There is an almost
identical statue of Maitreya in a
temple in Korea.

2 Hōryūji, a Buddhist temple to the
south of Nara. Founded by Prince
Shōtoku between 601 and 607, its
oldest existing buildings date from
later in the seventh century. The
buildings are in the Chinese style
(tile-roofed and raised on stone
plinths) which became the chosen
model for the palace and other public
buildings in eighth-century Nara.

3 Ganjin (Chien-chen). A memorial statue of the Chinese priest, invited to
Japan in the eighth century, who founded the Tōshō-daiji, a Buddhist temple
in Nara, in 759 and became its first abbot. The statue is attributed to two of
his disciples, who came with him from China.

4 *(top)* The Phoenix Pavilion of the Byōdōin at Uji, midway between Nara and Kyoto. Originally a Fujiwara villa, it was converted into a temple in 1052 and became a centre for the worship of Amida Buddha.

5 *(above)* Ladies of the Heian court. A scene from the Tale of Genji picture-scroll (*Genji monogatari e-maki*), showing court pastimes and the use of screens to break up the large open spaces of the palace rooms.

6 The Heiji incident. An incident during the twelth-century struggles between the Taira and the Minamoto in Kyoto, when the emperor was smuggled from the palace in disguise to escape from his Minamoto guards.

7 Minamoto Yoritomo in court dress. This portrait, long attributed to Fujiwara Takanobu (1142–1205), but now thought to have been painted after his death, was one of a series of studies of leading political figures of the time that set the style for later portraits of feudal overlords.

9 Feudal lord on horseback, fourteenth century. The figure wears full armour (of the kind often seen in museums) and is equiped with sword, bow and arrows. He has been identified as Ashikaga Takauji, but this is disputed.

10 *(right)* Nō mask. In Nō drama, as it developed in and after the fifteenth century, performers wore masks to indicate the nature of the character they portrayed. This one is for the *hannya*, a female demon.

8 *(left)* Kūya Shōnin (903–972). A statue, dating from the early thirteenth century, that shows him in his most famous role: as an itinerant preacher promoting the worship of Amida Buddha (hence the miniature statues of Amida projecting from his mouth).

11 Toyotomi Hideyoshi
(1537–1598).
A memorial statue
in court dress that
emphasises his
diminutive size
and unprepossessing
appearance.

12 Himeji Castle.
Held at one time by
Hideyoshi, later by
a senior Tokugawa
vassal, it was a
military stronghold
and administrative
centre that guarded
the approaches to
Kyoto from the west.

The most famous example of religious sculpture is the Daibutsu (Great Buddha) in Kamakura, a bronze figure of Amida over 11 metres high, cast in 1252. Since the building that housed it was destroyed by a tidal wave in 1495 and never replaced, the statue still stands impressively in the open. That apart, the city has little to show for a century and more of warrior rule, except a large array of shrines and temples. Of these, the Zen establishments showed signs of architectural novelty, deriving mostly from China. The Kenchōji, for example, is said to be a replica of the Ch'an headquarters at Hangchow. It had more elaborate gates – these became customary in medieval temples – and larger halls for communal contemplation than had been customary in Japan, but most of the points of difference from religious buildings of the past were to be found in the decoration and detail. Some features remained entirely familiar. In Kamakura, as in Heian, pagodas were distinctively unChinese, because the use of wood as a material, instead of brick or stone, required a modification of building techniques.

The Shogun's move to Muromachi after 1336 strengthened the link between court and warrior building styles. Across the road from the imperial palace, which had been moved to a new site in 1337 and made rather smaller, Ashikaga Yoshimitsu erected a splendid residence for himself, a symbol of his aristocratic – or conceivably monarchical – ambitions. (It may be recalled that he opened a correspondence with the Ming under the title 'King of Japan'.) As Daijō-daijin from 1394, always surrounded by court nobles of the higher ranks, he saw his palace as a suitable setting for both his official and his personal life. In 1397 he also acquired a villa on the northern outskirts of the city, known as the Gold Pavilion (Kinkakuji) from the fact that its central structure was covered in gold foil. It might be described as eclectically Chinese: the gold colour and the pond in which it is reflected have associations with Pure Land Buddhism, while the upper floor is Zen. The whole of what can now be seen is in any case a replica, for fire has wreaked its havoc several times, most recently as a result of arson in 1949.

Many find the Silver Pavilion (Ginkakuji) more attractive. It was built in 1482 by Ashikaga Yoshimasa as a retreat, lying below the city's eastern slopes, where he could escape the pervasive signs of weakness and civil war: a place of contemplation, provided with a separate tea-house, rooms for incense guessing and other courtly pursuits, and a notable landscape garden, designed by Soami, who also laid out the more famous rock-and-sand garden at the Ryoanji. Because of the Shogun's lavish spending on other projects, plus the financial depredations of civil war, the funds to provide the silver that was to cover the walls of the main pavilion never became available. Aesthetically, that was no bad thing.

Continuities of style between late Heian and Kamakura were maintained in painting, not only in portraiture, but in the picture-scroll (*e-maki*). Although Chinese in origin, this was undoubtedly a Japanese art form by the thirteenth century. The two basic styles, represented by the aristocratic interiors of *Genji monogatari* on the one hand, the crowd scenes of *Shigisan engi* on the other, were both to be found in thirteenth-century scrolls, as they had been in *Ban Dainagon* (Chapter 4). Most themes were narrative, either military or religious, while biography and accounts of con-temporary events made up a good proportion. Thus one finds scrolls that tell the story of Sugawara Michizane and of Ippen, a Jōdo monk; describe the building of the Kasuga Shrine in Nara; give a highly coloured account of the Mongol attacks on Japan (paying due attention to the exploits of the samurai who com-missioned the work); illustrate the ceremonies and processions held in the palace in the course of the year; depict in horrifying detail the range of human diseases, or the punishments inflicted in the Buddhist hells. There is even a scroll about a poetry contest.

The freshness and vigour shown in the earliest examples gave way in time to the repetitiveness of routine and occasional crude-ness of technique. Scrolls continued to be produced until modern times, often for purposes of record – there is one of a nineteenth-century reverberatory furnace, for example – but they were becoming more useful to the historian than attractive to the connoisseur. One reason is that illustrated books, block-printed in multiple copies, proved cheaper and more convenient after the sixteenth century. Another is that it became customary in the Muromachi period to provide the houses of the well-to-do with alcoves (*tokonoma*), where single scrolls of vertical format (*kakemono*) could be hung, often above a flower arrangement. This encouraged the production of individual pictures, which could fulfil some of the purposes previously served by scrolls. In Edo times the latter's role was also taken over in part by genre painting and the woodblock print.

Zen, by reason of its contacts with China, reinvigorated Chinese influence on other kinds of painting in Japan. The *suiboku* style, in which light colour wash was combined with brush strokes made in various shades of ink, appeared in the fourteenth century in sketches of Zen and Taoist religious figures – Daruma was a popular choice – as well as bird-and-flower studies, pictures of animals, landscapes. The largest designs were used on screens and sliding panels in religious establishments and the houses of the great, where they became a substitute for murals. Their manner was impressionistic, their subjects often imaginary. One notable 'portrait', for example, was of the three great teachers of the East Asian world, Buddha, Lao-tzu and Confucius. Not only were they dead many centuries since, but there were no 'true likenesses' for the artist to copy. Similarly, landscapes, including those by Japanese, were usually of places existing only in the imagination, or of Chinese mountains that the painter had never seen. Painting, in other words, did not have to rely on observation. This was not in itself a new phenomenon. In 1207, when the emperor Go-Toba commissioned four men to produce scenes of famous places on sliding screens for a newly founded temple, only one of the four expressed a wish to go and see his subject for himself.

Nevertheless, the best and most famous of Japanese artists of this school, Sesshū (1420–1506), did in fact visit China, as well as painting landscapes of real places in Japan. Born in the Okayama region on the northern shores of the Inland Sea, he studied painting as a monk in Kyoto in his early years, but in 1464 transferred to Yamaguchi, the Ōuchi centre, apparently to escape

the growing disorder in the capital. Three years later he joined a
trade mission sent to China by the Ōuchi, staying there two years.
It was after his return, when he moved to Oita in Kyushu, that
he painted most prolifically, producing work across the whole
range of figure studies, bird-and-flower compositions, and landscapes, both imaginary and real. Some were mounted as *kakemono*.
Others were painted on screens, usually designed as pairs or in
larger sets, appropriate to the kind of rooms that were favoured
by his patrons.

Sesshū's experience is a reminder that patronage was not only
available in the capital, especially in the later medieval years, but
it is none the less true that culturally, as well as politically, the
Bakufu was the principal heir to the court. The Kamakura Shogun
and the Hōjō regents, isolated in the Kanto, proved better friends
to Zen than they were to Chinese art, though Hōjō Tokimune
collected Chinese paintings, but the move to Muromachi under
the Ashikaga encouraged cultural borrowing across a wider range.
The Ashikaga presented themselves to the world as connoisseurs
of Chinese culture in many of its forms. They resumed the official
visits to the collection at the Shōsōin, abandoned by Kamakura;
gathered round themselves men knowledgeable in the arts; collected paintings, ceramics, tea utensils and incense burners, mostly
of Chinese origin or in the Chinese style; and acquired a flattering
reputation as painters and poets. Great lords from the provinces,
who were required to live in Kyoto as a matter of feudal duty,
followed their example. Parties were held, at which guests vied
with each other to produce linked verse (*renga*) in accordance
with complex rules, or gathered to admire *objets d'art*, recently
acquired.

Much of this lifestyle derived from the 'amateur' tradition of
China's official class, modified to suit a Japanese environment. It
called for a perceptive eye and a careful cultivation of taste, but
not the day-to-day application to study and practice marking
those who earned their living by the arts, nor the almost wholly
leisured existence that had made elegant dancers and musicians of
court nobles in the *Genji* years. The tea ceremony (*cha-no-yu*) is

perhaps the most apposite example. It had its origins in the Zen Buddhism of T'ang, which held it to be an aid to meditation. Introduced into Japan in the Kamakura period, it was at one time performed at rowdy 'tournaments' (for guessing types of tea), which had a reputation for riotous and alcoholic behaviour; but under the influence of Ashikaga Yoshimasa greater restraint was imposed, and the ceremony was transferred to special tea-houses in palace or castle grounds, where landscape gardens contributed to a more serene environment. In this context *cha-no-yu* provided an occasion for aesthetic appreciation, achieving popularity among both feudal lords and wealthy commoners. Politically, it was an opportunity to pursue discrete discussions. Socially, given the enormous prices paid for the most notable tea-bowls, whether imported from China or crafted in Japan, it made possible a carefully understated display of wealth.

Several of the 'lesser arts' that are associated with Zen, such as flower arrangement (*ikebana*), *bonsai* and landscape gardening, helped to provide the atmosphere of discipline and restraint in which the tea ceremony was expected to take place. Like the building of splendid villas, the patronage of drama and painting, and the support that was given to Zen, they played a part in making feudal rulers 'civilised', hence worthy and legitimate successors to the Fujiwara. Perhaps because of this, the Chinese influences that reached Japan in the Kamakura and Muromachi periods seem in retrospect to be less fundamental than those of Nara and early Heian. Nor is it surprising that this should be so. Japan had by then had several centuries to assimilate what it found most relevant in Chinese civilisation. The medieval phase did little more than bring its knowledge up to date by adding Sung to T'ang; and despite the importance of Zen as an instrument in this development, it did so as much in temporal as in religious terms.

CHAPTER 7

The Unifiers

The civil wars that broke out in central Japan in 1467 spread to most of the country in the next hundred years. Almost at once they destroyed what little remained of Ashikaga authority. In the longer run they also brought about a major change in feudal society. The greatest of the lords, engaged in struggles for power at a distance from their lands, all too often fell victim to rivals or ambitious vassals at home, destroyed in a recurrent pattern of *gekokujō*, 'low overthrows high'. As a result, all but a handful of those families that were great names in the land in 1450 were gone two centuries later. The Shimazu were the most notable survivors.

By 1500, in fact, a new generation of leaders had begun to emerge, men of a different stamp from those they had overthrown: able, bold, ruthless, as to be successful at such a time they had to be, but aware, too, that in order to lead large armies, better organised and equipped, they had to exploit their lands with more efficiency than those they had replaced. Many were innovators in methods of administration. Nearly all were brash and extrovert by comparison with the courtiers and Ashikaga nominees who ruled in Kyoto.

Fifty years later there were a handful, scattered through the country, who had the qualities and the ambition to aspire to rule Japan as a whole. Three stand out: Oda Nobunaga, Toyotomi

Hideyoshi and Tokugawa Ieyasu. Military leaders of a good deal more than average accomplishment, shrewd judges of what was politically feasible, they became in succession 'conquerors' of Japan. They then gave it a kind of political order that it had never possessed before. There is a Japanese saying, summing up their roles: 'Nobunaga mixed the cake, Hideyoshi baked it, Ieyasu ate it'. It was Tokugawa Ieyasu, in other words, living longer than the other two, who enjoyed to the full the fruits of their success. He took the title Shogun in 1603; passed it to his descendants, together with enormous holdings of land; and blocked out the shape of a governmental structure by which they ruled the country until the end of 1867.

Warfare and warlords (1460–1560)

The Japanese label for the period from 1467 to 1560 is Sengoku, 'the country at war'. Institutionally, the description is inadequate. The fact of warfare itself was nothing new, just as the issues that provoked it were familiar; but because its scale was greater than before, its techniques and tactics more advanced, the men who emerged as victors from it were holders of domains that are better described as princedoms than estates.

The first stage of the Sengoku wars, lasting until 1477, sprang from a quarrel between two great lords, resident in different parts of Kyoto, embroiled in a dispute over succession to the headship of the Ashikaga house. Ten years of fighting in and around the capital left the city in ruins, the Bakufu in disarray. Thereafter the war moved into the provinces, becoming a focus for every kind of political or territorial conflict at the local level, much as it had done in the struggle between north and south in the fourteenth century. Japan was plunged into chaos. The most powerful lords, little restrained by the Shogun's authority, fought each other for land, while their armies grew steadily in size, reaching 20,000 or even 50,000 men. Many of these were not samurai in the acknowledged sense, but foot-soldiers (*ashigaru*), armed with spears and fighting as organised units, whose proper employment on the battlefield called for new skills of military leadership. To keep them supplied with arms and provisions, to ensure that they were always ready for action, to direct them in a campaign, not just a battle, called more for organising talents than for panache. Not every lord possessed them. Nor did the landholdings they had brought together since the days of Ashikaga Takauji always provide a sufficient economic base.

Those who lacked the qualities that were needed in this situation – or simply failed to watch their backs – were replaced by ambitious deputies or other rivals, by whom they were assassinated, defeated in battle, or overthrown while attending to business that took them away from the centre of their power. In consequence, some of the largest holdings were broken up into smaller units. The Shiba, for example, a branch of the Ashikaga, who held large parcels of land, plus office as military governor (*shugo*), in several provinces to the east and north of Kyoto, eventually saw their territories crumble. In 1453 Asakura Toshikage, a Shiba vassal, was sent to Echizen (Fukui) to settle a local dispute on his lord's behalf. He became the *shugo*'s resident deputy there in 1459; used the prerogatives of his office to acquire land rights of his own; and in 1471 declared his 'independence' from the Shiba, which he proved able to maintain against attack. In Owari (Nagoya) another deputy *shugo*, Oda Nobuhide (Nobunaga's father), overthrew Shiba control throughout the province in the first half of the sixteenth century.

Within the regions where they were the leading figures, both the old lords and the new faced problems in enforcing their will. The upper levels of rural society by this time consisted mostly of a landed gentry, known as *kokujin*, many of whom had pledged a nominal allegiance to the *shugo*; but they were not bound so tightly to his interests as to accept without demur his demands for greater powers and greater revenues for the prosecution of his wars. They lacked the resources to oppose him individually. What is more, they were themselves coming under pressure from below, as the poverty and starvation that were the product of war prompted peasant revolt on a substantial scale. In some areas this led them to form leagues (*ikki*), coming together with others like themselves to defend their landed rights against rapacious lords and turbulent commoners. From such leagues several 'upstart' feudal leaders emerged. For example, when the head of the Ōuchi house was murdered by one of his vassals in 1551, it was not the latter who succeeded in taking his place. Instead, after a brief interval of fighting, victory went to Mōri Motonari, whose ancestors had come to prominence as the leaders of a *kokujin* league in the Hiroshima district. At the time of his death in 1571, Motonari was master of the ten most westerly provinces in the main island, Honshu.

Men lower in the social scale also formed *ikki*, usually as a defence against exploitation by the gentry and the religious houses who were their landlords. Since many villagers regularly carried arms, and some could claim a modicum of samurai status, they could be a formidable threat when brought together in large enough numbers. On occasion they would co-operate with *kokujin*, given sufficient cause, which made the rebellions they raised into something more than outbreaks of casual violence. One, in which *kokujin* and village samurai took a leading part, held Kyoto's own home province of Yamashiro in its grip from 1485 to 1492. Directed at first against the exactions of officials, it was brought to an end when the *ikki* itself became a symbol of oppression and a target of peasant revolt. Another, which proved to be still longer lasting, occurred in Kaga (Kanazawa) on the Japan Sea coast. Based on an alliance between peasants and *kokujin*, held together by the influence of the most influential of the local Buddhist sects, Jōdo Shinshū − known as Ikkō in this context − the *ikki* first intervened in a dispute over the choice of military governor in 1488; then grew steadily in power until the 1520s, when it dominated politics in the area; and for many years provided a structure of local administration, serving Ikkō leaders who behaved like feudal lords. Its power was not broken until Nobunaga overcame it in 1580.

One product of rural unrest was a modest growth in village autonomy. Some village elders, seeking to secure better living conditions while the attention of their lords was taken up with war against each other, won the right to handle local boundary disputes, determine the use of common lands, and draft and enforce village regulations. Something of the same kind occurred in towns. With the exception of a handful of political centres, like Kyoto, and the main ports engaged in the China trade (Sakai and Hakata), Muromachi towns were small, no more than local markets. They contained few, if any, wealthy merchants, had no impressive walls and could command no military force, even for defence. This meant they lacked the means to oppose their feudal masters openly, or even to buy them off in a majority of cases. A limited autonomy was the best they could achieve.

Sakai, just east of Osaka, is held to be the prime example of urban self-government in late medieval Japan. It had genuine wealth, plus a confusing sequence of different feudal lords. Taken together, these conditions enabled its inhabitants to set up a city council, having certain rights with respect to tax collection and the preservation of order in the market place, as well as in the organisation of festivals; but as the most important parts of its commercial business were carried on under official patronage (the China trade) or on behalf of feudal lords (the shipment of tax goods to market), it cannot be called a 'free' city in the wider European sense. When Nobunaga began to restore the country's central authority after 1568, he soon made it clear that the price of Sakai's freedom, such as it was, was submission to his will.

In setting out to discipline this increasingly insubordinate society, sixteenth-century lords, both old and new, had a number of advantages. One was the possession of overwhelming force, itself a consequence of war. Another was the fact that their potential opponents – *kokujin*, peasants, townsmen, priests – were socially divided and could be played off against each other. The lords best equipped to exploit this situation were therefore able to strengthen their hold until they had personal domains (later known as *han*) quite unlike the loose agglomerations of vassalage and land rights found in earlier periods. They were compact, except for a few outlying fragments surviving from the past; ranged in size from something less than a district (the majority) to something more than a province (a small minority); were subject to a single lord's control; and were administered from a central stronghold. These were the units – not in all respects complete in this form until the seventeenth century – into which Japan was divided for the next 300 years.

At the head of each domain was its daimyo, whose authority was absolute and whose 'office' was hereditary. If his territory were large enough, he would have a massive castle, strategically located at the heart of his lands. There the greater part of his vassals were expected to reside, forming an army, readily on call, which could not only guard his frontiers, but also keep order within them. Former warrior-gentry of the countryside (*kokujin*), now firmly subjected to vassalage, filled its higher ranks. Samurai of lesser standing provided its junior officers and élite guard units, always in attendance on their lord. Foot-soldiers (*ashigaru*), some resident in the castle, some still in villages, made up the rank and file. Commoners beyond the walls, both townsmen and villagers, though still granted a measure of autonomy, had now to submit to the castle's orders.

A daimyo's legal powers were no longer restricted to the governance of vassals, jurisdiction over land rights and enforcement of the warrior code. When he made laws, they were designed to regulate all inhabitants of the domain and every aspect of their lives, or at least all that had a 'public' character. Those which Asakura Toshikage issued in Echizen were typical. They set out rules to be observed in selecting advisers and officials; provided for regular inspection of the province, in order to remedy 'errors in government'; prohibited the building of castles and strongholds, other than his own; and even warned his followers not to waste time in choosing 'an auspicious day or a correct direction' when preparing for battle. They also touched on what might be called the foreign relations of the domain. Expensive actors should not be brought from Kyoto, when local young men could be trained to take their place. Confidential papers must not be entrusted to samurai from elsewhere. Agents were to be maintained in other provinces to report on conditions there. The list leaves little doubt that these were the orders of a self-styled prince, not just the possessor of large estates.

Nobunaga and Hideyoshi (1560–1598)

Although daimyo imposed unity on localities and even provinces, the effect was further to fragment Japan at large. A restoration of order in the wider sense required a rebuilding of the state, which had almost wholly slipped out of Ashikaga hands. This was the task to which Oda Nobunaga, Toyotomi Hideyoshi and Tokugawa Ieyasu turned in the second half of the sixteenth century. After nearly a hundred years of civil war there were at least half a dozen men who had the will and the capacity to undertake it, but some of them – the Shimazu in Kyushu, the Mōri in western Honshu, the Hōjō in Odawara – were too remote from Kyoto to intervene there easily. Others were distracted by local rivalries. In the event it was Imagawa Yoshimoto, lord of the coastal belt to the east of modern Nagoya, who set the process of unification in motion, but when his army departed for the capital in 1560 it was halted by a very much smaller force under Oda Nobunaga, whose domain lay across its path. The event was a turning-point, though it was only seen as such in retrospect.

Nobunaga spent the next few years consolidating his position in the region around his holding. An alliance with one of Imagawa's vassals, Tokugawa Ieyasu (who changed his family name from Matsudaira at about this time), gave him some protection from the east. Threats, or marriage alliances, persuaded other neighbours to open his route to the west. So when the emperor and Ashikaga Yoshiaki – an unsuccessful claimant to the title of Shogun – invited him to intervene in Kyoto in 1568, he acted promptly. His army was small, but well led and well equipped (he had been among the first to realise the potential of firearms, introduced by the Portuguese in 1543 and already being manufactured by Japanese). Making the most of these advantages, he seized the capital, installed Yoshiaki as Shogun and appointed himself as deputy. Before long this made him the Bakufu's senior member in name as well as reality, for Yoshiaki was removed from office in 1573.

In the remaining years of his life, Nobunaga tightened his hold on the central provinces. One step was to remove potential dangers from other feudal lords, which sometimes required him to fight against his former allies. Another was to reduce the temporal power of Buddhism, which had grown immensely during the years of turbulence. Tendai's Enryakuji, for example, had the temerity to oppose Nobunaga's attack on Asakura in Echizen. In September 1571 he turned his army against it. The temple complex on Mount Hiei was stormed and its buildings were put to the torch with massive casualties. Farther afield, force was also employed against the Ikkō sect in Kaga and other provinces, though it was not until the sect's main stronghold, the Ishiyama Honganji in Osaka, was taken in 1580 that success was at last achieved.

Victory in the central region left Nobunaga free to turn his attention to the more powerful lords in other parts of Japan. First on the list, because strategically the greatest threat, were the Mōri, controlling western Honshu. Hideyoshi, the most able soldier among Nobunaga's vassals, was therefore sent against them. Slowly he pushed them back along the shores of the Inland Sea, but he had advanced no farther than the outskirts of Okayama when Nobunaga's death in 1582 threw Japan once more into crisis.

The event was typical of the age. In June 1582, *en route* to join Hideyoshi, Nobunaga spent the night at a Kyoto temple. One of his senior vassals, Akechi Mitsuhide, leading a contingent of reinforcements in the same direction, suddenly turned aside from his road as he passed the city – for reasons that have never been entirely clear – and attacked him. A spattering of musket fire at dawn was the first indication of danger. Caught without a proper escort, Nobunaga fought his ground alone for a time, but at last, wounded, and seeing the temple in flames around him, he committed suicide. The news quickly reached Hideyoshi outside Okayama, 130 miles to the west. Keeping it secret, he came to terms with the Mōri, then made a forced march on Kyoto and defeated Akechi, who was killed by peasants as he fled. Within two weeks, setting aside Nobunaga's quarrelsome sons, Hideyoshi was master in the place of his former lord. It was a long step up the ladder for a man of his birth, no more than a village samurai in origin. Nobunaga, after all, had held thirty-two of the country's sixty-eight provinces when he died.

Hideyoshi's first aim was to ensure that what he had gained by speed he could hold by strength. Of possible rivals, the most dangerous was Ieyasu. The two came briefly into conflict in 1584–5, but chose to break off the confrontation before they came fully to grips, staying thereafter at arm's length. Other contenders were more brusquely treated. The settlement with the Mōri held, while a campaign in Shikoku in 1585 made the approaches safe from that direction. This gave Hideyoshi time to build political defences. A lavish residence was erected for him at Momoyama, on the out-skirts of the capital (Nobunaga had preferred his castle at Azuchi, overlooking Lake Biwa); he became a Fujiwara by adoption, taking the family name of Toyotomi; and he was appointed Kampaku, then Daijō-daijin. Dressed thus in the imperial authority, he was ready to bring the rest of Japan to heel.

It took two campaigns. The first, against Shimazu of Satsuma, who refused to give up the gains he had made in northern Kyushu during recent years, was launched in the spring and summer of 1587 by an expedition of 200,000 men under Hideyoshi's personal direction. Shimazu, driven back behind his mountain barriers in the south, where he was threatened by yet another 'imperial' force approaching from the sea, reluctantly sued for peace. Hideyoshi granted him generous terms. As a precaution, however, the map of the rest of Kyushu was redrawn, placing Hideyoshi's men at strategic points.

That left the Kanto and the north to be pacified. The key to them was the Hōjō domain,* ruled from Odawara; and when it refused to submit at the end of 1589, Hideyoshi set on foot another huge expedition, part of it led by Ieyasu. The Hōjō decided to stand siege, a choice of doubtful wisdom. Hideyoshi's two main columns, approaching along the coast and through the Hakone mountains, had western-style cannon, a knowledge of which, like firearms, had been acquired from the Portuguese, and they were well supplied by sea. By May 1590 they had enclosed Odawara castle within a double ring of earthworks. The besiegers, provided with comfortable quarters for themselves and their dependents, together with shops, singers, musicians and court-esans for their entertainment, settled down to starve the stronghold out. It did not take long. At the beginning of August the castle surrendered, the Hōjō leaders committed suicide and their lands were transferred to Ieyasu in exchange for his existing ones in Mikawa (based on Shizuoka). This made him, next to Hideyoshi, the most powerful daimyo in Japan.

Once these campaigns were over, Hideyoshi turned his military talents to overseas expansion (Chapter 8), while seeking at home to achieve stability. The court offices he held, it is true, helped him to overcome the disadvantages of birth, but they were not the instruments through which he chose to rule Japan. Instead, he treated the country much as a sixteenth-century daimyo treated his domain. The great lords were required to swear allegiance to him and send hostages to live in Kyoto under his hand. Restric-tions were imposed on the marriages and alliances they were permitted to conclude; their lands were increased, reduced or transferred as Hideyoshi decreed. He provided in this way not only an enormous holding for himself and his followers, but also a firm grip on those who might acquire ambitions to overthrow him.

Such specific controls were reinforced by a calculated mag-

---

* These Hōjō are sometimes known as Go-Hōjō, 'the later Hōjō'. They were not descended from the Hōjō regents of the Kamakura period.

nificence, underlining the overlord's connections with the court. At his Kyoto residence and his nearby castle, to which nobles and feudal lords were regularly invited, he indulged in lavish ceremonial and hospitality. In 1587 he celebrated his Kyushu victory with a tea ceremony at which there were over 800 guests. In the following year he entertained the emperor to a banquet that was made the occasion for poetry contests. One purpose of such display was to emphasise his place in the scheme of things, to make it plain that his accomplishments were not confined to military ones. Another, perhaps, was to give him a public persona more impressive than his private one. To judge by the portrait statues that survive, Hideyoshi was not a prepossessing figure of a man. Nobunaga had called him Saru, 'monkey'.

Despite the nature of his public life, Hideyoshi did not treat the court as an instrument of government to be taken over as his own. To carry out his policies, where they concerned the country at large, he appointed commissioners (*bugyō*) from his own immediate entourage. One dealt with matters concerning land. Another supervised shrines and temples, plus the administration of Kyoto. Three more handled finance, trade and public works, respectively. None had a large staff. By the standards of Nara and Heian it was a skeletal and highly personal establishment.

It was used nevertheless to bring about important changes in political society. As early as 1583, Hideyoshi ordered land surveys to be carried out in the areas under his immediate control, a practice extended to the whole of Japan in the next ten years. Supervised by his own officials and using a newly standardised set of measures – they were chosen as favourable to the tax-collector – they recorded not just the area or value of the land, as in the past, but its assessed yield (*kokudaka*), measured in rice. In each case a single cultivator was identified, who would be responsible for paying tax. This destroyed the last vestiges of the fragmentation of ownership into *shiki*, which had been characteristic of *shōen*. It also made it possible to list the exact value of a lord's domain as a measure of his wealth and military resources, since yield deter-mined the number of fighting men it could support. Uniformity was imposed on both fief and village, to the great convenience of their overlord.

More famous was the decree by which Hideyoshi ordered a so-called Sword Hunt in 1588. By denying villagers the right to carry arms, it disarmed the peasantry, reducing the danger of peasant revolt. It also separated samurai from the land, making them more dependent on their daimyo. Those warriors whose lifestyle had previously rested on the income from parcels of cultivated fields had now to choose between their weapons and their former means of livelihood. If they remained in the village, it was as an unarmed rural élite, deprived of samurai status. If not, they became full-time servants of their lord, living in the precincts of his castle and looking to him for maintenance (in the form of stipends).

It took time for these regulations to be fully enforced. Even then there remained exceptions: a few senior samurai who were still enfeoffed, a larger number of rural samurai (*gōshi*) who in some areas took part in cultivation of the land. Nevertheless, for the most part a line had been drawn across Japan's social structure. Those above it were samurai, armed and privileged. Those below it were commoners, who were neither their social nor their political equals. By a further decree of 1591 samurai, even if they left the service of their lords, were not allowed to take up residence in villages, while farmers were forbidden to leave their fields to emigrate to towns or engage in commerce. These were fundamental concepts that Hideyoshi bequeathed to the Tokugawa rulers who succeeded him. The task that was left for them to complete was the building of an administrative structure, less personal than Hideyoshi's, by which the daimyo, too, could be brought to order.

The Tokugawa settlement (1600–1650)

It was unfortunate for Hideyoshi that a son, Hideyori, was born to him in 1593, his fifty-sixth year, since the event persuaded him to make fresh – and in the event unreliable – arrangements concerning his successor. His nephew and adopted son, Hidetsugu, about whose personal habits there were doubts, was disgraced, then ordered to commit suicide in 1595. Hideyori became heir. Five regents (Tairō) were appointed to protect his interests, all of whom were daimyo.

One was Tokugawa Ieyasu. When Hideyoshi died in 1598, Ieyasu, despite the promises he had made, sought power for himself, disregarding Hideyori's claims. A military balance emerged: on one side Ieyasu, holding the Kanto and supported by lords in the north, as well as by two of Hideyoshi's most able vassals; on the other an alliance of daimyo from Kyushu and the west, which included Mōri and Shimazu. In 1600 their armies met at Sekigahara, midway between Nagoya and Kyoto, and Ieyasu emerged as victor. This was as much because of political skills as military genius, for two of his declared opponents had already come to terms with him before the engagement started. One refused without warning to take part in the battle. The other changed sides once the fighting began, launching his men against the flank of those who thought him their ally.

Hideyori, still a child, was allowed to retain his father's mighty castle at Osaka, but as the years went by it became clear that as long as he stayed there he would be a focus for anti-Tokugawa sentiment of every kind. Ieyasu decided therefore to remove him. At the end of 1614 a pretext was found to send an army against him, but it soon transpired that his castle's defences were too strong to be taken by storm. Having no wish for a protracted siege, which might give opposition time to surface, Ieyasu offered peace terms in January of the following year; and when they were accepted, he took advantage of the terms of truce to fill in more of the moats – in what was claimed to be a 'misunderstanding' –

than had been specified in the agreement. Inevitably, when he attacked again in June, success came easily. Clemency was sought; the appeal was ignored; and Hideyori committed suicide, removing any further danger from those who still looked back nostalgically to Hideyoshi's day.

Like Minamoto Yoritomo – and unlike Hideyoshi – Ieyasu chose to remain in the Kanto, surrounded by his followers and his lands, rather than move to Kyoto. Edo was to be his capital, giving its name to a period and a culture. He followed Hideyoshi, on the other hand, in using his supremacy to redraw the political map once more. After Sekigahara, Shimazu was allowed to withdraw to southern Kyushu and keep his position there on promise of good behaviour. Elsewhere, sweeping changes were made. Nearly a third of the land in Japan, measured by yield (*kokudaka*), was confiscated and redistributed, putting Ieyasu and his men in possession of a vast central stronghold, running from the Kanto to the provinces surrounding Kyoto. Vassal lords of the Tokugawa (*fudai*), plus cadet branches of the Tokugawa house, were given strategic domains within this region: defending Ieyasu's capital from the north; protecting the approaches to Kyoto from the east (Hikone), the west (Himeji) and the south (Wakayama); and controlling key centres (Hamamatsu, Nagoya) along the Tokaido, the road that joined Japan's two capitals. Farther afield were the wealthiest of the lords, known as *tozama*, who had not hitherto been vassals of the Tokugawa. The Maeda of Kaga (Kanazawa), who had not opposed Ieyasu at Sekigahara, were treated favourably. Others, like Mōri of Choshu, who had fought on the 'wrong' side in that battle, had their lands drastically reduced in size. Lesser men, unlikely to be able to resist, lost their domains altogether. Kyushu and Shikoku were divided for the most part between Tokugawa allies.

This process of land reallocation continued under Ieyasu's son, Hidetada, and his grandson, Iemitsu, justified on grounds of maladministration, suspected treachery, moral turpitude, even the lack of an heir. This implied that domains were held in trust from the Shogun on condition of good government, not simply by hereditary right. Indeed, the Tokugawa were well-nigh absolute. By the end of the seventeenth century, the head of the Tokugawa house, together with his enfeoffed retainers (*hatamoto*) below the rank of daimyo – the qualifying level for daimyo was a holding of 10,000 *koku* – and his numerous 'housemen' (*gokenin*), were masters of a little more than a quarter of the arable in Japan. Tokugawa relatives, plus the Shogun's vassal daimyo (*fudai*), shared another third. That left about a third to the 'outside' lords (*tozama*) and something under 2 per cent to the court and religious establishments.

Creating this overwhelming preponderance of land in the hands of the house head and his subordinates was fundamental to imposing order on Japan's feudal lords. It was bolstered by a number of institutional devices. In 1603 Ieyasu assumed the title of Shogun, signalling the end of an interregnum that had lasted since Ashikaga Yoshiaki had been deposed by Nobunaga thirty years before. Ieyasu is said to have possessed two genealogies in order to keep his options open. One showed descent from the Fujiwara, which would have qualified him for senior office at court. The other traced his line through the Nitta to the Minamoto, establishing a claim to be Shogun. It is by no means certain that either was genuine – false genealogies were a feature of sixteenth-century life – but the final choice of the second was a shrewd one, given that Hideyoshi had made a different one. It did not prevent Ieyasu from holding court rank and arranging an imperial marriage for Hidetada's daughter, but it strengthened his position *vis-à-vis* the samurai class, as it had done for Yoritomo. It provided a means, which he was quick to exploit, by which to make land grants under his own seal, to require written oaths of loyalty from daimyo, and to call for contributions from them for the building of Edo castle. They were made to attend him there. As Shogun he also took over the direction of foreign affairs, using for this purpose the title Taikun (since anglicised as Tycoon).

The prerogatives of his office were founded on custom, not law, but towards the end of his life Ieyasu committed them to paper. In August 1615, soon after Osaka fell, he announced a set of thirteen regulations, known as the Buke Shohatto, which was read to the lords assembled at Fushimi, just south of Kyoto. The ceremony took place in the presence of Hidetada (who had succeeded as Shogun in 1605, to make sure that he was well established before Ieyasu died). Some of the regulations were of immediate political relevance. Others looked to the longer term. Daimyo must not give sanctuary to lawbreakers (refugees from Osaka, for example); castle building and daimyo marriages were to be subject to the Shogun's consent; men of ability – by implication, those who qualified as such in the Shogun's eyes – were to be chosen as advisers. Samurai must be encouraged to study both the civil and military arts and to lead 'a simple and frugal life'. Reinforcing this were rules against drunkenness, licentiousness, 'wanton revelry', extravagant and inappropriate dress, and travelling with retinues that were needlessly large.

Ten days later a comparable document, the Kuge Shohatto, set out regulations for the court and its nobility. The emperor and his courtiers were to devote themselves to scholarship and the arts (that is, not to government). Appointments to high court office were to be made in accordance with rank and ability (implicitly, after consultation with the Shogun's representatives). Ranks and titles could not be conferred on feudal lords without the Shogun's approval, nor could imperial relatives be named without it to posts in the Buddhist establishment. In all matters of substance, instructions issued by the Kampaku (now a Bakufu nominee) and the Bakufu's own officials in Kyoto were to be followed without fail. The penalty for contravening them was banishment from the capital. To these were added further rules about dress, precedence and family succession, none entirely novel, but imposed for the first time by a 'military' ruler.

As these two documents indicate, Ieyasu's first principle was to control the men who exercised authority, whether as daimyo or court nobles, rather than seek to govern directly all those parts of Japan that were not within his feudal jurisdiction. Providing they followed his wishes, as made known to them in general terms, Fujiwara, serving as Sesshō or Kampaku, still made day-to-day decisions in the emperor's capital, while daimyo administered their domains. To represent him in Kyoto, Ieyasu sent a senior vassal lord as governor (Shoshidai), residing in the newly built Nijo castle. As a guarantee of daimyo compliance – reinforcing the ultimate threat of demotion or removal – he required lords to live for much of their time in Edo, much as the Ashikaga and Hideyoshi had done in Kyoto. Their wives and children remained as hostages when they withdrew to their domains.

Under Iemitsu these rules were spelt out in greater detail. By a revision of the Buke Shohatto in 1635, the arrangement became 'alternate attendance' (*sankin-kōtai*), by which daimyo spent half their time in Edo on a regular rota: that is, for six-monthly or yearly periods, depending on the location of their lands. This involved them in considerable expense, since they both lived and travelled in state. As a further restraint, a supplementary order of 1649 laid down the type and size of military force they could maintain.

It was mostly after Ieyasu's death in 1616 that clear political structures were devised to prevent his intentions from being undermined by the passage of time. Under Hidetada the court made Ieyasu a *kami* of the highest rank. Iemitsu, who was Shogun from 1623 to 1651, built him a magnificent shrine at Nikko. 'Ancestral law' was thereby given the extra sanction of divinity. More practically, Iemitsu took up the task of giving government a more defined and durable character, which would be less dependent on the qualities of the ruler and his subordinates. A council of ministers (Rōjū) was formalised in 1634 as a board of four or five members, each a *fudai* lord of 25,000 *koku* or more. Its members served as duty senior minister in monthly rotation. The same principle of rotation, allowing for differences of detail, applied to other appointments. The Rōjū were collectively responsible for advice on general policy and for matters concerning feudal lords. Below them was a junior council, similarly composed, but with more restricted duties. A number of commissioners (*bugyō*) came next, responsible for shrines and temples. Together these three offices comprised the upper division of the

Bakufu's administration. At the next level down were offices filled by *hatamoto*, not of daimyo status, who conducted most of the daily business of government. There were commissioners who supervised Edo and its largely samurai population; others whose concern was with Tokugawa estates and Bakufu finance; and several 'inspectors' (*metsuke*) who sought out maladministration and derelictions of duty. Outside the capital were stewards (*daikan*) on Tokugawa estates, plus governors in some cities, notably Kyoto, Osaka and Nagasaki, all graded in rank according to their responsibilities. Only Tokugawa vassals could hold these posts.

Since nearly all the men who filled them had assistants and clerical staff, the bureaucracy was a good deal larger and more complex than that of previous feudal regimes. Its conciliar structure and the rules it designed to divide responsibility in various ways also made it cumbersome. From the Shogun's point of view, this reduced the risk of attempts to overthrow him from below (*gekokujō*), but it certainly introduced a greater degree of centralisation than is customary in feudal states. Although no great effort was made to legislate for what was done within a daimyo's boundaries, it was taken for granted that his obligation to provide 'good government' would lead him to adopt the practices exemplified by the Tokugawa. Similar norms existed in other walks of life. Accordingly, despite the fact that the bureaucrats were hereditary vassals, not hereditary aristocrats, there was enough correspondence between what was taking shape in Tokugawa Japan and what had existed in Nara and Heian to make China's example and political philosophy of seeming relevance once more (Chapter 10).

CHAPTER 8

Relations with Asia and Europe

1500–1700

Japan's earliest relations with China had a powerful influence on the whole history of the country's culture and institutions, as we have seen. At the other end of the historical time-span, starting in the nineteenth century, Europe and America had a comparable impact. The years from 1550 to 1650 can be considered as in some respects the first indication of this change of focus. This was when the tribute missions sent to the Sung, interrupted by Chinese policy in 1549, then briefly by war in 1592, were replaced by a more arm's-length relationship, resting on an illegal maritime trade. It was also the time at which there were the first direct contacts with Europeans.

The nature of these has led to it being called 'the Christian century'; but this is in fact a misnomer, in so far as Christianity was in the end decisively rejected. Events indicated nevertheless that Japan's new feudal rulers were beginning to work out a fresh approach to the outside world. It was a world, they were forced to recognise, that included Europe, as well as Asia, within its boundaries, a change that was seen from the start as potentially a threat to Japan's domestic order.

The China trade

By the early years of the sixteenth century, the missions that the Ashikaga sent to China were in Japanese eyes of value very largely for purposes of trade. Most of the voyages sailed from Hakata under the aegis of the Ōuchi lords. The ships that took part in them, usually three in number, were small, and more than half the passengers they carried were merchants, paying for cargo space. The tribute goods they took as gifts for the Ming court consisted of consignments of raw materials, plus Japanese craft products such as decorated fans and screens, lacquerware, swords and armour. The 'supplementary articles', which had to be offered first to the Chinese government, but could then be put on the open market if refused, included camphor, sulphur, and copper ore, the last of which had recently become an item of increasing importance. Swords were also sent in considerable quantity, but were a source of some disagreement. A century earlier they had been much in demand, but the expansion of production to satisfy this demand had brought a sharp decline in quality, which was reflected in the prices on offer. Japanese resisted the trend, Chinese refused to pay more, disputes multiplied.

Return gifts from the Ming included large amounts in copper coins, which the Japanese valued – and regularly requested – because of their importance to domestic commerce. Other welcome gifts were rich silk fabrics and cultural objects, mostly books and paintings. Merchants, too, took home some of the proceeds from their sales in the form of copper cash, but they also bought silk cloth of a more standard kind, which had a ready sale in Japan, as well as tea-ceremony utensils in porcelain and bronze. It was a trade in small bulk, high-value imports, which yielded large-percentage profits.

Not unexpectedly, the so-called 'Japanese' pirates (*wakō*) – according to Chinese records, Japanese were often in practice a minority, outnumbered by Koreans, offshore islanders, or renegade Chinese – tried to obtain as loot much the same goods as made up return cargoes for the tribute missions. During the fifteenth century, the efforts of the Ashikaga and the Ming had succeeded to some extent in bringing their activities under control, but the Ming decision to put an end to Japanese official visits after 1549, imposing on trade with Japan the same restrictions as applied to other countries outside the tribute system, opened up new opportunities for the marauders. Large pirate fleets attacked the Yangtse region in 1553, then moved south to Fukien in 1561, seizing coastal settlements and stripping them of whatever could easily be carried away. Much of the booty went back to Japan for disposal, providing a source of supply that helped to make up for the loss of the tribute missions.

After 1560 renewed Ming efforts to build defences against the pirates began to have an effect, while removal of a longstanding Chinese ban on maritime trade in 1567 – though Japan remained a prohibited destination – made the inhabitants of China's southern coasts less willing to deal with *wakō* in an illegal commerce. More or less simultaneously, the restoration of a measure of order in Japan by Nobunaga and Hideyoshi (Chapter 7) was making Kyushu a less attractive pirate haven. In 1588, soon after his campaign against Satsuma ended, Hideyoshi prohibited piracy. He proved better able to enforce the law than his predecessors had been.

These circumstances favoured Portuguese attempts to gain a foothold in Japan. Already established in Goa and Malacca, they had first sent ships to Chinese waters in 1514, but it was almost thirty years later (1542 or 1543) that a party of Portuguese reached Tanegashima, an island just south of Kagoshima Bay. They came in a Chinese junk, escorted, it seems, by *wakō* from the China coast. Thereafter Portuguese ships themselves began to arrive in Kyushu, but it was not until China allowed Portugal to found a settlement at Macao (1557) and a Japanese feudal lord put Nagasaki under Jesuit jurisdiction (1571) that an ordered pattern of trading emerged. From that time on, these two ports became the terminals of a regular commerce between China and Japan, carried in Portuguese ships.

The *Great Ship*, as it was called, a carrack of between 600 and 1,600 tons, well armed and able to resist attack, sailed annually from China to Japan. It would reach Macao from Goa in time to load cargo in the early summer: silk floss and silk cloth, which were the staples of the trade; a quantity of gold, eagerly sought by daimyo for their war chests; rhubarb, sugar and similar items not readily available in Japan; and a few European products, chiefly firearms. Leaving for Nagasaki in June or July on the southerly monsoon, it would stay there for several months, selling to Japanese merchants. The return cargo for shipment to Macao, purchased with the proceeds of these sales, included camphor and copper, which Japanese had earlier taken to China, but above all silver bullion. During the sixteenth century, there had been a rapid development of silver mining in Japan, due to the adoption of Chinese (and later European) mining techniques. This provided a substantial surplus above domestic needs. Part of it, carried to Macao by the *Great Ship*, was invested there for the next Japan cargo. Part, representing Portuguese profit, went to Goa and Lisbon. A few other Japanese products, especially art objects, also found their way to Europe by this means.

The Portuguese were not left for long to enjoy their profits undisturbed. Spain, having captured Manila in 1571, soon began to trade to Japan. The Dutch, already challenging Portugal everywhere in Asian waters, were first brought to Japan by a ship that was wrecked on arrival in 1600, but were able to found a regular trading factory at Hirado (northwestern Kyushu) in 1609. The English, following the Dutch in the manner of a chain store determined to compete, came to Hirado in 1613. All three late arrivals found the Japanese market too deeply committed to trade with China to be easily changed. As Richard Cocks, the English East India factor, reported to his superiors in 1617, if England wished to trade successfully in Japan, 'then must we bring them commodities to their liking, as the Chinas, Portingales and Spaniards do, which is raw silk and silk stuffs, with Siam sapon [sappan wood] and skins'.

Lacking direct access to China's ports – Cocks tried to develop a junk trade with the China coast from Japan, but with little success – Spain, Holland and England all secured Chinese goods for Japan by tapping the trading network created by Chinese merchants in Southeast Asia. Spain worked through the Chinese community in Manila, repatriating its profits in Japanese silver, much as Portugal did (that is, by sending them to Mexico in the annual Acapulco galleon). The Dutch, based in Batavia (Djakarta), used Chinese merchants in Indonesia and on the adjacent mainland. The English tried to do the same, but were largely frustrated by Dutch competition. They withdrew from Hirado in 1623, their factory a commercial failure. In all these cases the trade goods obtained for Japan were the same as those carried by the Portuguese, concentrating heavily on silk, mostly Chinese, though including some from India and Vietnam. There was also porcelain, usually procured via Manila, aromatic woods from Siam and elsewhere, some European guns and 'novelties'. The greater part by value of the Japanese exports for which these goods were exchanged consisted of silver bullion: Japan was a major contributor to the world's silver supplies in the sixteenth century. To this were added the kind of craft goods familiar in Japan's trade with China. In other words, while the Portuguese enjoyed a direct trade between China and Japan, the other Europeans had to make do with an indirect one, only lightly touched by the markets of Europe and Southeast Asia.

Eventually the Japanese joined in this trade as well. The *wakō* – at least those who were Japanese – had been deprived of much of their livelihood by the measures taken against them by Hideyoshi and the Ming. Nevertheless, like Drake and his fellow mariners in England at the time, they had always been ready to ply a trade, instead of fighting, if that seemed more to their advantage; and late in the century some of those who survived began to engage in trading voyages to the south. Hideyoshi, still concerned about controls, required them after 1592 to have a licence, franked by his vermillion seal (*shuin*), for every voyage they undertook. Tokugawa Ieyasu continued the practice when he came to power. Their ships are therefore known as 'red seal ships' (*shuin-sen*).

A study of the licences issued before Iemitsu put an end to the traffic in 1635 shows that about 10 per cent were in the names of daimyo, chiefly in Kyushu; a quarter were granted to foreigners resident in Japan, both Chinese and Europeans; and the remaining two-thirds went to Japanese merchants in the ports and cities connected with the China trade (Nagasaki, Hakata, Osaka, Kyoto). They authorised visits to places scattered all through Southeast Asia. During Ieyasu's lifetime these were mostly in Macao, Luzon, Siam and Indo-China (Annam, Cochin China, Cambodia, Tongking). Later Taiwan was added, while some of the more distant destinations (Java, Malacca) dropped out of the list.

The imports carried by these vessels were much the same as those brought in by Europeans from those areas. Exports were more varied, since Japanese merchants found it harder to get silver for export and easier to find alternatives. It has been calculated that the red seal ships brought back between 50 and 70 per cent of the silk and silk goods entering Japan, which made them serious competitors for the Europeans. To help in obtaining their cargoes, they founded Japanese communities at a number of ports overseas, the largest, the one in Manila, having something like 3,000 residents in 1606. The settlements did not long survive Iemitsu's regulations of 1635.

By contrast, there were only twenty Chinese merchants living in Nagasaki by about 1600, the port's trade having fallen to a trickle as a result of the restrictions that the Ming had imposed since 1549, followed by Hideyoshi's wars on the Asian mainland (see below). Tokugawa Ieyasu, encouraged by the Kyushu lords, who had economic interests at stake, proved willing to seek better relations; but although a letter was sent by one of his senior retainers to the Chinese governor of Fukien in 1611, by the time a reply came – it took ten years – Hidetada was Shogun and the opportunity was lost. Nor did the conquest of the Ming by the Manchus (Ch'ing) after 1644 make any formal difference. China's new rulers were as adamant on the subject of tribute relations as the old.

The atmosphere in Nagasaki had nevertheless improved enough to encourage more Chinese to go there in contempt of Chinese law. In Hidetada's time there were 2,000 or 3,000 Chinese residents in the port, while between thirty and sixty Chinese junks arrived each year. Some were from southern China, some from Southeast Asia. The numbers increased again after 1639, when Iemitsu expelled the Portuguese, but fell back towards the end of the century. The regulations issued by Japan in 1714–15 permitted thirty junks to trade, twenty from Chinese territory (Nanking, Ningpo, Amoy, Canton and Taiwan) and a further ten from Southeast Asia, where Chinese from the south were beginning to settle. They brought, as they had always done, silk, medicinal drugs and cultural items (books, paintings, porcelain). They took out silver, previously carried chiefly by the Portuguese, plus other traditional Japanese exports. This was now the only direct trade between Japan and China.

After 1639 the Dutch alone survived of the European merchants trading indirectly between the two. The English had withdrawn in 1623. The Bakufu banned Spanish ships because of a dispute in 1624, while the Portuguese had fallen victim to the proscription of Christianity (discussed below). Accused of giving support to both Jesuit priests and Japanese rebels, they were ordered to leave Nagasaki for good in 1639; and when a mission was sent from Macao in 1640, asking that the order be rescinded, its leaders were executed to make it clear that the Shogun meant to be obeyed. The Protestant Dutch – they were not 'Christian' as the Japanese understood the word – had always held aloof from religious quarrels, but they, too, suffered from Japanese suspicions. In 1641 they were moved from Hirado to the island of Deshima in Nagasaki harbour, originally intended to house the Portuguese. Only in that one port were they to be allowed to trade thereafter, their movements kept under tight supervision, the amount and nature of the goods they could buy made subject to official regulation, as was the number of ships that could come from Java each year. All commercial dealings had to be conducted through a monopoly ring of merchants under the watchful eyes of the

Bakufu's local representatives.

The restrictions were worth enduring at first because of the high returns on the trade, but economic circumstance became steadily more unfavourable with the passing of the years. Japan developed a silk industry of its own, reducing dependence on China for all but goods of the highest quality. Silver production fell as the more accessible deposits of ore became worked out: after 1668 the amount that could be taken out of Japan was officially restricted, leaving copper as the staple of Dutch export cargoes. As a result of these two changes, the Dutch found it difficult to make a profit at all by the eighteenth century. It is said that they remained at Deshima only because those who took part in the trade – the factors, supercargoes and ships' officers – could enrich themselves, if not the Dutch East India Company, by a combination of 'private' trade and smuggling. It became a popular belief in Nagasaki that all the Dutch captains were fat, because of the habit they had of carrying goods ashore concealed in their clothes.

Korea and Ryukyu

The presence of Portuguese, Spanish, Dutch and English merchants in Japan in the sixteenth and early seventeenth centuries marks the beginning of a maritime, western strand in Japanese history. Yet the trade in which they all took part was essentially a link between Japan and China. In much the same way, relations with Korea and Ryukyu in these years took place within the familiar context of a China-centred institution, the tribute system. In the fifteenth century, when the Ashikaga acknowledged the Shogun to be 'King of Japan', that is, a Chinese vassal, the decision had also opened the way to dealing with the Yi dynasty, which ruled a united Korea after 1392, on a footing of equality. The Sō, feudal lords of Tsushima, were intermediaries between the two. They sent missions to Korea in the name of Japan, just as the Bakufu and the Kyushu lords did to China, exchanging official gifts. They also engaged in trade, exporting very much the kind of goods that went from Japan to Ningpo, importing skins, ginseng and honey, as had happened in the past, but also cotton cloth, which became more important than silk.

This trade, too, was beset by piracy. In 1443, in the hope of reducing the scale of *wakō* attacks on the Korean coast, the Yi concluded an agreement by which 200 Japanese ships could go to Pusan each year. A Japanese settlement was established there. The arrangement proved an uneasy one, however. Attempts by Japanese to expand their commercial foothold, much as they were doing on the China coast, brought about violent disputes, which led to a brief hiatus in the trade (1510–12); but peace was eventually restored and trade continued for most of the sixteenth century.

Hideyoshi did not wholly share the views of the Sō and the Tsushima merchants about what made Korea important to Japan. In 1586, when planning his Kyushu campaign (Chapter 7), he revealed to Mōri Terumoto that he had an ambition to conquer China. This was a task in which both Kyushu and Korea would have a part, the first as a base, the second as the route by which an attack would have to be made. He returned to the plan when the Shimazu and Hōjō had been defeated, believing, it appears, that an adventure overseas would give Japan's daimyo something other than civil war to occupy their minds. The Sō, convinced that their own interests lay in avoiding conflict with Korea, which would be bad for trade, did their best to head him off. They arranged a Korean mission to Japan, only for it to be bluntly told by Hideyoshi, when it appeared in Kyoto in 1590, that he intended to launch an attack on China, which would require him to move his forces through their country. Once victory was secured, he said, he would establish the Japanese emperor in Peking. More, in a letter to the Portuguese viceroy in Goa in the following year, he observed that China's conquest would also open the way to India.

Orders were given for an expedition to be prepared in April 1592. The bulk of the invading army was to be led by three of Hideyoshi's most trusted vassals, richly enfeoffed in Kyushu. One was Katō Kiyomasa of Kumamoto. The other two were the 'Christian daimyo', Konishi Yukinaga, holding half Higo province, and Kuroda Nagamasa of Nakatsu. Another army, provided by Hideyoshi and Tokugawa Ieyasu from central and eastern Japan, would be held in reserve in northern Kyushu. A headquarters was built at Nagoya in Hizen. Naval transports and escort vessels were to be manned in large part by former *wakō*, totalling several thousand in a force of something over 150,000 men deployed.

About a third of these landed in the neighbourhood of Pusan at the end of May 1592. The contingents commanded by Konishi and Katō captured Seoul on 12 June, but thereafter the Japanese forces were divided, Konishi taking Pyongyang (23 July), Katō pushing north towards the Yalu river frontier with Manchuria, Kuroda moving northeast. Other units spread out to occupy central and southern Korea. In readiness for an advance against China, supplies were commandeered, land surveyed and registered, taxes collected.

It was after this initial push that things went wrong. The Japanese naval forces proved unable to carry out their task. Faced by a formidable opponent in the Korean admiral, Yi Sun-sin, they were just about able to keep open a sea lane to Pusan, but failed to make an entry to the Yellow Sea, where they should have given support to Katō and Konishi. On land, the harshness of the Japanese occupation policies provoked local risings and attacks on communication routes, making it difficult to supply the armies in the north. Then the Chinese came to Korea's rescue. A small Chinese force, which had crossed the Yalu in July 1592, had been quickly driven back. But a much larger one followed a few months later, defeating Konishi at Pyongyang in February 1593 and driving him back on Seoul. He concluded an armistice, pending peace talks, and withdrew to Pusan. Japanese troops remained there for the next four years, living off the land.

The negotiations undertaken during this interval were exceedingly devious. Chinese envoys met Hideyoshi in Kyushu in June 1593, having been led by Konishi to expect a settlement within the framework of the tribute system. Hideyoshi told them to their astonishment that his terms included a resumption of the tribute trade, a marriage between Japan's emperor and a daughter of the Chinese emperor, and the cession to Japan of four provinces in southern Korea. This, they knew, was totally unacceptable to their superiors. Unhappily, no one had the courage to say so to Hideyoshi. Konishi therefore removed the talks to Korea again, seeking some form of words that would persuade the Chinese that Hideyoshi accepted vassal status, while concealing the concession from his awe-inspiring master. The process took time. It ended only when Konishi forged a letter in which Hideyoshi appeared to accept the title 'King of Japan'.

In December 1596 Chinese representatives again waited on Hideyoshi, this time at Osaka, prepared to invest him as king. Only then did Hideyoshi discover the deception that had been practised on him. He fell into a rage, expelled the Chinese from Japan, and set on foot preparations for another campaign. Large reinforcements were sent to Korea. Konishi and his fellow commanders took the offensive again (August 1597), though this time they set themselves a more modest objective, that of securing the four Korean provinces their master had demanded. The campaign even so was more difficult than that of 1592. The Koreans still had a naval advantage; their commanders were forewarned; a Chinese army was already in the field. Some progress was made towards Seoul before winter closed in, but the new year of 1598 saw the Japanese line come under increasing pressure. Konishi conducted a defensive campaign in the spring and summer to protect his base at Pusan, with little sign of achieving anything more than that. News of Hideyoshi's death (18 September 1598) finally brought his operations to a close. A truce was concluded. Japanese units, sometimes fighting their way out against heavy odds, began to leave Pusan for home.

The hardships suffered by Koreans under Japanese occupation left a legacy of lasting bitterness, but the Sō, taking up their role as intermediaries again, wanted to see the trade resumed. In 1605 they brought about a meeting between Korean envoys and Tokugawa Ieyasu at Fushimi. A more formal one with Hidetada followed at Edo two years later. Prisoners were exchanged. In 1609 trade was restored to its sixteenth-century footing, subject to a limit of twenty ships a year; a Japanese settlement, guarded by samurai, was established on the outskirts of Pusan; Korean missions to Japan began once more.

Behind the *rapprochement* lay a manipulation of correspondence by the Sō, who had followed the example set by Konishi. The embassy to Hidetada in 1607 had been the product of a letter they forged, in which the Shogun signed himself 'King of Japan'. Later letters coming from Edo did not lend support to this misrepresentation, but in forwarding them to Korea the Sō reworded them, giving the impression that Japan was content to act within the tribute system. The deceit was successfully maintained until 1635. In that year it became known to the Bakufu as the result of a dispute within the Tsushima domain, but too much was now at stake to justify a diplomatic break. Those directly concerned in the affair were punished, though not severely. A decision was taken in Edo that the Shogun would use an entirely different title, that of Taikun (Tycoon), in his dealings with Korea, so as to avoid any imputation that he was subordinate to China. The Koreans silently concurred. A Korean mission of congratulation to Japan in 1636 marked the end of the incident.

Korean missions to Japan continued intermittently until 1811. Edo treated them as bearers of tribute to the Shogun, a practice – coupled with a good deal of public show – that gave some substance to Japanese claims that the country now had a position in East Asia to compare with that long held by China. Writing of a world with 'two centres', Japan and China, Japanese scholars implied an equality between the two. Some even called Japan Chūgoku (*Chung-kuo*), 'the middle country', the label by which China identified itself as the centre of a Confucian universe.

Japan's relationship with Ryukyu (Loochoo to the Chinese) encouraged similar pretensions, though it was not of the same order. In the fifteenth century, because of Ming restrictions on the Chinese junk trade, Ryukyu had become an entrepôt for the routes between Chinese ports and Southeast Asia. The islands having acknowledged Chinese suzerainty, this gave them the right to send tribute missions and engage in trade with the mainland, but because of their distance from the Chinese coast they were able to ignore the ban on trading to the south. Since Satsuma also traded with Ryukyu, southern Kyushu was thereby provided with a 'secret' link, not only with China, but also with a shipping network that extended as far as Indonesia.

When Hideyoshi was planning his invasion of China, he called for help from Ryukyu as well as Korea. He was ignored. Nor did the 'king' of the islands respond to Satsuma efforts a few years later to persuade him to submit to Tokugawa Ieyasu. The result was a Japanese armed assault in 1609, authorised by the Tokugawa, but carried out by 3,000 men from Satsuma. Thereafter Kagoshima posted agents in the Ryukyu capital, exercising supervision over its ruler. They were careful not to break the link with China, since it furnished the legal cover for a profitable trade. The king, in fact, continued to receive his title from the Chinese emperor. On the other hand, Ryukyu also sent missions to Edo from time to time, smaller than those from Korea, and received with a degree less dignity, but serving the same purposes. Like those from Korea, they were treated as bearers of tribute.

In this way Japan enjoyed in both Korea and Ryukyu the commercial advantages of membership of China's tribute system, without formally belonging to it. Direct trade with China was carried on – illegally – through Chinese junks coming to Nagasaki, providing a channel through which to secure a knowledge of China's changing civilisation. Trade with Korea and Ryukyu, less valuable, left the Shogun safely removed from any shame that might be attached to vassal status. Indeed, he was able to enjoy a measure of prestige at home as the recipient of tribute on his own account.

Christianity and seclusion

Europe's trade carried no political implications of this kind. What is more, although it brought with it some pieces of useful information about the manufacture of guns, the mathematics of artillery, the practice of navigation and cartography, and the techniques of mining and fortification, while making minor contributions to Japanese painting and cuisine, it did not commit Japan in any important respect to European culture. The priests who came with the ships might have had a greater impact, had they been able to stay, but Christianity was rejected in the seventeenth century without having opened any important cultural doors.

The first Christian missionaries to arrive in Japan were three Jesuits, of whom one was Francis Xavier, brought to Kagoshima in a Chinese junk in 1549. Xavier himself left again in 1551, bound for Goa, with the intention of going to China, so he had little time to exert an influence in Japan; but by seeking access to the imperial court in Kyoto, then securing the patronage of the Ōtomo, who were emerging as powerful lords in the west of the country, he marked out a political framework for the mission. In the next thirty years his successors developed it. They were given permission to take up residence in Kyoto in 1560, which gave them access to the notional centre of authority. They won converts in the city and nearby provinces. Kyushu, where the trading ships came, nevertheless remained their main base. In 1563, in what was to prove a key event in the history of Christianity in Japan, they converted Ōmura Sumitada, daimyo of part of Hizen in the northwest of that island. He allowed them to settle in Nagasaki in 1571; ordered the compulsory conversion of the population in his domain in 1574; and put Nagasaki under Jesuit jurisdiction in 1580. The baptism of Ōtomo Sōrin and another daimyo at about this time, followed by that of those they ruled, raised the total of professing Christians in Japan to 150,000. By 1600 it was claimed to be twice that number.

This success owed as much to the religion's commercial as its doctrinal appeal. The Kyushu daimyo, anxious to protect their share of the trade with China, had taken note of the respect in which Portuguese captains held the Jesuits. It appeared to them that to tolerate Christianity, or show it favour, was a way of attracting Portuguese ships to Kyushu ports. The example of Nagasaki, which Ōmura's gesture made a regular terminal for the trade, confirmed them in this belief. In addition, the Jesuit priests were men of learning, whose expertise extended beyond religion into the fields of science and technology, including weaponry. This, too, made them men to cultivate.

The Kyushu campaign gave Hideyoshi his first personal knowledge of affairs in that region, including those relating to Christianity. As overlord, he objected to the administrative role of the Jesuits in Nagasaki, was alarmed by their interventions in local politics and was offended by tales of their intolerance to other religions; not only were their ideas alien, he believed, both in origin and in character, but their loyalties were directed to a foreign ruler, the Pope in Rome. These seemed reasons enough to bring them more closely under control. The difficulty Nobunaga had had in suppressing the Ikkō sect gave warning of what might happen if Christianity were allowed to spread.

On 24 July 1587, as soon as the Satsuma campaign ended, Hideyoshi issued a decree ordering Christian priests to leave Japan. Its text began with the time-honoured formula, 'Japan is the land of the gods (kami)'. From this it went on to accuse the priests of provoking attacks on shrines and temples, and stirring up 'the lower classes' contrary to law. Their presence was therefore a threat to civil order. In another decree the previous day, he had banned the practice of mass conversion on the order of feudal lords, which he held to be politically subversive. For the future, conversion must be individual, requiring approval either from representatives of authority (for samurai) or from household heads (for commoners).

These decrees were not apparently meant to be a prelude to suppression of the Christian faith, in that the only public anti-

Jesuit action taken in the next ten years was the seizure of Nagasaki. An official was appointed to govern the port in Hideyoshi's name in 1588. Starting in 1593, however, Dominican and Augustinian friars from Manila began to arrive in Japan. Confident of Spanish protection, they preached openly, in disregard of Hideyoshi's orders, spurning the more discrete means of propagation that the Jesuits had adopted, working through members of the ruling class. Annoyed, Hideyoshi gave the foreigners a sharp reminder of his wishes. In February 1597, twenty-six Christians, including three Jesuits and six Franciscans, were crucified in Nagasaki. It was the opening move in what was to become a full-scale persecution under the Tokugawa.

Tokugawa Ieyasu was wary, as Hideyoshi had been, of damaging foreign trade by acting too severely against the Christians, but he, too, found reasons to doubt their loyalty. After all, a good many of them rallied to Hideyori's cause at the end of 1614, fighting in defence of Osaka castle. Once the castle fell, therefore, he proscribed their religion and ordered the expulsion of the priests who had stayed in Japan in defiance of Hideyoshi's orders. All Japanese were henceforth to register as members of a Buddhist sect.

Hidetada and Iemitsu, the second and third Tokugawa Shogun, took still more drastic measures after Ieyasu's death in 1616. In the twenty years that followed, thousands of Christians, including many foreign priests, were executed, usually by crucifixion, or forced to recant by torture. Special commissioners were appointed to seek them out, taking, as it appears from missionary accounts, a sadistic pleasure in the task. Regulations, to be enforced by feudal lords as well as the Bakufu, were devised to remove all traces of the 'evil sect' among the population. True, small pockets of 'hidden Christians', preserving a form of the faith that was barely recognisable beneath its Buddhist accretions, were still to be found in Japan in the nineteenth century, but the campaign ensured that Christianity was not a force of any consequence in Japanese life while the Tokugawa ruled. When Japanese discovered different reasons for seeking a knowledge of the West, as they did in the nineteenth century, they did so through intermediaries of another kind.

Action against Christianity was made easier for the Tokugawa to contemplate because after 1600 the religion was no longer indispensable to foreign trade. With the appearance of competitors, both European and Japanese, the Portuguese had lost their near-monopoly of imports coming from China. Spaniards, Dutch and English all had a share in providing them. So did Japan's own *shuin-sen*. Chinese junks at Nagasaki, and Japanese junks from Tsushima and Pusan, were additional sources of supply. Of them all, only Portuguese and Spanish had links with missionaries. Apparently with these considerations in mind, Hidetada and Iemitsu felt free to adopt a more restrictive stance towards foreign trade as well as Christianity. In 1616 Hidetada banned trade at ports other than Nagasaki and Hirado, cancelling the more liberal access earlier granted to the English. In 1636 Iemitsu required Chinese to come only to Nagasaki. He had already in the previous three years ended the issue of permits for Japanese voyages overseas, apart from those to Korea and Ryukyu, and forbidden Japanese to reside abroad on pain of death. He thereby put an end to the trade of the *shuin-sen*. Only Chinese, Portuguese and Dutch were left to carry on the country's foreign commerce.

In the early months of 1638 a large-scale peasant revolt broke out in the Shimabara peninsula, not far from Nagasaki. Large numbers of Christians joined it, apparently driven to desperation by years of persecution. The Portuguese, who had more enemies than friends in Japan for reasons of commercial rivalry, were accused of helping the rebels, directly with arms, indirectly by smuggling in priests; and in 1639 this became grounds for ending the link with Macao. The Dutch – who, it has been said, gave some assistance to the Bakufu in suppressing the rebellion – survived the crisis, but were transferred from Hirado to the island of Deshima in Nagasaki harbour, where they could more easily be policed.

They remained in Deshima for over 200 years, having little impact on the Japanese economy, but a more important one –

after 1700, at least – on knowledge of the outside world. This state of affairs was traditionally held to have made Tokugawa Japan a 'closed country' (*sakoku*). Recent scholarship has tended to question this, pointing out that relations continued with Korea and Ryukyu, helping to keep open a door to China, but the traditional view still has something to recommend it. Bakufu policy after 1640, reinforcing the attitudes that censorship encouraged among Japanese at large, was to be much more inward looking than outward looking for generations to come. There was no longer travel from Japan to China, except for a handful of priests. Intermittent western attempts to open trade again were treated with scant respect, either rejected out of hand as contrary to 'ancestral law', or turned away by threats of force. Japan, in fact, came to view the outside world, or at least the European world, through a screen of hostility and suspicion. When confronted in the nineteenth century by an expanding industrial West, these emotions conditioned the response of both her government and people for several critical years.

CHAPTER 9

Edo Society

The Tokugawa tried to stop the clock of history. Until the end of the sixteenth century the feudal society of Japan had been a natural growth, broadly consistent from one part of the country to another, but varying locally in detail and nomenclature. The new Bakufu set out to impose an ordered structure on it. Starting from the policies Hideyoshi had devised, which rested fundamentally on an enforced distinction between an upper class, composed mostly of samurai, and a lower class of 'commoners', it elaborated the country's social differences to provide for further status subdivisions above and below that central line. The object was to ensure political stability, partly to perpetuate Tokugawa power, by putting an end to the constant repetition of *gekokujō*, the process of 'low overthrows high', partly to prevent a return to the more general disorders of the immediate past. What was overlooked was the long-term effect of economic development. As the generations passed and the distribution of wealth changed, the 'system' was marred by inconsistencies and contradictions.

The restoration of peace in the seventeenth century after more than a hundred years of civil war gave a major stimulus to the Japanese economy. Labour went back to the land; agricultural production expanded; there was a greater variety of crops (silk, cotton and the sweet potato were all brought in from nearby

countries). The resulting surpluses spilt over into domestic commerce. Towns grew larger and more numerous, providing greater
opportunities for merchants and artisans. As transport and communications improved, the products of distant regions became
available in the principal population centres. Inevitably these
conditions made for sharper disparities of wealth. Alongside
landed wealth, on which samurai in the last resort depended,
there emerged a commercial wealth in the hands of townsmen.
Emulation of the lifestyle of the urban rich brought many samurai
to debt, especially at the margins of the feudal class, and this in
turn led to a blurring of status lines. Marriage and adoptions were
arranged between samurai and well-to-do commoners, despite
being frowned on by the social code. Conservatives demanded
steps to check such practices.

It was not until the end of the Edo period that these problems
threatened a social or political revolution, but long before that
point was reached they had begun to undermine the accustom-
ed patterns of Edo life. As rulers sought to expand their sources
of revenue, while their more successful subjects looked for
status recognition, those who were losers in the economic contest – debt-ridden samurai, dispossessed farmers, the urban
poor – pressed for relief from their disabilities. By the end of
the eighteenth century, Edo society was marked by a rising
level of turbulence.

The ruling class

It was beyond all doubt that the Tokugawa ruled Japan after 1603,
but in formal terms the Emperor's court outranked the Shogun's
Bakufu. Among feudal leaders the Shogun alone reached Kyoto's
highest dignities. His senior vassals, like other daimyo, were no
more than in its middle ranks, despite their power and wealth.
The respect language in official documents reflected this. By
contrast, the higher-ranking courtiers had become by feudal

standards poor, since warriors had for centuries been eroding their rights in land. For appearance's sake, Edo subsidised the court on a steadily rising scale, but even in the eighteenth century its total contribution was no more than 120,000 *koku*, equivalent to the holding of a feudal lord of middle standing. About a third of it went to the imperial house. Another third was distributed as fiefs or stipends to members of the nobility. The most senior of these received between 1,500 and 3,000 *koku*: that is, something like the average stipend of a Tokugawa bannerman (*hatamoto*), serving as a Bakufu commissioner. Of the remaining 100 or more of leading families, nearly eighty had less than 200 *koku*, which in Edo would have classed them with 'housemen' (*gokenin*).

These were modest amounts, when one considers the rank of those who received them. A feudal lord, in order to be designated daimyo, had to hold land as vassal-in-chief that yielded at least 10,000 *koku*. If one accepts the traditional formula, that one *koku* of rice would support one person for a year, this made him master of a not inconsiderable body of people. The Shogun's own land amounted to over 4 million *koku*, yielding an annual revenue of about a third of that. Among the country's other daimyo, whose numbers rose from 200 in 1603 to just over 250 in 1850, there were sixteen whose domains were rated at 300,000 *koku* or more. Five were Tokugawa relatives, ten were *tozama*, or 'outside' lords, mostly in north and west Japan, and only one, Ii of Hikone, was a Tokugawa vassal (*fudai*) in the strictest sense. Daimyo of middle standing were those who had at least 100,000 *koku*, while those with less belonged to the lowest grade.

All the lords had samurai retainers, a small proportion of whom had fiefs and hence rear-vassals (*baishin*) of their own. Out of a total Japanese population of some 18 million in 1600, rising to 30 million in the nineteenth century, samurai, together with their families, accounted for 5 or 6 per cent. The head of the Tokugawa house had 22,500 samurai, plus another 60,000 *baishin*, though the numbers of the latter declined in the years of peace. The small apparent size of this armed following, compared with the Shogun's huge holding of land, reflects the result of victory in the civil wars, which had made possible a degree of generosity when enfeoffing warriors. The case of Ikeda of Okayama is similar. A Tokugawa ally, Ikeda had 21 upper samurai, nearly 700 middle samurai and over 500 lower samurai in a domain that was rated at 315,000 *koku*. In both examples there is on average one samurai (disregarding rank) for every 200 or 250 *koku*. At the other extreme, the defeated, like Shimazu of Satsuma and Mōri of Choshu, who had lost more land than vassals – vassalage was a highly personal bond, not easily broken – were left with far more men than resources. Their samurai were numerous but poor.

Each daimyo, if his domain were large enough, governed it through a structure much like that which served the Shogun in Edo (Chapter 7), but on a smaller scale. At its head were senior officials, drawn from upper samurai families, qualified for their posts by hereditary rank. Such men had fiefs, not stipends. Some were expected always to be in attendance to their lord, whether in Edo or his castle town, others would stay behind to administer his lands when he went to Edo in accordance with the rules of 'alternate attendance' (*sankin-kōtai*). There was also a range of middle samurai officials, carrying out duties equivalent to those of *hatamoto* in the Bakufu. These were of full samurai rank – entitled to attend personally on their lord on ceremonial occasions – but lower in the economic as well as the social scale than the senior councillors (*karō*). They had stipends, but these varied greatly in value. At the top of the range they might be as much as 500 *koku*, enough to sustain a comfortable lifestyle; at the bottom, they barely sufficed to support a respectable household. Below this level again were lower samurai and *ashigaru*, serving as guards, messengers and clerks on very much less.

Samurai, whether in Edo or the castle town, might perform their feudal service in either of two ways. There were on the one hand the traditional military duties of a warrior in time of peace: to garrison the daimyo's castle, to serve as his escort on journeys to and from Edo, and to provide a force he could use to police his lands. This was for the majority, though once the Tokugawa imposed order on the country in the seventeenth century most of these tasks became routine. Rarely did samurai need to take up arms after 1650. When they did so, it was usually to act against nothing more demanding than peasant revolt. As a result, they became more and more an unemployed soldiery, whose morale grew worse from one generation to another.

Other samurai – a minority, though a large one, tending steadily to increase – were employed in domain administration. Here a major preoccupation was finance: that is, raising the funds, whether in rice or cash, to pay stipends, to maintain an official residence in Edo, and to meet the cost of expensive journeys to and from the capital every year. Another was to administer the countryside, the domain's primary source of revenue. Since samurai were no longer resident outside the castle town, officials from the castle dealt with rural affairs through village headmen, or perhaps through a district office, manned by locally recruited staff. Occasional visits of inspection to the areas under their control, in order to keep a check on tax returns or supervise surveys, was all that was thought to be required by way of personal intervention. It was an authoritarian system, but not always an efficient one. Japanese farmers, like those elsewhere in the world, were adept at concealing and misrepresenting yields.

All this was a far cry from the medieval concept of the warlord as the leader of a warrior band, able to raise an army from his lands if the need arose. The daimyo of the Edo period held his territories from the Shogun, who required them to be governed in a manner that would bring well-being to their people: that is, in a way consistent with the peace and order of Japan at large. Not all, to be sure, lived up to this ideal, but for the most part they adopted the relevant vocabulary. Samurai, no longer simple warriors, assisted in this task, an army in waiting still, but comprising in the meantime the manpower of a government machine.

Since vassals might yet be required to fight, neither Shogun nor lords had any wish to discourage the samurai virtues of loyalty and courage, but quarrelsomeness and the pursuit of vengeance through vendetta, which were often the other side of the coin, were unwelcome in the kind of stable society that they were trying

to build. The Bakufu eventually banned them. An important step
in that direction came at the beginning of the eighteenth century,
when two lords, one of them a Bakufu official, quarrelled in the
Shogun's castle. Swords were drawn. The one who was held
to be the aggressor was ordered to commit ceremonial suicide
(*seppuku*), since resort to force was forbidden in the castle precincts. His domain was confiscated, making his samurai into
lordless men (*rōnin*). Forty-seven of them thereupon prepared
to take revenge on the survivor of the dispute, who remained
unpunished; but two years passed in plotting and dissimulation
before they found means to attack his Edo residence. This was in
1703. Their enemy was killed and his head was taken to their dead
lord's grave. The conspirators awaited the Bakufu's judgement.

It was not easy to determine. To punish the *rōnin* would
contravene tradition, since they had acted out of loyalty to their
lord. Not to do so would be to overlook a breach of the Shogun's
laws. In the end the *rōnin*, too, were required to commit *seppuku*,
incurring a punishment for breaking the 'public' law that was not
thought to threaten their 'private' honour. It was a landmark
ruling, which gave the incident lasting fame. On the one hand, it
became the subject of the longest of Kabuki plays, *Chūshingura*
(The Treasury of Loyal Retainers), which gives a much roman-
ticised view of the affair. On the other, it marked a stage in the
'civilising' of the samurai. From this time on, they were still
allowed as individuals to behave in accordance with their code of
honour, known as Bushido – indeed, its classical expression is in
a book entitled *Hagakure*, written about ten years later – and
even to pursue revenge in certain personal matters, such as the
unfaithfulness of a wife, but they were expected in other respects
to find satisfaction of their pride in public service. Duty to Shogun
or lord came first. A man would acquire the greatest respect, it
was made clear, by performing the tasks he was called on to
undertake by his station in life.

To encourage acceptance of the change, there were inducements. In the eighteenth century, additional emoluments were
paid to those in office, serving as a supplement to stipends.

Distinguished bureaucratic service became the grounds for an advance in rank, carrying with it possibilities of promotion. Samurai education was developed, in order to provide the ethos and the skills appropriate to an official career. Until this time most samurai, especially those of the higher ranks, had received their education at home, where they were given a knowledge of proper behaviour and a training in the use of weapons, flavoured with a dash of literacy. As a bureaucratic role in life became the norm, however, their superiors wanted something more. Like the aristocrats of Nara and Heian, they were deemed to need 'correct' moral attitudes if they were to play a part in government. This, it was held, they could acquire through the Confucian classics, so both Bakufu and domains began to establish schools at which these could be studied. Fifteen were founded by 1700, another seventeen in the next fifty years, seventy-five more by the end of the century.

In admitting students to the schools, preference was given to those of highest rank, who were likely to hold the most responsible offices. Middle and lower samurai might attend on a voluntary basis, or might even be excluded altogether, as were commoners as a rule. Teaching and organisation betrayed the same concern with status. Achievement as such was not greatly valued, except in military skills (which also formed part of the curriculum). An acquaintance with prescribed Confucian texts, acquired by rote learning, was all the philosophy that was given to most, while at the practical level an ability to read and compose official documents, perhaps with some help from those of greater literary accomplishment, plus a smattering of arithmetic, was as much as the school was ready to offer.

For some samurai, whose rank did not admit them to high office as of right, this was not enough. Society did not permit them to engage in trade or farming. Hence the pursuit of scholarship, or the possession of a more than local reputation for swordsmanship, or a recognised expertise in military science, all opening a path to employment by a lord – not necessarily their own – were among the very few ways of increasing their income with propriety. Most domains were willing to grant leave of absence for the purpose of acquiring the requisite knowledge, usually in one of the major cities.

It was because of this that private academies multiplied in and after the eighteenth century, matching the spread of official schools under feudal patronage. Most were founded by a scholar of some note, who supported himself by fees or regular gifts from students. The earliest academies, especially in Kyoto, catered for a more advanced study of the Confucian classics than was provided elsewhere. This remained their main attraction for many students, who came in time to include a sprinkling of well-to-do commoners. Some attention was also paid in them to mathematics. Separate schools were devoted to fencing (*kendō*) and various styles of swordsmanship. To these were added so-called 'western studies' (*yōgaku*) later in the period, inclining towards the practical and scientific: medicine, astronomy (which was related to cartography and surveying), western-style gunnery and the use and manufacture of explosives.

Advanced training of this kind provided outlets for ambition, but not on a sufficient scale to solve the larger economic problems of the samurai. Even feudal lords had difficulty in balancing income and expenditure. Revenue derived mostly from a percentage of the crop. It therefore remained buoyant during the seventeenth century, while production was rising, but after 1700, when population stabilised and the expansion of cultivated land was reaching its technological limits, yields no longer increased to any important degree. Growth became commercial growth. Since domains failed to devise effective ways of taxing it, they were left with little choice but to put further pressure on the farmers, in order to seek a higher return on land. Before long, tax demands exceeded capacity to pay, prompting resistance. In the second half of the Edo period, there was a rising level of peasant revolt, putting further constraints on revenue.

Expenditure, by contrast, continued to grow. Its principal component, other than the provision of samurai stipends, had always been the expense incurred in maintaining an establishment in

Edo and financing the daimyo's travels to it. Most of this commitment had to be met in cash. A proportion of tax rice was therefore sold to produce it, an undertaking that involved the domain's officials in financial dealings of which they had little previous understanding. Merchant advisers were employed to handle most of them. Since these were usually men who creamed off for themselves such profits as could be made from seasonal and annual variations in the price of rice, the domain saw little benefit. Indeed, when the treasury faced unanticipated needs, such as might arise from a Bakufu demand for contributions to the cost of public works, these 'official' merchants would furnish loans, the interest on which, invariably high, became a further burden.

The Bakufu was to some extent protected in this kind of situation by its possession of political authority. It could decree controls on prices and interest rates, even cancel debt in the last resort, though it sometimes found that meddling with the market in this way could make things worse in the longer term. Rank-and-file samurai had no such recourse. Like their lords, they were town-dwellers, whether in Edo or the provinces. Most had fixed incomes, payable notionally in rice. Since they needed cash for day-to-day expenses, and could obtain it only by marketing the rice that was due to them as stipends, the custom grew up of transferring the rice 'coupons' with which they were issued to a convenient merchant or moneylender, who would make a cash advance against them. This put the samurai in much the same position as the daimyo's treasury. Profit from selling the rice went to the financial agent. Any event for which no provision had been made – a marriage, an illness, a death – pushed the family into debt. Given that the temptations of urban life, due to the ever greater availability of expensive foods, clothes and entertainment, exercised a constant upward pressure on household budgets, the samurai's expenditure year on year exceeded income. On rare occasions there might be a moratorium on samurai debt, but much of the time the Shogun and the lords were just as likely to cut hereditary stipends in their search for economies that might benefit themselves. Official assistance proved a slender straw at which to clutch.

In the course of time, the tension between wealth and rank arising from these changes caused an erosion of the status structure of the ruling class. Daimyo granted samurai rank to a few merchants whose services they especially valued. In larger numbers, middle and lower samurai sought financial support by entering into family ties through marriage or adoption with affluent commoners. More widely still, they used family and household labour to produce craft goods for sale, so setting up a kind of upper-class by-employment. Those in the greatest distress might even seek permission to abandon their rank, whether on a permanent or a temporary basis, in order to take up farming or trade.

The result was a decrease in the cohesion of Edo society. The changes inevitably aroused resentment, directed both at successful social climbers and at those who could in one way or another be held accountable for the problems that society faced. Lords and upper samurai were accused of not having done enough to remedy hardship among those whose loyalty to them had been tested over many lifetimes. The merchants were blamed for feudal debt, because it was thought to stem from their greed and manipulation of prices. Villagers, on whom samurai income depended, saw the root of their misfortunes in the growth of towns. Even so, the system still held together tolerably well in 1850, if less from inherent strength than for lack of an impetus to bring it down. Some new factor, it seemed, was needed to provide a shock to the structure before it would fall apart.

The village and the town

Hideyoshi's Sword Hunt (Chapter 7), reinforced by Tokugawa polices, ensured that Japan's villages were under the jurisdiction, not of local samurai, but of their lord, who controlled them through the officials of his castle town. The main exception was to be found in the Shogun's lands, because they were too large to be governed as a unity. In them, domain-sized sections were put under the supervision of resident stewards (*daikan*), chosen from Tokugawa vassals, who served as both daimyo-substitutes and the Shogun's representatives.

Everywhere there was a form of indirect rule that left a good deal of influence in the hands of those with whom the officials had to deal: village headmen, village elders, and those of slightly higher status who held office in more than one village. All were non-samurai. One of their duties was to allocate the burden of tax within the community, since the lord assessed it on the village as a whole. Another was to adjudicate in such misdemeanours as seemed of too little consequence to call for samurai intervention. They also regulated festivals and other communal events. In return they were accorded benefits and social recognition which set them above their fellows: perhaps a small salary, privileges with respect to tax and labour dues, the right to bear a family name, to carry a sword, to wear superior clothes. They were likely, too, to possess the better fields and have a larger house than was permitted to other farmers. Given that such positions were hereditary, these were men who might be described in some respects as quasi-samurai, which is certainly how their neighbours and their superiors saw them. If officials were oppressive or inefficient, peasants expected the headman to take the lead in seeking redress. Should his protests in their turn prove too insistent or threatening, the domain would punish him, usually with severity.

With few exceptions – mostly of ex-samurai houses – peasant holdings were small enough to be worked by family labour, though there was an under-class of day-labourers, landless or with not enough land to support themselves, who found employment on the larger farms. Early in the period, village economies were nearly self-sufficient. Only enough of the crop was sold, or exchanged by barter, to secure necessities that were not produced in the locality, such as salt, iron (for tools) and cotton (for clothing). The proportion of the crop that was paid in tax varied with local custom and political conditions. On Bakufu estates it was commonly 30 to 35 per cent, though it became a little more in the eighteenth century. On daimyo domains the average was nearer 40 per cent. Even higher figures are sometimes cited, but these, if true, seem to have been exceptional. At all events, the burden was a heavy one, leaving little margin for investment to improve the land, none at all for luxuries. Most finance for land reclamation and better irrigation came from outside the village, initially from feudal lords, who had reason to expect that revenue would rise with an increase in cultivated area, later from commercial (possibly urban) investors.

The situation changed in the course of the seventeenth century as a result of the growth of domestic commerce and the towns it bred. Farmers, especially in the vicinity of urban areas, began to produce for the market: silk, cotton, vegetables, vegetable oils, even rice, as conditions made it favourable. Some turned over all their land to this kind of production, relying on their profits for the purchase of the rice they owed in tax. Since prices were unstable, despite intermittent Bakufu efforts to control them, the process necessarily produced both winners and losers. The successful could invest more heavily in fertiliser, farm animals, better strains of seed. With higher incomes, they sought entry to the village élite, if they were not already members of it. Those who failed fell into debt, became tenants or day-labourers, perhaps moved to the towns. By the eighteenth century, the ideal of village life envisaged by early Tokugawa thinkers – a kind of equality in poverty, affording margin only for the payment of tax – had broken down.

The social disruption caused by economic change, plus the pressure of taxation, as feudal lords tried to maintain or increase their revenues, brought unrest to the countryside. Though never absent altogether, rebellions averaged fewer than two a year in the seventeenth century. In the next fifty years, the number doubled; in the hundred years after 1750, it doubled again. A few of the outbreaks were on a major scale, especially after 1800, involving large bodies of peasants from many villages. Others, though little more than protest marches, were nevertheless put down with the same severity. At the local level, rioters usually directed their anger against the nearest targets: village headmen and other non-samurai officials, or well-to-do farmers, who had taken up money-lending as a supplementary source of income. The early nine-teenth-century revolts were more likely to be prompted by wider issues, concerned in some way with feudal government, hence politically more worrying. Grievances cited by the rebels ranged from the imposition of new taxes and the use of false instruments in surveys of the land to the introduction of monopoly arrange-ments, in which the domain entered into partnership with urban merchants, putting its power to tax at the service of exploitation for the sake of revenue.

To understand more fully the nature of these developments, one needs to look at the growth of towns. Medieval towns, other than political centres like Kyoto and Kamakura, had been the site of markets serving a limited area. In the Edo period, the castle town became the norm. It had its origin in the need felt by emerging daimyo to establish a stronghold from which they could both defend and govern their lands; and it was therefore a garrison town, where a force of samurai was required by duty to reside (in effect, the whole of a lord's following, once Hideyoshi decreed his Sword Hunt in 1588). To provide this force with weapons and other supplies, a daimyo would offer legal and taxation privileges to artisans and merchants who settled there: the makers of weapons, the financial agents who collected and marketed tax rice, those who devised and managed transport facilities. Within the urban area, the samurai nucleus, grouped according to rank, was housed near the castle's walls. The most favoured commoners, divided by occupation, occupied the districts round the samurai perimeter.

To this military and governmental core, non-samurai of lesser standing were attracted in the course of time. A community composed of members of the ruling class, plus privileged suppliers, was a consumer market rich enough to bring together retailers, shop assistants, servants and porters in substantial numbers. To them were added the entrepreneurs and workers of the construction industry, engaged in extending the urban boundaries, plus the men who fought fires (an important group where houses of wood and paper huddled together), those who collected night-soil (for sale as fertiliser to farmers in nearby villages), and entertainers of every kind. Many of the unskilled among them were immigrants from the surrounding countryside, 'released' from cultivation into penury or alternative livelihood by improvements in agricultural methods and techniques.

These towns quickly became district centres with an economic as well as political function, places to which farmers sent their tax rice and such items as they had for sale, from which they bought the foodstuffs, clothing and tools they could not produce themselves. Because the lord and many of his retainers spent half their time in Edo, as required by the rules of 'alternate attendance', the castle town also had to develop links with other parts of Japan. Tax rice was shipped to Osaka for sale, if that city were reasonably accessible. A large part of the proceeds was then sent to Edo to pay for the domain's official residence there and the costs incurred by lord and samurai staying in it. All this helped to establish a national network of commercial and financial operations, in which domains were inextricably involved. The raising of loans, when revenue proved inadequate, was part of it.

In the larger domains, these conditions led to the growth of towns of significant size. By 1721, when an official census was taken, Japan had five cities with a population of over 100,000. The greatest was Edo, castle town of the Tokugawa lands and headquarters of the Bakufu. Because of 'alternate attendance', half its inhabitants – estimated to total as many as a million in the eighteenth century – were samurai. Another place with political functions, though smaller, was Kyoto. It had become for the most part a cultural and commercial centre after Hideyoshi's death, but was still the seat of the emperor's court. Next came Osaka, a wholesale market for the products of west Japan, already on its way to being the cotton textile capital of the country. The other two in this category, qualified by their size, not their national role, were the castle towns of Kaga (Kanazawa) and Owari (Nagoya).

There were a further five cities with populations of 50,000 or more: Nagasaki, the sole remaining port for foreign trade, together with the castle towns of Kii (Wakayama), Aizu (also called Wakayama), Aki (Hiroshima) and Satsuma (Kagoshima). Of the ten so far listed, four, including Edo, were in the domains of the Tokugawa and related families, three were the castle towns of *tozama* lords, the rest (Kyoto, Osaka, Nagasaki) were directly under the Bakufu's administration.

No fewer than sixteen other towns had a population of 30,000 or more. By the nineteenth century, in fact, Japan's urban population in centres of at least 10,000 people amounted to about a sixth of the national total. This is two-and-a-half times the estimate for 1600. In the Kanto and the provinces round Osaka and Kyoto, the proportion ran as high as a fifth.

Townspeople, like villagers, varied in status, though the gradations were related to housing and commercial wealth, not land. The most senior were the headmen and elders of the wards into which the towns were divided, performing duties that were much like those of their rural counterparts; but because the town was the home of the lord and most of his retainers – and in the case of Edo of high-ranking visitors – they were much more tightly supervised by samurai officials. Magistrates of middle samurai rank (higher in Edo, Kyoto and Osaka) intervened in almost every aspect of urban life. From an initial concern with the preservation of order and the prevention of fire, their jurisdiction was gradually extended to cover rules about debt and the implementation of the sumptuary laws, together with the regulation of the entertainment quarters, in which theatres, houses of prostitution and the venues for sports like *sumō* were to be found. The Confucian rationale for this was not that personal morals were the ruler's business – Edo society was anything but prudish – but that luxury, gambling and loose living of every kind attracted criminals and wrongdoers, raising issues of public order. Bakufu officials set an example of intervention in civic affairs in seventeenth-century Kyoto by banning the performances of *kabuki* plays by women. When troupes of boys replaced them, substituting male for female prostitution, these were required to be licensed. Their members were forced to live in designated quarters of the city, where they could more easily be supervised (towns, although they had no walls, were divided into districts by gates, which had to be shut at night). Similar restrictions were imposed in Edo as it grew, while the officials of daimyo followed suit in their castle towns. Books, plays and pictures were all subject to censorship (though this did nothing to prevent a very large output of pornography).

The punishments inflicted for breaking laws were in all cases severe, but more so for commoners than for samurai. Torture was freely used to extract confessions. Samurai who committed serious offences, especially political ones, might be beheaded, but they were more likely to suffer the 'lesser' penalty – it carried no loss of status or stipend for their family – of ceremonial suicide (*seppuku*), usually known in the West by its less formal name, *harakiri*, or 'belly cutting'. Even this type of execution was miti- gated by custom in the end. By the later years of the period, the offender was allowed to call on the services of a friend, who would cut off his head simultaneously with the first incision of the sword (sometimes even before it). Lesser crimes were remitted to the samurai's lord for punishment, which could often mean nothing more than a year or two of house arrest. The same penalty might be imposed on daimyo.

Commoners were treated more roughly. Leaders of a peasant revolt, or even a protest demonstration, could expect crucifixion. Other forms of punishment were equally gruesome. There was a case in Kanazawa in the 1660s of a woman who had robbed several employers and set fire to their houses to conceal what she had done. She was boiled to death in a cauldron (perhaps because she had committed the anti-social offence of arson). Also from Kanazawa comes an example of discrimination according to status. In 1690 four samurai were found guilty of hiring a group of prostitutes and holding wild parties. The townsmen who provided the women were beheaded, or had their ears and noses cut off before being banished from the city. The women themselves were sent to a rural district to be servants for life to local farmers. The samurai were at first exiled to the countryside, later pardoned.

Incidents like this, coupled with evidence of poverty and hard-ship among the lower classes of both town and village, make it tempting to paint a dark picture of society in the Edo period. Yet to do so would not be entirely accurate. In the cities, at all events, many Japanese were able to find an escape from the oppressive hand of government in a 'floating world' (*ukiyo*) of theatres, geisha houses and restaurants. There wealth, not status, governed human relationships, except in so far as the residents evolved a status system of their own. Much of the period's art and literature describes the life they led (Chapter 10). The escape was more psychological than legal, but it may well have acted as a safety-valve, preventing urban discontents from becoming revolutionary.

Some commoners, not only in towns, were in any case better off as a result of commercial development. As the scale and complexities of domestic trade increased, bringing a growth of wholesale markets, banking facilities, money exchange, insurance, inns and post-stations along the main roads, and shipping routes that linked not only Edo to Osaka, but also both to the rest of Japan, so prosperity reached large sections of the country. Urban entrepreneurs made their way into rural areas to fund and organise production for the market, providing by-employment for farm families. Commerce spread beyond the towns. Its profits, more-over, opened up new opportunities. A few commoners were admitted to domain schools. More secured an education in the private academies, where sons of the rural élite – village headmen, doctors, priests, well-to-do farmers – joined those of merchants in the kind of studies once thought proper only for samurai. Even those of lower rank could acquire a knowledge of 'letters and numbers'. After 1800 hundreds of so-called 'temple schools' (*terakoya*) were founded by community leaders to provide a basic training in literacy and arithmetic, plus some homely moral phil-osophy, for those who in the past would have had no education at all. Perhaps 40 per cent of boys – though far fewer girls – had reached a modest standard of literacy by the time the Tokugawa were overthrown.

There was also a gain in standards of living. Japan's dense population and relative lack of resources had long encouraged the kind of material culture – and attitudes towards it – that emphasised simplicity and lack of waste. Because of this, it took only a minimum increase in national wealth to have an important impact. The greater range of goods from different regions of the country, available in the shops of the towns from the late seventeenth century onwards, was early evidence of it. Sumptuary laws, issued by the Bakufu in accord with Confucian doctrine, were a sign of rising consumption. So was the spread of social habits like gift giving and restaurant entertaining. Among foods, rice remained the preference for those who could afford it, but many could not. The poor still had to make do with cheaper substitutes (now including the potato). Sugar, too, was a luxury, only grown in the farthest south. On the other hand, fruit and vegetables were being commercially produced, especially near the cities, making possible a healthier diet for many; protein was available in the form of bean-curd and fish; sake (rice-wine) had a national market. The use of cotton, introduced from Korea in the sixteenth century and soon planted as a staple crop in central Japan, brought a huge improvement in the quality of clothing and bedding: silk had always been a fabric for the few. Cotton, indeed, was the first non-food item to achieve importance in the Osaka wholesale market.

In all these respects, the components of Japanese everyday life were becoming those that are now regarded as 'traditional'. Tradition in this sense is not much older than the Edo period. Housing is an example. Since the later Muromachi years, samurai and others of rank had lived in single-storey dwellings, divided into an earth-floored working space, which included the kitchen, and a living space with a raised floor made of thick straw mats (*tatami*) packed into oblong frames. There was a covered entrance (*genkan*), at which a visitor could step up onto the *tatami* floor, leaving outdoor footwear on a shelf or rack. The principal reception room would have an alcove (*tokonoma*) for the display of the owner's works of art or other treasures, set off by a flower arrangement. The building itself had wide overhanging eaves; was divided into smaller rooms, as required, by sliding panels, decorated, or made of translucent rice-paper to provide more light; and was heated, if at all, by small quantities of charcoal, burnt in braziers (*hibachi*). It was a type of housing better designed for summer heat than for winter cold. An early (and superior) example of it is the Katsura villa on the outskirts of Kyoto.

In theory, sumptuary laws prohibited commoners from having houses of this kind, though the wealthy were often able to ignore the rule. Few farmers, other than village headmen, could afford them. Most had buildings with greater working space, earth-floored throughout, at least until the later part of the period. Merchant houses were to a quite different plan. They had a narrow frontage on the street, abutting those of their neighbours. At the front of it was space for a shop or other business; living quarters were farther back; the kitchen and storerooms were at the rear. The city poor as a rule had no street frontage at all, occupying the middle of an urban bloc, where they shared toilets and water with neighbours; but the introduction of public bath-houses, another Edo innovation, made life a little more hygienic for them.

The Edo period was the last stage of Japanese history before the country and its people came under the influence of the modern West. Since this was to bring about a far-reaching trans-formation, it is natural enough that to the present-day observer the institutions and values that are associated with the Edo past should seem to be 'typically' Japanese. Yet one needs to be wary of treating Edo Japan as an undifferentiated whole. There were, as we have seen, important differences between the beginning of the period and the end of it, touching political authority, social structure, economic achievement and lifestyle. So there were between regions in dress, custom and spoken language. Beneath a surface uniformity, in fact, there was still variety and change.

CHAPTER 10

Edo Culture

The Edo period is nowadays seen as the high-water mark of Japanese cultural tradition (except by those who have a sentimental attachment to Heian). Two centuries and more in which there was much greater movement of goods and people between different parts of the country, linked variously to commerce, 'alternate attendance', the travels of students seeking profitable expertise, and a habit of pilgrimage to famous temples and shrines, ensured that culture did not remain exclusively metropolitan or upper-class. Geographically it was becoming countrywide. Socially, on the other hand, divisions remained, corresponding for the most part with the line between samurai and commoner.

Samurai and court nobles shared a taste in philosophy, literature and painting that was essentially 'Chinese', or at least classically Sino-Japanese. It was both reinforced and modified by a growing knowledge of China under the Sung and Ming. By contrast, the non-samurai residents of the towns preferred novels, pictures and plays that owed more to the 'popular' strand in medieval life, as developed in Kamakura and Muromachi. For this reason the town-dwellers (*chōnin*) of the 'three cities' of Edo, Osaka and Kyoto added a distinctive element to Japanese culture. It was to remain characteristic of the age.

★

Chinese thought, Japanese thought

During the Kamakura and Muromachi periods, Buddhism had been a dominant influence on Japanese religion and culture. Amidist sects spread the faith to the greater part of the population; the great Buddhist houses accumulated lands, which gave them a quasi-feudal power; Zen played a major part in bringing to Japan the civilisation of China under the Sung and Ming. Medieval Japan was therefore in many respects a Buddhist society. By the time the Tokugawa were Shogun, some of this ground had been lost. Armed force, used against the most popular sects by Nobunaga and Hideyoshi, had weakened the religion's political independence, making it little more than an instrument of feudal government. True, Buddhism was still part of the fabric of daily life – many of its temples had the patronage of feudal lords; all Japanese were required to register at one, since they were instructed by the Bakufu to keep population records; most houses contained small Buddhist altars (*butsudan*) – but this gave it no more than a residual prestige. There was no doctrinal or social innovation to impart fresh vigour, no new sects, no charismatic Buddhist figures of the calibre of Hōnen and Shinran, of Eisai and Dōgen. For lack of any overriding structure of authority – there was no Buddhist 'church' with an acknowledged head – doctrines were diverse, the discipline exercised over the clergy weak.

Against this background, Japanese turned increasingly to the less other-wordly beliefs of Confucianism, a philosophy that addressed the social dimension of human life. It had a number of 'schools'. One, associated in China with the name of Wang Yangming (1472–1529), envisaged a cultivation of the moral self as the primary duty of the individual, designed to reinforce a code of behaviour towards one's fellow members of society in accordance with justice and benevolence. Another, which was central to what became known as Neo-Confucianism, as developed by the Sung scholar Chu Hsi (1130–1200), emphasised its 'state-ordering' role:

that is, creating and preserving a well-ordered society. Both strands became influential in Japan during the seventeenth century, though it was the second that had the greater prominence.

Chu Hsi placed emphasis, first, on the idea that human society must reflect the existence of an orderly universe. From this it followed that study of the universe – in a search for underlying principle, not merely an understanding of phenomena – must be part of the moral training of the statesman. Second, since the universe itself was hierarchical, so must social structure be: the concept of inequality sprang from the relationship of Heaven to Earth. Of the five human relationships, four (leaving aside that between friends) were necessarily unequal, those of ruler–subject, parent–child, husband–wife and elder–younger. Finally, since the fundamental wisdom of the sages, which remained universally valid, was to be found in the Classics, later men must seek guidance from their study.

Although Neo-Confucianism incorporated a number of religious elements, involving ancestor worship and a cult of Confucius himself, it was in essence a temporal creed. Humanity, righteousness and decorum all had a place in the virtues it identified. To Chu Hsi, however, loyalty and filial piety were the primary ones, defining the duties of low to high. To the feudal rulers of Japan, faced with the task of restoring order after generations of civil war, this gave the doctrine more appeal than the characteristically inward-looking ideas of Buddhism. An emphasis on the attitudes that ruler and subject should adopt towards each other – benevolence from the first, submission from the second – together with a stress on agriculture as the heart of the economy, could readily be accepted in a feudal society. Confucius had lived in one, after all. In addition, the duties that Chu Hsi ascribed to the bureaucrat could just as easily be applied to the functions of the samurai in time of peace. For both reasons, Neo-Confucianism was welcomed. This is not to say that it became an orthodoxy, officially prescribed, but it certainly attracted the favour of the country's ruling class.

Fujiwara Seika (1561–1619), a Zen priest in Kyoto, who was

drawn to it by what he learnt from Korean scholars at the time of Hideyoshi's campaigns, is given the credit for establishing Neo-Confucianism in Japan as a distinct political philosophy. He also brought it to the attention of Tokugawa Ieyasu; but it was his student, Hayashi Razan (1583–1657), Confucian tutor to Ieyasu after 1608, who entrenched it in the Edo establishment. Until the nineteenth century, successive members of his family were to have responsibility for the Bakufu's official school.

In the intervening 200 years, Confucian thought in Japan became diverse. One group of scholars, of whom the most famous was Kumazawa Banzan (1619–91), looked more to Wang Yang-ming than Chu Hsi, putting innate virtue before the needs of the state. Another, linked usually with the name of Ogyū Sorai (1666–1728), turned, as some recent Chinese philosophers had done, to the study of the ancient texts, seeking thereby to disentangle what was 'classical' from the commentaries of later times. This led to a greater concern with laws and institutions, which was a Legalist rather than a Confucian concept in ancient China, closely bound up with the development of imperial autocracy. Ogyū himself, denying that the actions of the ruler should be determined by a moralistic philosophy, conceived of the Shogun as an absolute ruler on the Chinese model, served by officials selected for their ability, not their birth. It was an argument in which Maruyama Masao has detected the seeds of modern thought.

To men like Kumazawa and Ogyū, one of their duties as advisers to the Shogun or feudal lords was to put forward programmes of reform for the times in which they lived. In practice, however, it was not always easy to apply a system of thought devised in China to the circumstances obtaining in Japan. Rationalising the role of Shogun and samurai, in particular, was a problem. Both owed their place in the order of things to the military prowess of ancestors, who had transmitted it to succeeding generations as of hereditary right. In this respect Ogyū had reason on his side when he compared the Shogun's position to that of Chinese emperors. There were nevertheless two difficulties. One was that Japan also had an emperor, supposedly of higher standing than the Shogun.

Another was that the officials of Japan's central government were samurai, chosen by the Shogun on the basis of their status. They did not depend on imperial appointment and approval. Nor did they face a Confucian test of attitudes and capability, as Chinese bureaucrats did through their country's state examination system. Hence the situation did not fit readily into Confucian categories.

In considering such matters, a good many scholars chose to ignore the claims of the emperor and treat the Shogun as a Confucian ruler in his own right. A group in the service of the Mito branch of the Tokugawa house, writing at the end of the eighteenth century, preferred what might be called a 'laddered' approach: the samurai, they argued, owed loyalty to his lord, the lord to Shogun, the Shogun to emperor. The implications of a dispute arising between these different levels were not thought through. Arai Hakuseki (1657–1725) probed a little more deeply. In a history of Japan entitled *Tokushi yoron*, which he completed in 1724, he arranged his material so as to trace the transfer of authority from emperor to Fujiwara, from Fujiwara to Taira and Minamoto, and then to succeeding houses of Shogun. This inevitably raised the question of legitimacy. Arai's response was to apply the Confucian test of good government as a touchstone, in effect adopting a modified version of the Chinese theory of rebellion, applied – as caution required – to the past, but not the present.

Yamaga Sokō (1622–85) was more concerned to reconcile the role of the samurai with Confucian doctrine. Even in time of peace, he maintained, those parts of the samurai's code that enjoined austerity, self-discipline and a readiness to sacrifice his life in performing his duty remained relevant to his functions as an official. In addition, however, he must be a moral exemplar, bringing the Confucian ethic to the lower orders. In carrying out this task, the ancient Chinese texts, introduced to Japan and endorsed by the founding emperors, were of greater value than the more recent works of Chu Hsi; but because they were difficult and required extensive study, for which farmers, merchants and artisans, occupied with the needs of daily living, were unable to find the time, it was for samurai to act as their interpreters. The samurai, in fact, had to be Confucian scholar as well as warrior in order to fulfil his obligations to society.

In the hands of such men as this, Confucianism was capable of being politically radical, not always intentionally. They sought ways, for example, to overcome the malaise that was beginning to affect Japan as a result of economic change, especially where it influenced the life of samurai. Kumazawa urged a return of samurai to the land, in the belief that this would restore both their morals and their morale. Ogyū put his trust in sumptuary laws and controls on urban spending. Arai sought to make government more Confucian – and therefore more Chinese – conceiving of a revision of rituals and titles as the means to this end. All three, as befitted men who had risen to positions of influence because of scholarship, gave support to the essentially Confucian doctrine of 'promoting men of talent'. Taken to extremes this might have been thought to be an attack on status. It was therefore redefined in Japanese terms to mean the selection of able men for office among those who qualified by birth, much as had been done in Nara and Heian, though then with reference to the court nobility.

Confucian scholars were the intellectual leaders of Japan in the first half of the Edo period. Their influence was pervasive, filtering down to all levels of the population through official schools, private academies, even *terakoya*. It determined the substance not only of the country's political philosophy, but also of the standards approved for social and ethical behaviour. Accompanying it – as had been true of Buddhism in Japan's early centuries – were a range of ideas and activities that were not so much Confucian as Chinese: theories about medicine, mathematics and science; a view of the material world, obtained through 'the investigation of things' (geography, geology, botany, astronomy); the application of technology to irrigation, sericulture, mining, printing and the making of porcelain.

In the eighteenth century, this renewal of Chinese cultural influence prompted some Japanese to react against it. Most conspicuously, there was a revival of Shinto. That religion's long subordination to Buddhism, which had lasted for a thousand years, had been disturbed from time to time by attempts to assert its independence, usually by doctrinal innovation, but on this occasion the impetus to change had its locus in popular sentiment. It began with efforts by Shinto priests, especially those of Ise, to encourage pilgrimages to the major shrines. Since these were carried out by organised groups of residents from villages and towns, to whom they offered congenial company and a welcome break from the disciplines of daily life – it was one of the few purposes for which farmers, for example, could obtain permission to travel – they grew rapidly in popularity. It is said that well over 3 million pilgrims from many parts of the country worshipped at Ise in the spring of 1705. In later years the enthusiasms so engendered gave rise to occasional popular outbursts of religious fervour, identified with the slogan *ee ja nai ka*, 'isn't it good?'.

The movement was given an intellectual grounding by three men, Kamo Mabuchi (1697–1769), Motoori Norinaga (1730–1801) and Hirata Atsutane (1776–1843). Kamo took as his model the work of those Confucian scholars – exemplified by Ogyū Sorai in Japan – who had turned to ancient texts in order to discover the 'true' meaning of what the sages wrote, freed from later accretions. In Shinto terms, Kamo believed, this involved a re-examination of the *Kojiki* and *Manyōshū*, in order to remove the distortions introduced by Buddhism and Confucianism, but as a preliminary there had also to be a study of the language in which these texts had been set down. He made this his special task. In addition, he set out the conclusions he reached from his reading, which became the central tenets of the so-called Shinto Revival. His work was taken a further stage by Motoori in a multi-volume commentary on the *Kojiki*, a monumental piece of scholarship that remains at the heart of Shinto thought to the present day. Hirata was the publicist who adjusted its findings to nineteenth-century circumstance.

Motoori, intellectually the most significant of the three, was a man of samurai descent who practised as a doctor in Ise province. His followers were mostly well-to-do farmers, townspeople and

Shinto priests, persons of some influence locally, but not unshake-ably committed to the interests and ideology of the ruling class. Hirata, however, aimed at a wider social base, which included samurai. In keeping with the changes of his time, he identified the 'alien' influence that had to be rejected as not only that of China in the past, but also that of the West in the present (though he excepted western military science and technology from his condemnation). In his hands, in fact, Shinto became potentially nationalist. Its scholarship came to be known as Kokugaku, or National Learning.

Central to it was the assertion that the emperor reigned by virtue of divine descent from the sun-goddess, Amaterasu. It was her decree that the imperial line would rule the nation 'until the end of time'; and Japanese must therefore owe the emperor absolute obedience, regardless of whether he be 'good' or 'bad'. An ethical sanction, as applied in China, was irrelevant. Nor did the Japanese in general need an ethical code: because, like their emperor and the land in which they lived, they, too, were in origin divine, albeit descended from lesser deities, it followed that they were innately good. The clinching evidence for all these claims was historical. Japan's unbroken ruling line, contrasting as it did with China's turbulent dynastic record, showed where virtue had invariably resided.

As long as the Tokugawa seemed unshaken in their power, it was likely to be difficult for those who held authority to take this argument seriously as a threat to their position. They were wrong. A century later it was the official doctrine of the Japanese state, embodied in a written constitution and taught in every school.

Literature and the arts

Most of the books about Confucianism in Edo Japan were written in Chinese. So were many works on history, law and Buddhism. Depending on subject, government records were kept in Chinese or in a kind of hybrid Sino-Japanese (*sōrōbun*). There was poetry in Chinese – though less than in Japanese – while a number of volumes of prose fiction were based on Chinese models, or heavily influenced by them. There is a parallel with the place of Latin in medieval Europe.

The situation was in many ways like that which had existed in Nara and Heian, combined now with a popular literature that owed more to Kamakura and Muromachi. Most of the new readers were to be found in the cities, reaching lower in the social order than before as books became cheaper. Printing, carried out at first by movable metal type, then by the more economical, if more time-consuming method of carving page-sized wooden blocks, made multiple copies available, increasing sales. Writers, finding they could support themselves without relying on feudal patronage, began to produce a very large range of different kinds of work: manuals for use in every aspect of education, some of them specifically for women; works of fiction, making use of the simple *kana* script to attract a wider public; and reprints of the classics of the past, such as *Taiheiki* and *Heike monogatari*. By 1700 over 10,000 titles were in print and available from bookshops. Some were made available for rent to those who could not afford to buy; pedlars carried others to the villages. Nearly 300 publishers were engaged in the trade.

By the end of the seventeenth century, urban society was already large, varied and, for at least some of its members, affluent. A good many merchants had the wealth to enjoy the theatres and the houses of assignation that had multiplied in the pleasure quarters, priding themselves on their aesthetic taste, but relishing, too, the less refined entertainment that was offered in the theatre of melodrama and burlesque. Authority indulged them to a degree, despite its habits of censorship, since the things that pleased them did not fall within the bounds of the political. Authors, publishers and producers of plays regarded them as valued customers.

Three names dominate Japanese literature in these years, those of Ihara Saikaku (1642–93), Matsuo Bashō (1644–94) and Chikamatsu Monzaemon (1653–1725), respectively novelist, poet and playwright. Saikaku was the son of an Osaka merchant, who abandoned business to become a poet and only turned to writing novels in the last years of his life, starting in 1682. He wrote about what he knew: the life of merchants, the making and spending of money, the 'passing world' (*ukiyo*) of the city pleasure quarters. His books, though presented as novels, were more like collections of short stories, centred on a single person or theme. Their prose was informed by a poet's brevity, a few vivid phrases serving as a rule in place of description and analysis. Three in particular are famous. The first, which appeared in 1682, has been translated under the title *The Life of an Amorous Man*. It told of the sexual adventures of a wealthy rake, the son of a Kyoto merchant, who in the end at the age of sixty set off to seek the fabled Island of Women. A second such book, *The Life of an Amorous Woman* (1686), purported to be the memoirs of a woman, looking back when old on a life of lovemaking, usually for pay, some of it in the pleasure houses of the city, some of it, more degradingly, outside them. It is the portrait of a human being's decline, touched with sadness. The third book is *The Japanese Family Storehouse* (1688), a collection of tales about ingenious ways of making money. The same kind of themes recur in a number of other works, including one on homosexuality, all earthy, rather than directly pornographic. Their villains almost always come to a bad end.

Bashō, by contrast, was of samurai background. He lived most of his life in Kyoto and Edo, but travelled extensively in other parts of Japan, belonging to a circle of intellectuals whom it is difficult to classify as either samurai or commoners. Unlike Saikaku, whose early reputation as a poet rested on the speed with which he composed 'linked verse' (*renga*), usually in public competitions, Bashō devoted himself to developing the *haiku*, a seventeen-syllable poem in lines of 5–7–5. In his hands it became an independent lyric form. Its brevity imposed limitations, making it more suitable to express a flash of insight than a train of thought, but he made it reflect an acute awareness of nature, as witnessed on his travels, and a consciousness of the human dimension of what he saw. In these respects it was the quintessence of the Japanese tradition in poetry.

Chikamatsu wrote principally for the puppet theatre. This had developed in the early seventeenth century from what were in effect recitals, accompanied by the *samisen*, a stringed instrument newly imported from Ryukyu. Puppets were used to illustrate the narrative. After 1650 a more rhythmic style of recitation was adopted, identified with the name of its originator, Takemoto Gidayū (1651–1714); larger puppets were devised, two-thirds human size; and plots became more dramatic. The last of these changes was largely Chikamatsu's work. Some of his plays were historical, drawing freely on books like *Heike monogatari*. Others depicted the life of his own time, often based on real-life scandals and *causes célèbres*, of which his audiences would have been aware. Where the historical pieces (*jidaimono*) were about honour and loyalty, the contemporary ones (*sewamono*) chose themes that explored the conflict between sentiment (*ninjō*) and duty (*giri*), especially in the context of love and marriage. Love suicides were a favourite subject. To a degree, therefore, such plays provided a commentary on the ruling philosophy of the day as it impinged on different social groups, though more for the purpose of entertainment than critique. In manner they were melodramatic, usually with a touch of the supernatural.

Some of Chikamatsu's plays were also performed in a new kind of drama, known as Kabuki. It had originated in performances at the Kitano shrine in Kyoto at the beginning of the Edo period, moving later to a theatre in the centre of the city, then spreading throughout the country. Travelling companies took it to provincial areas. The earliest troupes of players included women, who engaged in prostitution in addition to their duties as actresses, but the Bakufu banned them in 1629. Thereafter men-only companies became the norm, some members of which, the *onnagata*, showed immense skill in playing female roles. Male prostitution replaced female prostitution in their unofficial repertoire. Most plays – other than Chikamatsu's – consisted of a series of almost independent scenes, having a general unifying subject-matter or character, but no integrated plot. In most cases they were written by a group of authors attached to a particular theatre, drawing their material, like the puppet theatre, from historical texts or current events. If the latter were deemed to carry political overtones, like the story of the forty-seven *rōnin*, the action might be transferred to an earlier century in the hope of escaping Bakufu censorship.

Whereas in Nō and the puppet plays the dialogue was provided by reciters or chanters of the text, in Kabuki the players spoke their own lines. For the most part these were simple, even banal, making little claim to intellectual depth or literary merit. The attraction of Kabuki lay rather in its spectacle and the opportunities it offered for actors to display their techniques, both of facial expression and of acrobatic movement in fighting or dance. In fact, the players and the production were more important than the plot. Actors were lionised, their appearances widely advertised, fan clubs formed. Portraits of them were sold in quantity to their admirers.

Nō drama still drew audiences, especially of samurai and those who followed their fashions, but in the eighteenth century literature became much more like Kabuki in tone. Novelists, taking their cue from Saikaku in their choice of subject-matter, dwelt more and more on the humour and the coarseness of urban life. The humour was anecdotal, wry rather than bitter, poking fun at human weaknesses, but not in the manner of the social critic. The canon of ideas approved by government was generally treated with respect. One can interpret this as an acceptance of society-as-it-is, or simply as a response to fear of punishment; but in either case it meant that the nature of the social system was never seriously debated outside works of Confucian scholarship.

Like literature, the visual arts appealed differently to different status groups. Painting showed more variety of style and subject-matter than that of earlier periods, some of it looking back to the aristocratic traditions of Heian, some extending the medieval interest in Chinese models, now a 'samurai' preference, some catering to the livelier tastes of the newly rich in towns or those of their poorer neighbours. There were many more artistic schools than there had been in the past, just as there were in swordsmanship, the tea ceremony and flower arrangement. One result of such diversity was that the boundaries between what was 'Chinese' and what was 'Japanese' became more blurred. Another is that the art of Edo Japan is not easy to describe in a narrow compass.

The most striking qualities it inherited from the late sixteenth century were ostentation and display, contrasting sharply with what is thought of as the Zen tradition. The military leaders then coming to power looked to the decoration of their castles as an element of prestige, complementing the size of the buildings and the towering height of their central keeps. For functional reasons, castles had to be stone walled, heavily timbered and grim, lacking the elegance of Kyoto's palaces and villas. Their state rooms, though large, were usually gloomy. Lords tended therefore to favour bright colours and lavish decoration for them, quite different from the monochromes and restraint of Muromachi. Murals, painted on multi-leaved screens and sliding panels, were of subjects – birds and flowers, trees, animals, stylised landscapes – that lent themselves to bold designs, covering large expanses. They were enhanced by an extravagant use of gold leaf, set off by gleaming black lacquer.

Nobunaga set the fashion when he built his castle at Azuchi. It was completed in 1579 and burnt down in 1582, so not very much was known about it until a copy of the builder's plans was discovered in 1974. Nevertheless, some record exists of the paintings, which were the work of Kanō Eitoku (1543–90). Eitoku already had a reputation as a painter in Kyoto, where his grandfather and great-grandfather had been artists producing murals for Buddhist houses; but from the time he undertook the Azuchi commission he made a shift to temporal employers, working on the rooms of Osaka castle after Nobunaga died and contributing to the fashion for large-scale decorative painting. His grandson, Sadanobu, moved to Edo in 1621; and one of Sadanobu's sons, Tanyu (1602–74), became the most influential artist of his day, introducing the Kanō style – red, blue and white paint, gold leaf, black lacquer, rich sculptural decoration – into the magnificent shrine erected to Ieyasu in Nikko. Their successors served the Shogun until the nineteenth century.

A more characteristically Chinese school, deriving from the Sung landscapes and black-and-white figure studies associated in Japan with Sesshū and his contemporaries, continued to attract Japanese artists under the Tokugawa. One who helped to establish this particular continuity was Hasegawa Tōhaku (1539–1610), a painter of murals, mostly for Buddhist temples, which had none of Kanō's rich colour. Among his portraits is one of the famous tea master, Sen no Rikyū. Later painters were more influenced by China's so-called 'literary' school, which flourished in southern China and became known in Japan through books and paintings brought by Chinese merchants to Nagasaki. Ike no Taiga (1723–76) is said to have learnt it by studying a Chinese album. For all that, some of Taiga's landscapes, like those of Sesshū, were of places in Japan. His friend, Yosa Buson (1716–83), a poet, who did not start painting until he reached middle age, showed greater interest in the kind of rural scenes in which people – unmistakably Japanese – had a more prominent place. One is tempted to wonder whether Bashō's poems had something to do with this.

Some of Buson's work has affinities with Yamato-e, 'Japanese' painting, which is known as such in large part because of the subjects it chose. It was carried forward into the Edo period by artists of the Tosa family, who continued to produce scrolls (e-maki) and album illustrations in the established manner. A seventeenth-century artist, Tawaraya Sōtatsu (d. 1643), about whose life little is known with any certainty, translated the style to the painting of large screens, using strong colours typical of Heian. Maruyama Ōkyo (1733–95), who began by studying in the Kano school, was more eclectic. In his large and varied corpus of work – it includes screens, scrolls and woodblock prints – one can trace the influence of Ming painters (in his use of ink) and of western art (in his treatment of perspective), as well as of Yamato-e. Western-style perspective also appears at about this time in paintings and prints by several other artists, reflecting a growing interest in what was called 'Dutch studies' (Rangaku). This is a topic to which we must refer again (Chapter 11).

The subjects chosen by these painters, including Buson, were in many cases related to the popularity of genre painting in Edo Japan. Illustrating aspects of everyday life had long been an element in *e-maki* – witness the village scenes in *Shigisan engi*, the pictures of fighting against the Mongols in *Mōkō shūrai ekotoba*, and the accounts of court ceremonial and the building of temples in various other scrolls, some of them produced by members of the Tosa house – but it was not until the second half of the sixteenth century that it became more widely a concern of Japanese artists. They expressed it in a number of styles on screens, murals and hanging scrolls (*kakemono*). There were scenes of Kyoto street life (expensive souvenirs for daimyo visitors); studies of upper-class pastimes like horse racing and mounted archery; sets to illustrate different trades and accomplishments; mementoes of theatrical performances and religious festivals; pictorial records of the arrival of Portuguese ships and the people they brought to Japan. Any event that was likely to attract the interest of many, but could be seen by only a few, had a potential market. Artists from both the Kanō and Tosa schools, plus some from neither who remain anonymous, were happy to meet the demand.

In the rapidly growing urban areas of the seventeenth century, customers could also be found for works that were less expensive. Wealthy merchants could afford original paintings, like their social betters. Town-dwellers of more modest means, whatever their tastes, could not; but the development of woodblock printing soon made it possible to supply at least some of their needs at moderate cost. This was done first by the publication of illustrated books, then by that of independent prints (*hanga*), of which 200 or more could be made from a single set of blocks. Because the format did not lend itself to the treatment of large and complex genre subjects, such as were found in murals or on multi-leaf screens, the printed repertoire was narrower in its range and simpler in its style. For commercial reasons it catered necessarily to interests that were widely shared. As a result, it focused in particular on the pleasure quarters, much as Saikaku and other writers did in their novels: lists of famous persons in the theatre and the world of courtesans, annotated as well as illustrated; guidebooks to the cities; sex manuals in the manner of contemporary Chinese publications, by some of which Japan's artists may well have been inspired. The erotic was a recurring theme. Sexually related illustrations, known as 'spring pictures' (*shunga*), were to be found among the works of even the most famous print designers of the day.

The first prints were in black and white, similar to those that had earlier been evolved to provide simple devotional pictures for the Buddhist faithful. The blocks provided black outlines, colour, if used, being added by hand. The style was made famous by Hishikawa Moronobu (*c.* 1625–95), who had studied under both Tosa and Kanō teachers. His prints, mostly for books, included portraits of actors, courtesans and legendary warriors, plus incidents from literature, but he also produced paintings in the genre tradition. A pair of sixfold screens of a theatre performance provide a notable example. Little change in technique occurred until late in the career of Okumura Masanobu (1686–1764), when the prints he designed began to appear in colour. Soon after his death came the first fully polychrome prints, known as 'brocade pictures', or *nishiki-e*. From that time on the black outline vanished, to be replaced by shapes in different colours; the artist became a member of a team in which designer, colourist and engraver worked together; and the finished product was sold in sufficient numbers to make counterfeiting a worthwhile occupation.

During the last hundred years of the Edo period, woodblock artists worked in highly divergent styles. Suzuki Harunobu (1725–70) is famous for willowy beauties, whose figures have an improbable grace; Kitagawa Utamaro (1753–1806) showed a preference for head-and-shoulder studies of courtesans, their features simply sketched in the manner of *Genji monogatari*; Sharaku, about whom almost nothing is known, appeared briefly on the scene at the end of the eighteenth century to publish some very striking heads of actors; Utagawa Toyokuni (1769–1825) favoured historical subjects (often taken from Kabuki). In the opinion of most art historians, figure studies declined in quality after Toyokuni. On the other hand, Katsushika Hokusai (1760–1849) and Andō Hiroshige (1797–1858) brought the design of prints much closer to that of painting. Hokusai's views of Mount Fuji and Hiroshige's several sets depicting the way-stations along the Tokaido, the road linking Edo with Kyoto, were outstanding landscape prints. The two men also produced vivid prints of birds and flowers. This showed that the art of print making was still capable of development, in both subject and technique. Despite that, it remained within the boundaries of the traditional. For all the impact it was later to have on modern European art, painting in Japan had not yet cut itself off from its past.

CHAPTER 11

The Coming of the West
1840–1873

Occasionally in the history of a country there comes a time when a number of different social and political changes reach a critical stage together. This is the signal for a 'revolution', using the word in its widest sense. For Japan the middle of the nineteenth century was such a turning-point. It was marked by entry into multifaceted relations with the West; the choice of Europe and America as institutional models, instead of China; the first steps in the introduction of capitalist industry. These developments coincided more or less with the overthrow of the Tokugawa Bakufu and its replacement by an emperor-centred form of government. As a result Japan's national life was transformed, much as it had earlier been in the Asuka and Nara periods.

The trigger for these events was the action taken by the western powers to open Japanese ports to foreign trade, itself part of a wider process of imperialist expansion in India and on the China coast. It once more bound Japan into a close political and commercial relationship with China, this time under the aegis of the West, acting through 'unequal treaties'. It also exposed her for at least a generation to the full weight of economic and military pressure that modern industrial states could bring to bear. Her response was to determine much of the region's modern history.

Unequal treaties

The immediate background to the western threat to Japan was the trade of the maritime powers with China. From the outset it had met with difficulties. Chinese officials, conditioned by centuries of the tribute system, took it as axiomatic that there should be an acceptance of Chinese law and methods of taxation among the foreigners coming to their country. Europeans and Americans did not always agree. There were occasions when Chinese custom seemed to them to be barbaric or unjust. There were also problems about balance of payments. By 1800 the world had acquired a taste for Chinese tea and silk to a value very much greater than that of China's demand for western products. To avoid using bullion to make good the difference, an alternative was found in selling opium to China; and when the Chinese government, denouncing opium as a danger to its people's health, banned the import of the drug, there was the making of a serious conflict. The opium trade became a smuggling enterprise. Since its proceeds found their way in large part to Canton, where they financed the legal purchases of tea and silk, western governments soon found themselves involved in its ramifications.

Crisis came in 1839. A conscientious Chinese viceroy at Canton, determined to uphold the law, chose to hold foreign merchants at the port as hostages until the smugglers, their fellow-countrymen, surrendered all opium held in ships offshore. In the short term, the move succeeded: the trade came to a halt, the opium was handed over and destroyed. The British Foreign Office, however – much the largest part of the opium traffic, as well as of the purchase of tea, was in British hands – held that the viceroy's action was no more legal than the smuggling he was trying to suppress. It therefore authorised the use of force to support the merchants' claims for compensation. Since China refused to accept the argument, the result was war. Desultory naval engagements in the Canton estuary in the winter of 1839–40 spread northwards up the China coast in the next two years; Britain seized the islands of Hong Kong and Chusan; China sued for peace at Nanking.

The treaty signed there in 1842 was taken by Britain as an opportunity to settle not only the issues from which the war arose, but also the general management of the trade. Hong Kong became a British colony and naval base. Four more ports in southern China were opened to trade, in addition to Canton. Consuls were to be appointed to them, having access to Chinese officials of equivalent rank; foreign merchants were to reside in designated settlements, subject to their own national laws, administered through consular courts; customs duties were to be charged on a scale laid down by treaty (that is, not fixed by China of its own volition). These privileges were made available to all the powers that came to terms with China, by means of the inclusion in each agreement of a most-favoured-nation clause. Together they defined the 'treaty port system'. It was expanded in 1858 by the addition of extra ports in the north and along China's river system, plus the right of diplomatic residence in Peking.

To Japanese, when they learnt of them, the arrangements seemed ominous. One Japanese scholar, writing in 1847, after accounts of the Opium War had been brought to Nagasaki by Dutch and Chinese merchants, was moved to ask, 'how can we know whether the mist gathering over China will not come down as frost upon Japan?'. He had reason on his side. Western governments, consuls and commercial establishments, largely ignorant still of this part of the world, were easily persuaded that the structure they had devised to regulate their trade with China would serve just as well in dealings with other 'orientals'. This attitude did much to ensure that the treaty port system was eventually imposed on Japan with the minimum of adjustment.

In 1844 the Dutch, fearing for the future of their rights at Deshima in the international situation produced by the Opium War, approached the Edo Bakufu to seek a relaxation of the seclusion laws. The overture was rejected. A British plan to send an expedition to Japan from the China coast in 1845 came to nothing because an 'appropriate' naval force could not be found to carry it out. In the next few years, occasional warships from Britain, France and the United States found occasion to call at Ryukyu (Loochoo) and Nagasaki, but none of these visits was followed up.

It was events in America that in the end brought a more determined effort to 'open' Japan. In 1848 the United States acquired California from Mexico, securing a substantial seaboard on the Pacific. There was talk of a transcontinental railroad, even, perhaps, a steamer route across the Pacific to Shanghai, where American trade was second only to that of Britain. Since the Japanese islands lay on the great circle route from San Francisco to the China coast, and were known from Dutch accounts to possess deposits of coal, they might, it was thought, serve as a staging-point for steamers, which at this stage of their development had limited range. For the first time, therefore, Japan's ports became of more than passing interest to one of the maritime powers.

By 1852 it was widely known that an American naval expedition was being prepared to undertake negotiations with Japan. In July of the following year, it anchored off Uraga at the entrance to Edo Bay. The two steamers and two sailing vessels that made it up were cleared for action. Its commanding officer, Commodore Matthew Perry, was very clear that he would admit no visitors to his presence but Japanese of suitable rank, while the letter he brought from President Millard Fillmore – it called for better treatment for shipwrecked seamen, the opening of ports of refuge where foreign ships could obtain coal and stores, plus permission to carry on trade – must be received with proper ceremony. On 14 July the elaborate boxes in which the President's letter and Perry's credentials were enclosed, escorted by a landing party from the squadron, were handed over at nearby Kurihama in the presence of 5,000 Japanese troops. The commodore added a letter of his own. If these 'very reasonable and pacific overtures' were not accepted at once, it said, he would return for a reply next spring, this time 'with a much larger force'. To underline the point, before he left for China he took part of his command into Edo Bay to survey the approaches to the Tokugawa capital.

True to his promise, Perry returned with eight ships early in 1854. In the interval Edo's policy-makers had been consulting the country's feudal lords. The results had not been helpful. One small group, whose spokesman was Tokugawa Nariaki of Mito, head of a senior branch of the Shogun's house, held that so insulting a demand must be altogether rejected, if necessary at the cost of war. Anything less would not only impugn the national honour, he claimed, but also undermine the Bakufu's prestige at home. Another equally small minority, led by Ii Naosuke of Hikone, the most powerful of the Tokugawa vassal lords (*fudai*), took a very different view. To seek to buy time, even if it meant compromise, was in their opinion only politic in view of Japan's military weakness. The time so gained could be used to prepare for war, above all by the adoption of western weapons and technology. The great majority of the lords, however, were less forthright. Most of their replies were nothing more than reiterations of the duty that followed from 'ancestral law', or plaintive calls for peace. They did little to suggest how the one could be upheld or the other secured.

Faced by these inconsistencies, Abe Masahiro, the senior member of the Tokugawa council, decided to accept the substance of Perry's proposals, if all else failed. It did. In meetings at Yokohama under the guns of the American ships, Perry showed himself unmoving. In March 1854 a convention was signed. It opened Shimoda and Hakodate as ports of refuge, gave undertakings about the future treatment of castaways and provided for the appointment of an American consul at Shimoda. It made no specific mention of rights of trade, which was Edo's only diplomatic achievement.

Despite the disappointment over trade, the agreement prompted efforts at emulation. The Dutch obtained better terms for their commerce at Deshima. The British and Russian naval commanders in the north Pacific, engaged in desultory operations against each other – one of the remoter aspects of the Crimean War – found time to secure conventions much like Perry's. British officials on the China coast, believing all that had been done so far to be inadequate, began to formulate plans for a 'proper' treaty with Japan. So did the new American consul at Shimoda, Townsend Harris, who arrived there in September 1856.

At this point Japan's dealings with the West became entangled once again in the affairs of China. Towards the end of 1856, when the Crimean War was over, fresh hostilities, arising from disputes over trade, broke out between China on the one side, and France and Britain on the other. Canton was captured, large Anglo-French forces were assembled for a campaign in the north. Both Dutch and American representatives in Japan made it plain to Edo that these forces, once victory set them free, would undoubtedly be used to support a demand for trade rights in the Japanese islands. The Bakufu, it was pointed out, would be able to offer no effective resistance, so its only hope of averting a catastrophe was to sign a commercial treaty first with countries whose demands would be less exacting. This could become a model for what would follow.

The Bakufu council, led now by Hotta Masayoshi, acknowledged the attractions of this argument. By October 1857 the representatives it sent to Nagasaki had concluded agreements not only with the Netherlands, but also with Russia, removing the upper limit long imposed on the value of the Nagasaki trade. High customs dues were retained, however, as were other Bakufu rights of interference. It was a formula Townsend Harris, a former businessman, was quite unwilling to accept. These treaties, he recorded in his journal, were 'disgraceful to all parties engaged in making them ... [and] not worth the paper on which they were written'. Instead, he proposed negotiations on a different text, which was more in line with the demands that France and Britain were currently making on Peking.

Getting it agreed by Edo proved uphill work. During the winter Harris was subjected to 'interminable discourses' by the Japanese, refusing 'points they subsequently grant, and meant to grant all the while', as well as 'many absurd proposals made by them without the hope, and scarcely the wish, of having them accepted'. Nevertheless, he persisted. He also hammered home the warning, based, he said, on his correspondence with the governor of Hong Kong, that the arrival of a British fleet could be expected at any time. By the end of February 1858 a draft was ready for signature.

Apart from the omission of a most-favoured-nation clause, it reflected the West's experience in China, applied now to Japan. The ports of Nagasaki and Kanagawa (Yokohama) were to be opened to American trade in 1859, Niigata in 1860, Hyogo (Kobe) in 1863. Foreign traders were to be admitted to Edo in 1862 and Osaka in 1863. An American minister would be resident in Edo. Customs duties were to be specified by treaty, as in China, and settlements set aside at the treaty ports, where Americans would be subject to American law.

Not surprisingly, the sweeping concessions that had been made by Bakufu officials encountered opposition in Japan. When the draft was put to feudal lords for comment, the same arguments against it emerged as had been voiced in 1854. More dangerous, the issue became enmeshed in dynastic politics. One of Tokugawa Nariaki's sons, Yoshinobu (Keiki), an adult with a reputation for ability, was widely favoured as a candidate to succeed the ailing Shogun, Iesada. Ii Naosuke, who remained at odds with Nariaki over foreign affairs, preferred a different choice, a child, but closer to Iesada by blood. The rivalry quickly acquired ramifications. Both sides canvassed the imperial court; objections to the treaty, stated in private by the emperor, became publicly known, lending more support to Nariaki than Naosuke; ostentatious efforts were made to change his mind. At last, in an attempt by Edo to still the turmoil, Hotta Masayoshi was removed from office and Ii Naosuke appointed regent (Tairo). It was a post, only filled in times of crisis, that gave him powers to override the Bakufu council.

Within weeks he had to use them. Lord Elgin, Britain's special ambassador, and Baron Gros, his French colleague, having signed treaties with China at Tientsin in June, which granted all their principal demands, decided to go at once to Japan (though not in company). The news was carried to Townsend Harris at Shimoda. Harris travelled at once to Kanagawa to warn the Shogun's representatives that the catastrophe he had predicted was about to become reality; the council of elders met; and Ii Naosuke, persuaded by Harris of the need for haste, decided to sign the American treaty, despite the fact that this would be to disregard the emperor's wishes. He also named the Shogun's heir – his own preferred candidate, Iemochi – and took steps to stifle opposition. Several great lords, including Nariaki, were sentenced to house arrest. A number of samurai, who had acted as their agents in the succession dispute, were executed or imprisoned.

The arrival of Elgin proved an anti-climax. He brought a single warship, not the fleet of which Harris had warned; made no secret of his lack of knowledge of conditions in Japan, borrowing Harris's secretary to advise him on the American treaty's terms; and generally behaved as if the whole expedition were a welcome relief from the grimmer duties he had faced in China. His entourage went shopping. Elgin himself, taking the Harris treaty as his model, but adding a most-favoured-nation clause, completed his negotiations in a mere two days. Having signed the document (26 August) and given a banquet for the Japanese representatives, at which they made their first acquaintance with the ritual of the loyal toast, he set off for China again, content, as he reported in a letter to his wife, to see 'an illumination of the forts in our honour'.

Treaties were also very soon signed with France, Russia and the Netherlands, bringing the total number of treaty powers to five. They incorporated Japan into a treaty port system 'made in China'. The first two British ministers appointed to Japan, Rutherford Alcock and Harry Parkes, had both been consuls in Shanghai. On leaving Japan they were promoted to Peking. Several of the British consuls in the newly opened Japanese ports had a similar background; the consular courts over which they presided looked to those in China as courts of appeal. Moreover, most of the foreign merchants who established themselves in the Japanese ports, not only the British ones, were representatives of firms on the China coast, or had gained commercial experience there. Often they brought with them their Chinese compradores and household staff, who became Japan's most numerous 'foreign residents'. Even the trade took on a Chinese character. Instead of providing China with the Japanese goods that had traditionally found a market there, Japan began to export silk and tea to the West. This made her China's competitor, no longer her trading partner.

Nationalism and politics

The events of the summer of 1858 marked the beginning of modern nationalism in Japan. Among samurai, at least, there was already an incipient national consciousness, bred by dealings with the mainland in the past, but enforced acceptance of the treaties brought a new awareness of a foreign threat directed at something larger than the villages or domains that most Japanese described as 'home'. The treaties, after all, applied to everyone; and in imitation of the West, Japan acquired a national flag – the Hi no Maru, a red sun on a white ground – which for formal purposes replaced the separate banners of the Shogun and feudal lords. A recognition of political unity slowly spread, first from major centres to the provinces, then from samurai to other sections of the population. It was given focus by the call to 'honour the emperor'.

The response to the foreign crisis was highly emotive, breaking through the bounds of acceptable behaviour. Men felt anger: anger against the foreigners, who had brought dishonour to Japan by the content and the manner of the demands they made; anger against the Shogun and feudal lords, who had failed in their duty to prevent it. These attitudes did not at once become universal, but already by the opening of the ports in 1859 there were some – the *shishi*, or 'men of spirit' – who were willing to act on such beliefs. To them it was not enough to lament the country's fate.

They found a spokesman in a young Choshu samurai, Yoshida Shōin. In 1854, convinced that Japan could not be saved unless the samurai spirit were harnessed to the military science of the West, he had tried to smuggle himself aboard one of the American squadron's ships at Shimoda, his intention being to travel to the United States, in order to learn the secrets of western strength. Frustrated in this aim by Perry's refusal to flout the Bakufu's laws, he was taken into custody and sent back to his home in Hagi under house arrest. There Choshu after a time allowed him to found a school. Gathering a group of students, mostly, like himself, from the lower ranks of the samurai class – they included several who were to be famous leaders of Japan in the second half of the century – he taught them that the fate of the country rested not in the hands of those now in authority, but with 'grass-roots heroes', willing to sacrifice themselves in the emperor's name. Nor was he content with words. In 1858 he became involved in a plot to kill one of Ii Naosuke's senior colleagues, a step designed to mark a protest at the regent's action in choosing to sign the treaties. The plot was discovered and Shōin was arrested once more. He was executed in the following year.

The notes he had written in prison to justify what he had done were circulated privately by his friends and students, spreading his ideas among the young hotheads of the samurai class. Already embittered by the 'shame' of the treaties and by Ii Naosuke's 'purge', many of them, taking as their slogan *sonnō-jōi*, 'honour the emperor, repel the barbarian', turned to terrorism as the only means they had by which to demonstrate commitment to the anti-foreign cause. Violence was at first directed against individual foreigners in the newly opened treaty ports. Townsend Harris's secretary was a victim. Some ships' officers were killed. Unsuspecting Japanese who entered foreign service also found themselves at risk. A former castaway, recruited in Shanghai to be Rutherford Alcock's 'linguist', was murdered outside the gate of the British legation. Gradually the *shishi* grew more ambitious, seeking to force action from the Bakufu itself, or to precipitate a conflict with the West that might overturn the treaties. In March

1860 Ii Naosuke was cut down at one of the gates to Edo castle. In March 1861 a night attack on the British legation left two of its staff with wounds and several marauding samurai dead.

Edo's response lacked Ii's ruthlessness. To the fury of most western envoys in Japan, their protests about the attacks on foreigners were met by contrived delays and bureaucratic shuffle: since the culprits, when identified, often proved to be retainers of powerful lords, they were for all practical purposes outside the Shogun's jurisdiction. In the political context, a compromise was sought with the imperial court, in the hope that this might pacify the samurai. As evidence of it, a marriage was arranged between the emperor's sister – who showed reluctance – and the Shogun; but it came at an embarrassing price, for to win the court's consent the Bakufu had to promise to abrogate the treaties or expel the foreigners within the next ten years. In flat contradiction of this promise, Edo arranged to send a mission to Europe to persuade the powers to postpone the opening of any further ports and cities, the treaty provisions notwithstanding. Its argument that the rising tide of unrest in Japan was as much a threat to foreign trade as it was to Bakufu authority eventually proved persuasive. A protocol was signed in London in June 1862, granting a respite until 1868.

Nevertheless, the settlement broke down within a year. The arguments put forward by the anti-foreign activists struck a chord with many other samurai in Japan. Those of Satsuma and Choshu, in particular, whose domains had been defeated by the Tokugawa at Sekigahara in 1600, had been encouraged to cherish resentment ever since. The loss of land after that defeat had had the effect of keeping their stipends at a lower level than average, leaving them more subject than most to the pressures caused by economic change (Chapter 10). This left them restive. Brought up, moreover, like samurai elsewhere, to think of themselves as a political élite, responsible in some degree for the country's fate, they had become alarmed by 'the trend of the times' since the arrival of Perry. It was a dangerous situation for a regime that depended in the last resort on samurai loyalty.

Two incidents underlined its dangers in 1863 and 1864. In September 1862 Satsuma samurai, escorting the father of their lord, attacked a party of British merchants near Yokohama, claiming that they had failed to show the customary deference to his procession. One of the party, a visitor from Shanghai, was killed; others, including a woman, were wounded. The British government demanded apologies and compensation from both lord and Shogun. After a winter of bad-tempered diplomatic argument, the Bakufu paid. The lord of Satsuma did not. A British naval squadron was therefore sent against him in August 1863, its orders to enforce compliance. On arrival it seized several Satsuma ships; shore batteries opened fire on it; and in the action that followed, part of the town of Kagoshima was set ablaze. The squadron, having suffered damage, withdrew, but Satsuma came to terms in talks at Yokohama a few weeks later.

While this crisis was being worked out, Edo faced another from a different direction. During 1862–3 the *shishi* had become active on a larger scale. Hundreds of them swarmed in the streets of Kyoto, attacking Bakufu officials, fighting Bakufu guards, putting up posters that called on the emperor to lead a crusade against the foreigner. Responding to the pressure, the court called on the Shogun to take some positive action about the presence of foreigners in Japan; and the Bakufu, desperate to avoid hostilities with the West, which it could neither afford nor hope to win, attempted once again to escape through verbal compromise. It agreed to a decree in favour of 'expulsion', which was to take place in June 1863. Privately it decided that this was to mean no more than fresh negotiations to close the port of Yokohama. But the device proved unsuccessful. Choshu, whose samurai made up a large proportion of the Kyoto malcontents, chose to take the decree's wording literally. On the appointed day its steamers attacked an American vessel in the Shimonoseki Straits. In the next few weeks its shore batteries several times fired on foreign ships that were passing through. By the end of July the most direct sea route from Yokohama to Shanghai was closed.

This time the treaty powers took action jointly. Home governments were consulted, a process that took some months; then there was a further delay while the envoys awaited the result of Bakufu overtures to France; and it was only when these had proved abortive – a year or more after the original incidents – that a fleet of seventeen ships, furnished by four different countries, set out from Yokohama for Shimonoseki. It bombarded the coast batteries in the straits, landed men to dismantle them, then concluded a truce (14 September 1864), under the terms of which Choshu was to open the passage through the straits again and pay a large indemnity.

The bombardments at Kagoshima and Shimonoseki changed the character of Japanese relations with the West. Demonstrations of western naval might had proved enough to convince the majority of samurai, even the 'men of spirit', that something more than personal self-sacrifice would be required if Japan were to challenge the treaties with any expectation of success. Calls for the immediate use of force began to recede. Instead, plans were made to acquire the most up-to-date western weapons and a knowledge of how to manufacture them. Satsuma tried to order Armstrong guns of the kind the British squadron had used at Kagoshima. The Bakufu, Choshu and Satsuma all sent students abroad to acquire technological skills. In addition, Satsuma turned to Britain for diplomatic support – with equivocal results – and signed contracts with a Belgian entrepreneur to develop the trade that would pay for ships and guns, while the Bakufu strengthened its links with France for similar purposes.

There is a direct line from these events to the overthrow of the Tokugawa. The Bakufu was finding the suppression of unrest expensive. So, indeed, was the conduct of foreign relations. Coast defence had been an increasing burden since the Opium War. Opening the ports, providing facilities for trade, creating a rudimentary diplomatic service and sending missions abroad all added to the charges on regular expenditure. Those arising from the clashes with the treaty powers in 1863 and 1864, which resulted in the payment of indemnities, were larger still. The treaties therefore helped to empty government coffers. When the cost of western–style rearmament spiralled after 1864, the financial strain became unbearable. By 1868 both Edo and a number of domains were heavily in debt to foreign creditors, who had underwritten their purchases of ships and guns.

Inflation accelerated. Since rice was still the principal unit of account for tax, as well as a staple food, public insolvency translated quickly into living costs, provoking further popular unrest. Even so, the results were not 'revolutionary' in the sense of breeding an ideology and a political movement aimed at achieving social change. Feudalism still had a grip on Japan. In fact, the struggles that were to follow between 1865 and 1867 had much in common with the sixteenth-century civil wars. The great domains of Kyushu and west Japan, led by Satsuma and Choshu, emerged once more as contenders for national power; the Shogun was accused of ineffective leadership at a time of danger, sacrificing thereby his right to office; the emperor was acclaimed as a symbol of unity. It was a view in which both lords and dissident samurai could join.

In the late summer of 1864 Edo, seizing what it saw as an opening created by the foreign attacks on Kagoshima and Shimonoseki, set out to restore its authority over emperor and domains. Armed patrols were sent out on the streets of Kyoto, and samurai loyalists arrested or driven from the city. When Choshu was persuaded by some of them to send its troops to restore their influence, these were repulsed in heavy fighting. Many of the 'men of spirit' were killed, others committed suicide. The survivors sought refuge in Choshu, reinforcing the local loyalists to the point at which their leaders were able to seize control of the domain.

The result was open confrontation. On the one side was the Bakufu, which turned increasingly to western armaments and western methods of administration in an effort to defend itself against its enemies at home. On the other, Choshu and Satsuma began to come together in a co-operation clearly directed against the Tokugawa. The Bakufu decided at last to seize the nettle. Choshu was declared rebel. When its newly established loyalist leaders rejected the terms offered by way of settlement, a punitive expedition was announced and troops assembled in Osaka to carry it out. This forced Japan's daimyo to show their colours. Satsuma made secret alliance with Choshu. A few others, chiefly from the north, took their stand with the Shogun. Many more held aloof, guarding their frontiers.

The climax came in the summer of 1866, when an attack was launched on the Mōri lands in western Honshu. It was repulsed on all fronts. The defeat marked a critical loss of Bakufu prestige. To be fought to a standstill, not by the might of the treaty powers, but by a single domain (Satsuma's role was secretly to supply Choshu with arms), had an effect that was the reverse of what Edo had intended. A new Shogun, Yoshinobu (Keiki), Nariaki's son, the unsuccessful candidate in 1858, succeeded on Iemochi's death towards the end of the year; but although he presided over frantic measures to restore the Bakufu's strength, calling on the French minister, Léon Roches, as adviser, chaotic finance and low morale proved too much for him. In November 1867, in the hope of saving something from the wreck, he offered to resign.

His opponents were not willing to let him off so lightly. To leave a former Shogun undisturbed in possession of his lands and fighting men, they argued, would ensure that Tokugawa power continued, if in different form. Exploiting their links with friends at court, and calling on several other powerful domains to join them, the leaders of Satsuma and Choshu planned to 'seize the jewel' – that is, the emperor's person – as a decisive weapon. The young Mutsuhito (Meiji), come only recently to the throne, was persuaded to give them countenance (his maternal grandfather was one of the conspirators). This done, Satsuma forces, led by the domain's most famous samurai, Saigō Takamori, and joined by contingents that were furnished by four other lords, including two who were Tokugawa relatives, took over the gates of the imperial palace in the early morning of 3 January 1868. A council was summoned, its membership carefully chosen; a decree was approved, stripping the Shogun of his office and his lands; and the direct responsibility for national government was placed once more in the emperor's hands. In the strict constitutional sense, this was the Meiji Restoration (*ōsei-fukko*), a reassertion of the prerogatives of the ancient ruling house.

Study of the West

To consider, not the events that led to the overthrow of the Tokugawa, but the changes that followed from it (Chapter 12), brings into focus a different aspect of Japan's relations with the outside world: namely, the country's knowledge of the West. During the seventeenth century, while memories of the persecution of Christianity were fresh, that knowledge had been very limited. After 1700, by contrast, there developed a vogue for Rangaku, 'Dutch studies', based on information provided by the Dutch at Deshima. Often it reflected no more than casual curiosity about 'concoctions from abroad', but there were also investigations of a kind that had more practical purposes. Japanese doctors, for example, began to study European medicine, especially surgery, not only because it became fashionable, therefore profitable, but also because it produced more convincing results than the Chinese methods in which they had been trained. Astronomy came into favour for its relevance to calendars, though the first clear illustrations of heliocentric theory came in fact from an artist, Shiba Kōkan. Much of what was done was in the 'amateur' tradition cherished by Chinese literati. Inō Tadataka (Chūkei), who was by trade a sake-brewer, turned in later life to the study of surveying. Using western instruments, he prepared a remarkably accurate map of the whole of Japan in the first few years of the nineteenth century. Other aspiring scientists, taking advantage of the visits made to Edo by the Dutch factors from Nagasaki, bombarded them with requests for clocks, telescopes, barometers, even Leiden jars. Colour prints of Dutch life at Deshima found a ready sale.

As news began to spread about European advances in India and on the China coast at the time of the Napoleonic wars, the emphasis changed. A good many samurai, persuaded that their country faced a danger of attack from overseas, sought a knowledge of western military science. Navigation and gunnery were their principal interests, together with the design and siting of coastal batteries, but a number also took up the more theoretical branches of the subject, including the mathematics of ballistics and the chemistry of explosives. Some learnt, at first from Dutch books, then by experiment, how to build reverberatory furnaces and manufacture cannon made of iron, instead of bronze. When Perry arrived in 1853, bringing a variety of technological gifts, he found to his surprise that there were Japanese who appeared to understand the steam engine, at least in principle. Within a year or two the first steamships were being launched from Japanese yards.

On the face of it, the opening of the ports in 1859 increased Japan's access to information about the West by providing opportunity for travel. In practice, not many Japanese were allowed to avail themselves of it. For several years only those whom the Bakufu sent abroad on diplomatic missions or for military training, plus a handful who were willing to take the risk of travelling illegally, visited the countries of Europe and America. These continuing restrictions were not welcome to the treaty powers, who believed that the spread of knowledge would be good for trade. They therefore pressed the Bakufu to ease its rules; and in 1866, having demonstrated the superiority of their armaments in 1863 and 1864, they won their point. The revised customs treaty of that year laid down that 'all Japanese subjects may travel to any foreign country for purposes of study or trade', if provided with passports. From then on, Japanese travellers overseas multiplied, some sponsored by feudal lords or others in authority, some financed privately. The process was to continue until the end of the century, allowing many hundreds of men and women to attend schools and colleges in the countries of the West.

The Bakufu itself sent missions abroad, some with diplomatic functions, narrowly defined, others with a wider brief. The one sent to the United States in 1860 to ratify the Harris treaty was intended to be of the more restricted kind, but in the event the lavish American hospitality it received and the round of educational visits arranged for it did a great deal to give its members an understanding of American society. Because of this, when a mission to Europe was being planned in 1862, primarily for the purpose of negotiating a delay in the opening of Hyogo, Edo and Osaka, the French and British resident ministers in Japan urged that it be instructed to seek a knowledge of Europe's wealth and strength as well, thereby redressing the international balance. The men whom Edo appointed to carry out this task included several of Japan's 'Dutch scholars', who went about it with enthusiasm. The result was a surprisingly detailed account of European society in the 1860s.

Between April and October 1862 the thirty-six members of the mission, travelling at the expense of various European governments and carrying with them a supply of soya sauce in champagne bottles, journeyed from Marseilles to Paris to London, then to the Hague, Berlin and St Petersburg. From there they returned to Paris by train and on by sea to Lisbon before sailing for Japan via the Mediterranean and Indian Ocean. In addition to their diplomatic duties, on which more time was spent in London than elsewhere, the envoys were ceremonially received and entertained by Napoleon III, the kings of Prussia and the Netherlands, and the tsar, though not by Queen Victoria (who was in mourning for Prince Albert). To these extremely formal activities were added numerous visits to military establishments, dockyards, factories, government departments, banks, hospitals, exhibitions, museums and newspaper offices, all assiduously recorded in the notes and sketches of the mission's secretariat. Little interest was shown in art or music.

The value of this information gathering was put in question once the party returned to Edo. During the weeks in the early part of 1863 when a report was being drafted, anti-foreign violence in Japan was reaching its peak. Reluctant to provoke the terrorists any further, senior officials formally received the document, then buried it in the files. There it remained unused, as far as one can tell, until superseded by the much longer and better-informed report of the Iwakura embassy of 1871–3. Despite this, the mission was not without influence on Japanese knowledge of the West. The doctors and interpreters attached to it included men who were to be opinion-formers of significance: Terashima Munenori, Foreign Minister in the early Meiji years; Fukuzawa Yukichi, Japan's foremost writer on western civilisation during the rest of the century; Fukuchi Genichirō, editor of one of Tokyo's first daily papers.

Yet it must be said that this was not what the Bakufu itself had meant by learning about the West, which is better revealed by the reasons it gave for sending students overseas. The first group of these went to Holland in 1862. All but two of its members were to undergo naval training in specialist fields, ranging from navigation and gunnery to engineering and ship construction. One, apparently on his own initiative, became an explosives expert. The two exceptions were sent to Leiden to study law and economics, which were properly 'governmental' subjects in Confucian eyes. Later parties were sent to Russia (1865) and Britain (1867) with similar intentions, plus that of training interpreters.

It is doubtful whether the daimyo of Choshu and Satsuma, who also sent samurai to the West to study, had any very different motivation. Itō Hirobumi, one of five students from Choshu who went to England in 1863, described their purpose as being to make themselves 'living weapons of war'. Nevertheless, both they and the Satsuma men who followed them in 1865 had a quite different insight into western life from that of their fellow-countrymen under government sponsorship. Not for them the world of government receptions and military academies. With merchants as the go-betweens in making their arrangements, they were encouraged to follow courses in law, politics, economics and civil engineering, or even literature and the humanities, such as would qualify them for careers in business or the civil departments of their country's government. Most of the 'private' students who

13 A daimyo fulfils his duty of 'alternate attendance' (*sankin–kōtai*).
His escort, greeted with respect and curiosity by local residents,
enters the outskirts of Edo, en route to his residence there.

16 Geisha writing letters, a woodblock print by Utamaro (1753–1806). The hairstyle is a symbol of status (as entertainer and courtesan, not simple prostitute). The evidence of literacy carries the same implication.

14 (opposite above) Nijō Castle in Kyoto, the Shogun's private apartments. Though the castle was completed by Tokugawa Ieyasu to watch over his interests at the emperor's court, Ieyasu and his successors rarely left Edo to visit it. When they did, they occupied these apartments, protected by the 'nightingale' flooring of the corridors outside, which made it impossible to approach the rooms undetected. The style of the wall panels is that of the Momoyama period (late sixteenth century). Compare the Heian palace (plate 5).

15 (opposite below) Kabuki theatre. By the end of the seventeenth century, as Japanese cities became larger and more complex, Kabuki drama was being performed in regular theatres in Edo and Osaka. This print by Okumura Masanobu (1686–1764) shows the interior of one, together with a section of the audience. By this time (c.1740), Japanese artists had begun to use the western-style method of depicting perspective.

17 *Sumō* wrestlers in the nineteenth century. Before the modern period *sumō* tournaments were held in the open, like prizefighting in England.

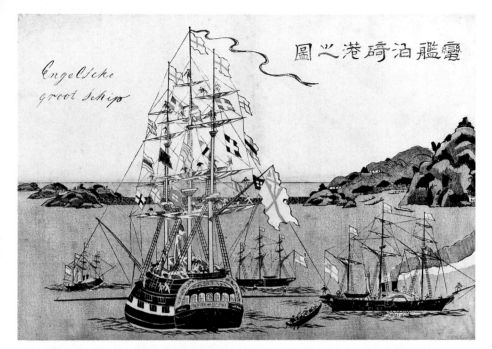

18 *(top)* A British squadron in Nagasaki's outer harbour, 1855. It was engaged in naval operations against Russia during the Crimean War, but its presence was seen as a threat by Japanese. Reflecting the port's traditional role in foreign relations, the print is labelled in Dutch and Chinese, not in Japanese.

19 *(above)* Japan's expansion overseas. The First Division leaves Tokyo for service in Manchuria, 1936.

20 Surrender. The Japanese delegation wait to sign the surrender agreement aboard USS *Missouri* in Tokyo Bay, 1 September 1945.

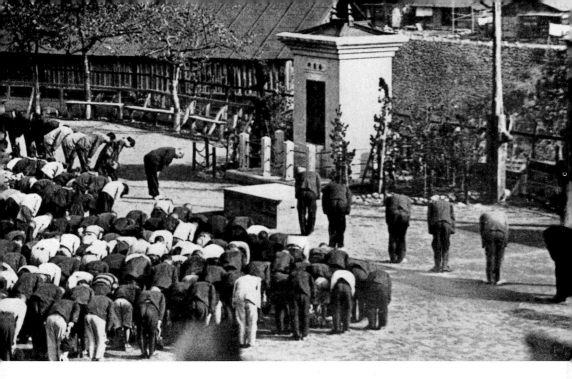

21 Prewar education. In the 1930s the school day started with a collective act of respect towards an enshrined portrait of the emperor.

22 Postwar education. To get a good start on the educational ladder, children under the age of twelve attend special 'crammer' schools (*juku*) in the school holidays.

23 *(top)* International recognition. One result of the postwar 'economic miracle' was Japan's membership of international bodies like the Group of Seven. Here Nakasone Yasuhiro (prime minister 1982–87) talks to the leaders of the United States (Ronald Reagan), Germany (Helmut Kohl) and France (François Mitterrand). Tokyo, 1986.

24 *(above)* The survival of tradition. A popular outing for the residents of Edo, later of Tokyo, was a visit to the Asakusa district of the city and its famous temple, especially during festivals. The temple was destroyed by bombing in the Pacific War, but when it was rebuilt (in ferro-concrete) such outings were resumed. The road leading to the massive gate is lined with small shops selling traditional souvenirs and crafts.

went abroad in later years did much the same, increasingly in the United States. They returned to Japan to take a vital but fairly low-profile role in the Meiji period's transformation of Japanese society: as middle-ranking bureaucrats, technical experts and managers in business and industry, translators and interpreters, and educators at every level.

The chief exceptions were those who went in the earliest groups, especially those from Choshu and Satsuma. By the intercession of the Jardine Matheson company, which arranged their travels and finances, the five from Choshu who arrived in London in 1863 found places at University College London. Three of them, together with a handful of others who joined them later, acquired a training in science and engineering. Two, Inoue Kaoru and Itō Hirobumi, went home in the spring of 1864 to play a part in the negotiations between Choshu and the treaty powers before the Shimonoseki bombardment, having little more to show for their experience than a knowledge of English and a nodding acquaintance with mid-Victorian Britain. Even so, this was enough, when added to the part they played in anti-Tokugawa politics in the next few years, to guarantee them office in the Meiji government after 1868. They rose rapidly within it to become outstanding political figures of their time, rewarded with the highest ranks.

The Satsuma students, who arrived in London in 1865 under similar auspices – those of a Scottish merchant in Nagasaki – also found their way to University College London, where they stayed for several years. Some were then called home, while others went on to America to study. These men, too, took positions of some importance in Meiji society. In addition, two of the older members of the Satsuma party, Terashima Munenori and Godai Tomoatsu, who did not enrol as students, acquired a different but equally valuable kind of knowledge. Terashima had been ordered to try to persuade the British government to give some backing to Satsuma in its growing rivalry with Edo. This led to contacts with diplomats and politicians in London, which opened the way to his own career as a Meiji diplomat. Godai's instructions were to make arrangements with a western business firm by which the domain might raise the funds to purchase arms. He did so with a Belgian entrepreneur. The scheme was not particularly successful, but in the course of the travels and talks that led to it Godai learnt more than most Japanese about industrial society. Industry, he became convinced, was the source of western strength. After the Bakufu was overthrown he spent some time in the Meiji government's finance department, but later abandoned an official career to become an entrepreneur himself, largely in railways and mining. He was for many years President of the Osaka Chamber of Commerce. Other travellers, including some who served the Tokugawa, took a similar course. Shibusawa Ei'ichi, for example, whom the Bakufu had sent to France in 1867 as financial comptroller to the mission that represented it at the Paris Exposition, quit official life in the early Meiji period to become a highly successful banker and entrepreneur, who did much to develop the modern textile industry.

Awareness of the importance of industry to a country's ability to defend itself brought a fresh slogan into prominence in Japan: *fukoku-kyōhei*, 'enrich the country, strengthen its army', or Wealth and Strength. It was in origin a Chinese tag, dating from the time when 'wealth' was land and soldiers were farmers; but in the late Edo and early Meiji periods it came to signify instead the need for a military establishment, based on western organisation and technology, which would be paid for from the resources that commerce and industry made available. As a corollary, so at least men like Godai believed, Japan would need a change of political leadership to bring it about.

Such thinking became another strand, distinct from *sonnō-jōi*, in the ideas of those who opposed the Tokugawa. It was represented in the regime that replaced them after 1868 by a number of the younger samurai, most of whom had been abroad. This ensured that study of the West would not be neglected, despite the disappearance of those feudal patrons who had so far sponsored it. Students were still sent overseas under government auspices, or given grants if they were already there; small 'expert' missions were dispatched to Europe and America to examine aspects of western governmental practice; a number of foreign advisers were hired; and the Iwakura embassy took over the task of the Bakufu mission of 1862, albeit on an altogether more impressive scale. Led by three senior ministers from the Council of State and taking with it a large body of attendant bureaucrats, it left Yokohama at the end of 1871 to circle the world, partly in an effort to win recognition for the imperial government, now that there was no longer a Shogun, partly, as it announced to its foreign hosts, 'to select from the various institutions prevailing among enlightened nations such as are best suited to our present condition'. In other words, it avowedly sought not only information that would be of military value, but also 'enlightenment'. Crossing the Pacific first to San Francisco, it spent several months in the United States, then visited in turn most of the capitals of western Europe before returning via the recently opened Suez canal in the spring of 1873. Along the way it carried out a programme of surveys and inspections more extensive by far than that of 1862. It was better served by its interpreters, too. As a result, the embassy's report, published in five western-style volumes a few years later, was more detailed and very much better informed than anything Japan had possessed before about the outside world, while the rank of the men responsible for it ensured that it would not be overlooked. It was, in fact, a draft for the building of an entirely remodelled Japan, reflecting the current wisdom of the West.

CHAPTER 12

The Modern State

The *coup d'état* of 3 January 1868 did not immediately settle the
fate of the Tokugawa house. The Shogun Yoshinobu accepted
defeat without demur. Many of his followers did not. Some fought
battles against the 'imperial' army – troops from loyalist domains –
on Kyoto's outskirts in the next few days. Others carried on a
determined campaign in the north for several months. A squadron
of Bakufu naval vessels escaped from Edo to Hokkaido, where its
commanders planned to create an independent princedom for
their lord. They did not surrender until the early summer of 1869.

The new rulers had therefore been in power for eighteen
months before they could settle with any confidence to the
business of deciding how to govern Japan. The completion of the
process took them twenty years – that is, nearly half the Meiji
emperor's reign (1867–1912) – and by the end of it they had
turned to the West for models, believing that a modern state
needed institutions appropriate to the world in which it would
compete. The monarchy itself was an exception, but in other
respects the government of Japan until the middle of the twentieth
century was based on that of Europe in the age of Bismarck. Even
after defeat in 1945 the changes that were made can be described
as modifications to the pattern, not an attempt to dismantle it
entirely.

The kind of centralised state that was created between 1870 and 1890 inevitably brought about a social revolution, too. Feudal privilege was destroyed; an education system was introduced, capable of training recruits to government service in the skills that were now required for it; and western-style industry was developed, providing a substantial segment of the population with novel ways to make a living, as well as a lifestyle that reflected them. Some of these changes were disruptive. With a view to preserving national unity, therefore, which was a prime consideration of its policy, the Meiji leadership brought in laws concerning censorship and the suppression of dissent. It also set out to reinforce tradition, or at least such parts of it as might contribute to good order. Meiji Japan, ideologically as well as institutionally, became a hybrid, part western, part Sino-Japanese.

Political institutions

During 1868 the emperor, still resident in Kyoto, was served, as his distant forebears had been, by a council, the Daijōkan, and several executive departments bearing Nara-period names. At the highest level they were staffed by daimyo and senior members of the court who had played a part – not necessarily an important one – in bringing the Tokugawa down. Sanjō Sanetomi and Iwakura Tomomi, nobles who had the emperor's ear, were the most distinguished. As assistants they had several samurai leaders from the loyalist domains, notably Kido Takayoshi (Kōin) of Choshu, together with Saigō Takamori and Ōkubo Toshimichi of Satsuma. These were all men with genuine power. In lesser posts there were a large number of other nobles and samurai, most of them chosen, or so it would appear, to reconcile opinion to the new regime, not for any acknowledged competence. Certainly they had little to do: the only areas directly subject to imperial rule were those surrendered by the Tokugawa; elsewhere the feudal lords retained their former rights. Indeed, had the duties of the emperor's representatives been more onerous, the system might have broken down, for it was cumbersome and inefficient.

The central group of office-holders, who had organised the *coup d'état*, found this situation unsatisfactory. Once victory had been won in the civil war, they took steps to change it. In 1869 the court was moved to Edo, renamed Tokyo (Eastern Capital), where the Shogun's castle became the emperor's palace. Many men of undoubted dignity, whose formal rank exceeded their ability, were removed from office, clearing the way to a more effective form of imperial rule. Opinions about what would be desirable still differed widely. Some feudal lords favoured a baronial council, responsible to the emperor. Passionate loyalists, especially in the palace, urged that the emperor, despite his youth, be made in fact what he was in name, a personal autocrat. Samurai like Itō Hirobumi of Choshu and Godai Tomoatsu of Satsuma, who had been abroad and were now beginning to find a place in official-dom, set out the case for the abolition of domains and the building of a centralised state on western lines. This was also the advice that came from certain western diplomats and sympathetic foreign residents. It clearly had attractions for the ambitious.

The first step in that direction came in March 1869, when the samurai officials of Satsuma, Choshu, Tosa and Hizen persuaded their lords to submit a joint memorial, putting their lands and people at the emperor's disposal. It was an ambiguous document, leaving it open to him to confirm the state of affairs inherited from the Tokugawa, if that seemed politic; but in July the offer was accepted and the rest of the lords were ordered to follow suit. In order not to give too great a shock to feudal opinion, daimyo were then appointed 'governors' of the territories they sur-rendered, a step that seemed to leave the government with nothing more than a right to interfere. In August 1871, however, all former daimyo were summoned to an imperial audience, at which they were told – without discussion – that henceforth the domains would be replaced by prefectures (*ken*), administered from the centre in the Chinese manner. A month later all armed forces, other than those that owed allegiance to the throne, were summarily dissolved. To sweeten the pill, lords were allowed to keep a tenth of the revenue from their lands as private income, while samurai retained their stipends, subject to review.

There remained the task of devising an institutional structure to replace the highly personal one that had previously bound the daimyo to the Shogun. Within a few months an imperial embassy, led by Iwakura, who was accompanied as deputies by Kido and Ōkubo, left on its travels to America and Europe (Chapter 11). One of its functions was to investigate western governmental models, in order to identify any that might be applicable to Japan. Before it left, two initial decisions about the country's government had been taken in general terms, to be put into force as soon as details were decided. A conscription law, announced in December 1872 and published in January 1873, was the first. It provided that men, regardless of social origin, were to be called to the colours at the age of twenty to serve three years, followed by four years in the reserve. This gave the regime an army of its own, replacing the feudal class. Training and organisation were to be western-style, planned and initially supervised by officers from France and Germany. An army officers' school was founded, soon followed by an arsenal, an ordnance factory and an artillery practice range. A General Staff was added in 1878. The development of a navy came more slowly, because its technical skills depended to a large extent on study overseas, but by 1894 it had a fleet of twenty-eight ships, amounting altogether to 57,000 tons.

The expense of these reforms was to be met by the introduction of a land tax, the second important measure worked out in the embassy's absence. It was announced in July 1873. The key to it was to be found in Finance Ministry recommendations, insisting that the Meiji government needed to enjoy a revenue at least as large as that which Shogun and feudal lords together had received. To achieve this, the law, as issued, prescribed that the owner of land, responsible for paying tax, was to be the former landlord or cultivator, as local enquiry might determine. He was to pay tax in cash, calculated as a percentage of capital value. The rate was initially set at 3 per cent (plus a supplement for local expenditure).

Farmers found some of these conditions harsh. There was no relief for years of bad harvest, for example, such as had sometimes been granted by feudal lords, while the need to pay in cash posed problems for those who still engaged in subsistence farming. As a consequence, rural unrest did not come to an end. By contrast, the government was broadly satisfied. It could now determine policy on the basis of a regular and predictable revenue.

Armed forces and a tax system were fundamental to the very existence of the state. Anything more elaborate by way of administrative machinery had to await the findings of the Iwakura embassy, which returned in the summer of 1873. Decision was then delayed by a serious dispute over priorities. While the embassy was away, the 'caretaker' government, led by Saigō Takamori, had become embroiled in conflict with Korea, which Saigō and his colleagues wished to resolve by force. Kido and Ōkubo strongly opposed the decision. In the first place, war, they believed, would present the powers, especially Russia, with an opportunity to interfere in the region's affairs. It would also pre-empt resources which, as the embassy's experience in America and Europe showed, would be better spent on institutional reform, if Japan were ever to be able to take a stand against the West.

The 'war party', as it is called, lost the subsequent argument, but the disagreement split the ruling group. Some of its members resigned in order to organise a 'consitutional' opposition. Others, including Saigō, put themselves at the head of samurai discontent, occasioned by resentment of Meiji policies that seemed designed to destroy the remaining vestiges of samurai privilege. There were a number of local rebellions in western regions in the next few years. The largest, that in Satsuma, which Saigō joined in 1877, took the whole strength of army and police to overcome it. Saigō himself committed suicide in the face of imminent defeat. In the following year, sympathisers of his cause assassinated Ōkubo, seen to be the architect of their rebellion's failure. Since Kido had died in 1877, the result was a generational change in national leadership.

Ōkubo, who as Home Minister had been the regime's strongest figure after 1873, had done much to strengthen Tokyo's control of the country in his final years. A network of prefectural and local officials, recruited for the most part from former samurai, had been made responsible to his ministry. Their appointments and promotion were decided in the capital, their duties covered almost every aspect of provincial life. Tokyo ruled, in fact, more firmly than Edo had done for generations. The younger men who took over in the 1880s, of whom the most important were Itō Hirobumi and Yamagata Aritomo of Choshu, continued Ōkubo's work. They gave it, however, a more distinctively western flavour. Both had been abroad, Itō several times. Yamagata had studied military science in Germany. A significant number of their senior colleagues had a similar background. Such experience became a test of suitability for office.

Authoritarian regulations, issued in December 1880 and revised in 1886, were introduced to govern the workings of the central bureaucracy, echoing the Nara codes in their attention to detail. The powers and duties of ministers and their subordinates were spelt out, the limits of departmental budgets defined, a host of rules laid down concerning archives and accounts. Recruitment and promotion were made subject to examination, as in the distant past, though the tests were now in elements of 'western' learning, such as law, politics and economics, not Confucian philosophy.

The coping-stone of the structure was a western-style cabinet, established in December 1885 to replace the Council of State. Its members were departmental ministers, appointed by the emperor and responsible individually to him. The co-ordination of their work and the presentation of general recommendations on policy were duties that fell to the prime minister (replacing the Daijō-daijin). From April 1888 there was also a Privy Council, composed of senior advisers, men not currently in office, who were to be consulted by the emperor on legal and constitutional questions. The Council was specifically instructed not to 'interfere with the executive'.

Japan's legal system was also reformed. Local and regional courts, presided over by appointed judges, had been created in 1871 to replace the judicial arrangements of the Bakufu and domains. A Supreme Court was added in 1875. In 1886 the justice minister's power to remove or dismiss judges was restricted, and from 1890 judges were appointed for life, subject to competitive examination. To this extent the judiciary was made independent of politics. The law was meanwhile being changed to bring it as far as possible into line with that of the West. A criminal code was drafted under a French adviser between 1875 and 1877, though it took another five years to get it through the processes of scrutiny. For commercial law Japan looked to Germany for advice. A draft was prepared in 1881–4, then promulgated in 1890 after review by the Justice and Foreign ministries. A new civil code took even longer to agree: the parts that touched on marriage, inheritance and other family matters proved too politically sensitive to be hurried. The first version, based on the French civil code, was rejected in 1878 as being too 'foreign'. A revision completed in 1888 met at first with similar objections; and discussion of it lasted until 1898 before there was wide enough agreement to make its promulgation possible.

The adoption of western institutions in this way brought Japan a measure of international respectability, which proved a useful adjunct to diplomacy in efforts to revise the unequal treaties (Chapter 13). It was reinforced by the introduction of a written constitution in 1889. Some of the men who had broken away from the ruling group in 1873 had made it their business to demand one, hoping thereby to weaken the power of those who had defeated them, but neither Iwakura nor Ōkubo was prepared to let authority be undermined while Japan still faced rebellion and other domestic unrest. Although Kido was more sympathetic – as the Iwakura embassy's 'constitutions' specialist, he had come to believe that representative government, cautiously framed, could contribute to national unity – ill health and early death combined to reduce his influence. Itō Hirobumi, who subsequently emerged as the senior Choshu representative in government, eventually took over his role, but with more than a touch of Ōkubo's steel. In discussions with Iwakura during 1881 he worked out an agreement on the kind of constitution that might meet the leadership's needs, rather than those of its opponents. It should have a cabinet responsible to the emperor, they decided; a bicameral assembly with an elected lower house, though this should have no power to initiate legislation or in the last resort to deny the government funds; and an electorate defined by a property qualification. The plan remained secret, except in so far as an imperial decree, issued in October, announced that a constitution would be granted by the end of the decade. Even this was careful to state that those who campaigned for it were not to agitate for 'sudden and violent change'.

Itō himself took on the task of supervising the preparation of a draft. In 1882 he made another long visit to Europe in order to flesh out the skeleton that he and Iwakura had already outlined, spending most of his time in Vienna and Berlin. He brought back two German advisers, Alfred Mosse and Hermann Roesler. In 1886 they settled down in Itō's country residence, together with Itō and his Japanese staff, to put together detailed proposals. These were brought before the Privy Council in May 1888 and formally proclaimed by the emperor in the palace on 11 February 1889.

The text conformed to the principles agreed some eight years earlier. Central to it was the doctrine of imperial divine descent, reference to which was introduced at Itō's insistence. This would serve the purpose, he believed, of reinforcing patriotic unity, while putting those who served the emperor beyond the reach of elected representatives. The German contribution, following the Prussian example, was to try to make the monarchy strong enough to serve as a defence against the danger of social disorder. Disorder, after all, was to be expected in Japan, as it was in Europe, from the growth of an industrial economy. For this reason the emperor was given extensive powers: supreme command of the armed forces; the freedom to adjourn or prorogue the national assembly (the Diet); the right – at least in theory – to choose the cabinet and senior members of the bureaucracy. Since the constitution was his gift, he could also veto changes in it. Such provisions greatly impaired the influence that could be exercised by elected members of the lower house. Since the authorities also had at their disposal extensive powers of censorship and law enforcement, embodied in a Press Law (1875) and a Peace Preservation Law (1887), they were confident of their ability to deal with critics. Police intervention in the election of 1892, to cite the worst example, left twenty-five dead and nearly 400 injured.

There is controversy about the long-term impact of the Meiji Constitution on Japanese politics. Defenders of the actions of Itō and his colleagues (Iwakura died in 1883) have argued that to have tried to move Japan in a single generation from feudalism to a fully representative parliament would have invited serious protest from significant elements in the population. Nor did the document itself prohibit further change, though it made it difficult. Their opponents, both at the time and since, have held that the provisions of the constitution, coupled with official measures of 'thought control', made domestic conflict inevitable in later years. By blocking or impeding full participation in policy making by social groups that were of growing importance – entrepreneurs, industrial managers, technicians, as well as trade union leaders – they undermined the standing of established institutions as a whole. They also created dangerous tensions. Political parties, no matter how law abiding, were able to make little headway. The most that Diet members could do was to create disruption, then try to exact a price for ending it. Hence the parliamentary process became mere political bargaining. Trade unions, which long remained illegal, could do no more than strike or riot, so weakening their public support. Much of Japanese opinion was accordingly unrepresented. The armed forces, by contrast, committed from an early stage to an ideology that treated 'liberals' as subversive, were able to use their special relationship with the emperor – their commander-in-chief – to free themselves more and more from civil control. This made them in the twentieth century a source of national policy distinct from that of cabinet and Diet. The consequences were disastrous, both at home and abroad. To that extent the 'emperor system', as the complex of Meiji institutions has come to be called, was at the heart of subsequent turbulence.

Social change

The abolition of domains in 1871 left Japan's former ruling class in disarray. Whereas court nobles could still find posts in the palace, or connected with culture and religion, while feudal lords at least had satisfactory incomes, most samurai found life hard. If they lacked the ability and political connections to guarantee appointments in central and local government, they were expected to live on their stipends. These had been subject to successive cuts since 1868, and were less able now to support a satisfactory lifestyle than they had been in the last years of the Tokugawa. Some tried their hand with varying success as entrepreneurs. Others farmed, or found employment in the towns, once the Edo rule forbidding them to do so was abolished in December 1871. Very few prospered. They also suffered loss of status. In 1872 the announcement of the conscription law made it clear that samurai were no longer to be treated as a military élite. 'After living a life of idleness for generations', the document said, 'the samurai have been authorised to take off their swords ... ' True, many continued to serve in army or police – they were, after all, the only men with relevant training – but it was no longer a birthright, or a guarantee of quasi-officer rank.

The final stage in their decline was the abolition of stipends. Even at their much reduced levels these had proved to be a heavy burden on government finance. From December 1873, therefore, samurai were permitted to commute their annual stipends for a capital sum, payable in interest-bearing government bonds. Not many found the offer attractive. In August 1876, as state revenue came under heavy pressure from inflation, commutation was accordingly made compulsory. For the very largest pensions, those of feudal lords, bonds were to be issued equal to the total of five years' income, bearing interest at 5 per cent. At the other end of the scale, the calculation was based on fourteen years and 7 per cent. Thus for the wealthiest, income was to be a quarter of what it had been, for the poorest as much as 98 per cent; but since the bonds were capital, which could be held or sold at will, there was nothing to prevent the recipients from squandering it, or losing it in ill-considered ventures. Given the samurai's acknowledged lack of financial expertise, it is not surprising that many did so, ending with neither capital nor income.

For those non-samurai who lived in the countryside, the land tax brought similar opportunities and dangers. Landlords, who had won legal recognition of their holdings in the tax law, were free to use their wealth in ways more profitable than in the past. So were the richer farmers, many of whom had long engaged in moneylending and commerce. By contrast, those who were nearer subsistence level were likely to find that the burden of paying regular tax in cash to the representatives of a distant ministry left them in no better case than before. Many fell into debt, lost their lands, became tenants, much as they had done in the Edo period. Others migrated to towns.

One result was continuing armed unrest among peasants after 1873. The government suppressed it by force (another task for the modern army and police). At the same time it took steps to bind men of higher standing to its interests. New dignities were devised. In July 1884 the emperor announced his intention of honouring 'high-born descendants of illustrious ancestors', plus those who had contributed to 'the restoration of my rule'. They were to be formed into a western-style peerage. This had five ranks, ranging from prince (or duke) at the top to baron at the bottom. Of the 500 titles first bestowed, the great majority went to former members of the court and feudal nobility in what might be described as compensation for loss of perquisites. The rest – it was to be a growing proportion as time went on – were for the principal samurai leaders of the anti-Tokugawa movement and those who now held senior posts in government or armed forces.

The existence of such a peerage made it possible not only to reward the emperor's most distinguished servants, but also to include a House of Peers, well stocked with friends of the regime, as the upper chamber of the Diet. What it did not do was to make political office hereditary, or subject to inherited status, as had been customary in the past. After Itō's civil service reforms of 1886, birth, though it might well be influential in a man's career – women did not have careers – carried no entitlement to office. In this respect the Meiji system was more 'Confucian' than that of Nara had been. In practice the keys to bureaucratic advancement, both civil and military, were family 'connections' and education: that is, education in accordance with a western-style curriculum.

Education was one of the subjects most closely studied by Japanese missions to the West both before and after 1868. In addition, several western employees (*o-yatoi*) were brought to Japan, either to teach in official schools or to advise on educational organisation, bringing with them a variety of experience from Europe and America. Their influence was evident in the Education Code of 1872. This provided for a system of primary schools to be established throughout the country, giving instruction in subjects that ranged 'from language, writing and reckoning for daily use to knowledge necessary for officials, farmers, merchants and artisans' (the four designated classes of Edo society, substituting 'officials' for 'samurai'). The schools were to be attended by children from the age of six, who would be taught for sixteen months; were to conform for the most part to a western curriculum, using translations of western texts; and were to charge fees (small ones, but sometimes more than the poorest families could pay).

From this beginning there followed a steady expansion in the number of schools, the percentage of children attending them, and the length of the compulsory course. By 1886 attendance was some 46 per cent of the relevant age group and the course had become four years. Other educational facilities also expanded. Normal schools for the training of teachers had been founded in 1872. Middle schools were added in 1881, higher middle schools in 1886 (renamed high schools in 1894). High schools for girls came in 1889. At the more advanced level, several institutions, deriving from the Tokugawa Bakufu's Confucian academy and institute of western studies, were amalgamated into a university in 1877, then reorganised as Tokyo Imperial University in 1886. A similar body was established in Kyoto in 1903. Others later followed in Sendai, Nagoya and Fukuoka. Among private foundations, Fukuzawa Yukichi's Keiō Gijuku, dating from just before the Restoration, also acquired university status, as did Ōkuma Shigenobu's Semmon Gakkō of 1882, which was renamed Waseda. Tokyo Higher Commercial School (1887) was the nucleus from which Hitotsubashi University developed.

By the time of the Meiji Constitution of 1889, Japan provided an eight-year period of primary education, half of it compulsory, plus a middle school course of four years for those who had the ability and resources to go beyond the primary stage. Middle school graduates were likely to qualify for jobs in the lower reaches of the bureaucracy and business management. Entry to high schools was for a small minority, mostly destined to go on to university. After that, careers in senior posts in government would be open to them, or a life as members of the country's growing body of intellectuals. Tokyo University, usually through its Law Faculty, was the main source of recruits to the higher bureaucracy. Keiō and Waseda were advantageous points of entry into business, journalism and the law.

Since access to high school and university, while it did not depend on birth, required the resources to pay for modest fees and living costs, the poorest needed financial help – not provided by the state – or private patronage in order to make use of it. Even so, this was a much more open system than anything Japan had had before. It was not only the children of former samurai, but also those of landlords, well-to-do farmers and merchants who could be confident of qualifying for the most senior levels of employment in government and business, if they had the academic ability. This made education a solvent, eating away at the formal class divisions bequeathed to the Meiji period by Edo. It also spread the skills and training characteristic of bureaucracy into many other walks of life, including the largest firms.

If education was one important instrument of social change, industry was another. Since success in it – and the wealth it brought – depended on non-traditional kinds of knowledge, together with commercial acumen, careers were likely to rest on individual achievement (reinforced, perhaps, by adoption), rather than social origin. On the other hand, the growth of Japan's industrial economy was by no means due exclusively to private enterprise. Ōkubo Toshimichi, writing as home minister in 1874, observed that manufacturing, which he considered vital to the country's future, required 'the patronage and encouragement of the government and its officials'. Few were likely to question the statement. The Bakufu and feudal lords had financed gun foundries and shipyards even before 1868; the Meiji government took over the plants they had established, then extended official initiative into railways, telegraphs and telephones. A Ministry of Public Works was established under Itō Hirobumi in 1870 to supervise the programme. It hired a large number of foreign technicians and advisers.

In an attempt to overcome inflation and an unfavourable balance of payments, the government also gave its attention to banking. The Bank of Japan (1877) was given the task of regulating the banking system, while the Yokohama Specie Bank took over control of foreign exchange. A more direct attack on balance of payments problems was made by instituting rules to standardise the quality of silk for export. Two model silk-reeling factories were established at government expense to demonstrate western machines and manufacturing methods. Import substitution in other fields was encouraged by similar action with respect to machinery (1871), cement (1875), glass (1876) and bricks (1878). In 1881, however, the Finance Ministry decided that the programme had served its purpose. It therefore set out to recover as much as possible of its capital outlay by offering the various model plants for sale. Bids proved few, prices low. As a result the successful purchasers – 'friends of government', for the most part, including Mitsui and Mitsubishi – received what was in effect a subsidy for their entry into heavy industry. The use of tax advantages and government contracts later extended subsidies into other fields, notably shipping. They became a regular part of economic policy.

Many of the entrepreneurs who took the lead in this phase of Japan's development were former samurai. Some, such as Godai Tomoatsu of Satsuma (railways and mining) and the Bakufu's Shibusawa Ei'ichi (banking and textiles), had been overseas as students or members of missions. Others had experience in running the monopolies or other commercial undertakings of their domains. Iwasaki Yatarō, for example, developed Tosa's late-Tokugawa shipping organisation into the core of what was to be the Mitsubishi company. Yet for all their importance, such individuals were a minority within the Meiji industrial leadership. After 1880, when Shibusawa's cotton-spinning factory began to show significant profits, a much wider spread of Japanese capital, much of it accumulated by merchants in the Edo period, moved into the textile industry. The number of spindles in use rose to nearly 400,000 by 1894, mostly in small, less capital-intensive firms, which used cheap labour as a substitute for the more advanced – and therefore expensive – technology available from Europe and America. Cotton thread, followed by the coarser grades of cotton cloth, soon became export goods, finding markets at first in nearby countries, then farther afield in Asia and Africa. These products became one of the two staples of foreign trade in the first half of the twentieth century. Silk for the West was the other.

Industry brought wealth to a large number of entrepreneurs, employment to managers and technicians, and job opportunities to an unskilled workforce, recruited, at least in part, from groups that had been disadvantaged by reform, or driven out of the villages by hardship. In the next generation it was to change the face of Japanese society. The change was not invariably for the good. The bourgeoisie emerged as a political force, enfranchised, but voting for parties in the lower house of the Diet whose members had limited power. The most successful businessmen tended to turn away from parliamentary politics in the search for influence. Lower in the social scale was a new kind of urban poor: the lowest-paid among industrial workers, housed increasingly in slums, and beset by unemployment and illegal strikes whenever there was financial crisis. These were conditions – familiar enough elsewhere in the world – in which the extremes of political left and right could flourish.

Tradition and modernity

To many Japanese after the middle of the Meiji period, modernity became a cult. What they meant by it was a complex of behaviour and ideas that they associated with the contemporary West, brought home by Japanese travellers, or exemplified by foreign residents in Japan. In the provinces, especially in the countryside, life went on very much as it had in the past, but in the centre of Tokyo and one or two other cities the evidence of foreign influence was everywhere, mingled with the familiar homes and shops and kimono of tradition. Public buildings, railway stations, banks and some offices were now being built in brick or stone. There was gas lighting in the streets, telegraph wires overhead. A considerable number of Japanese were to be seen in various forms of western dress: soldiers and police in uniform; officials on their journey to or from the office, wearing frock coats and tall hats; businessmen in bowlers and suits; the wives and daughters of the rich in bonnets and long skirts. The court had adopted western ceremonial dress at the end of 1872. As early as 1873, we are told, a group of Satsuma samurai, coming to the capital in the clothes and hairstyle that had always been proper for their class, were 'stared at as foreigners had formerly been'.

There was the same mixture of old and new in literature and the arts. Western music was performed in the 1880s at the Rokumeikan, a hall built in Tokyo to provide a meeting-place for 'official' Japanese and foreigners. Lessons in ballroom dancing were given there by a German instructor. Some of the West's more serious music became a polite accomplishment in the capital. It was taught at the Tokyo School of Music, founded in 1887. In 1903 came Japan's first opera performance in Japanese, a translation of Gluck's *Orpheus*, staged with the help of a foreign conductor and pianist. Martial music had a wider appeal. After 1905 it was played by army and navy bands in turn at the bandstand in Hibiya Park, as well as in many other locations. Yet while concert halls made much of the works of Beethoven and other great names of nineteenth-century Europe, Japanese music was still studied and performed by individuals throughout the country. The two cultures also existed side by side – at arm's length from each other – in drama, attracting different audiences. The modern theatre put on translations of Shakespeare, Molière and Ibsen (though not very well). Kabuki remained popular, as it has done since. Nō plays suffered eclipse for a time, but later revived as an intellectual fashion, cultivated by theatre clubs.

In the visual arts, the division was less distinct. Japanese painters who went abroad often came back as representatives of American or European schools, rather than Japanese ones, while others, remaining at home, asserted loyalty to traditional styles; but the latter also reflected piecemeal the influence of western methods and techniques, as some of their Edo predecessors had begun to do. Woodblock prints, for example, which remained very popular, not only chose non-traditional subjects, like treaty port scenes, or the naval engagements of the Russo-Japanese War, but also drew perspective and human figures in the western manner. Despite this overlap, however, 'western' art and 'Japanese' art centred on different institutions. Traditional techniques were taught at the Tokyo Art School (Bijutsu Gakkō), directed by Okakura Kakuzō, while exhibitions of painting in the western style were organised by the Fine Arts Society (Bijutsukai). Both were founded in 1889. It was not until 1907, when the Education Ministry established an annual exhibition, that both schools presented their work together, competing for prizes.

The transition to modern taste was in some ways easier for Japanese novelists. To write in straightforward colloquial prose about the self and the individual, or about contemporary manners and society, was not too sharp a departure from what had been done by Ihara Saikaku and his followers in the Edo period. On the other hand, the changes now taking place in Japanese life suggested a different choice of themes: nostalgia for the past, perhaps, or a zeal for social reform. Nagai Kafū (1879–1959) wrote with evident regret about the passing of the old Edo. In *Sumida-gawa* (The Sumida River, 1909) he explored the problems of a student torn between the attractions of old and new: that is, between his mother's wish that he should have a modern education for the sake of its job opportunities and his own desire to make a career in the traditional theatre. Natsume Sōseki (1867–1916), who studied for a time in England, took changing social life as his subject, drawing material from his work as a teacher and his own environment. *Waga hai wa neko de aru* (I am a cat, 1905) described his home life from the viewpoint of the household cat; *Botchan* (1906) was about a young middle school teacher. Shimazaki Tōson (1872–1943) produced similar work in his early years, but later in his life he wrote a major historical novel, *Yoakemae* (Before the Dawn, 1929–35). It was a semi-fictional account of his grandfather's village in the Restoration years.

Most of the developments in literature and the arts can be described as spontaneous: that is, were a response by individuals to changing circumstance. Their variety and appeal increased in the twentieth century, as new means were found – illustrated magazines, radio, television – to bring them to a wider audience. As a consequence, 'the culture of the masses' became predominantly western-style within a generation or two; tradition became more and more traditionalism, a conscious evocation of the past. Neither the Meiji government and its censors, nor their successors, made much attempt to check the trend, despite the grumbling of conservatives. Nevertheless, officialdom had a cultural agenda of its own, related to ideology. In the fields of religion and education it took steps to strengthen the people's loyalty to the emperor, as well as patriotism and commitment to the social order. Its principal instruments were Shinto and Confucianism.

Since the myth of imperial divine descent was a part of Shinto thought, it was logical to give Shinto a special place in the Meiji state. In 1868 the Council of Religion (Jingikan), which was primarily concerned with Shinto ritual, was made in theory the highest organ of central government, taking precedence over the Council of State. This somewhat unrealistic arrangement did not survive the reforms that followed the abolition of domains in 1871. Despite that, the country's most important shrines remained in a special category, officially approved and subsidised. In 1882, when the popular sects of Shinto, linked with fire walking, faith healing and shamanism, were put on a private financial and organisational footing, along with other religions, the national shrines retained their separate status and finance. They continued to have a ceremonial role in festivals concerning the monarchy and the imperial family, and were served by priests appointed by the state.

Itō Hirobumi's determination to endorse the doctrine of imperial divine descent in the text of the 1889 constitution was of a piece with these decisions. To bolster them, emperor worship, together with Confucian morality, was actively promoted among the people at large. In 1872 the Bureau of Rites, the downgraded successor to the Jingikan, set out to propagate the Great Teaching (*taikyō*), an amalgam of Shinto, Confucian and Buddhist thought, by which Japanese were called on to respect the gods, revere the emperor, love their country and observe the traditional moral code. As a means of promoting habits of civic duty this proved ineffective, but it established a precedent, not least for the teaching of a compulsory ethics course (*shūshin*) in schools.

In 1879 the emperor was persuaded by some of the men about him, led by his Confucian tutor, Motoda Eifu, to issue a rescript condemning 'indiscriminate emulation of western ways' in Japan's teaching of the young. In 1890 there followed the more famous Education Rescript, insisting that loyalty and filial piety, plus respect for the constitution and the law, be put at the heart of the educational system. Thereafter the textbooks prescribed at every level – not only in the ethics course – set out to ensure that morality, patriotism and 'the spirit of reverence for the emperor' were given pride of place in the curriculum. Books used in schools were carefully scrutinised for undesirable foreign influences. A portrait of the emperor and a copy of the Education Rescript were put in a position of honour in every educational establishment.

Outside the schools, the law permitted, and the police attempted to implement, a policy of thought control, which continued on a rising curve until 1945. All the same, one would find it hard to argue that there was total uniformity, even in matters most subject to it. There were still teachers who interpreted 'ethics' in the light of current intellectual fashion or their personal beliefs. Some remained unorthodox or uncooperative. Christians, for example, though their numbers were not large, often felt bound to challenge the official doctrine where it contradicted religious faith. Newspapers and serious magazines, available throughout Japan, canvassed or encouraged discussion of alternative ideologies, many of western provenance. It was not until much later, mostly in the years between 1930 and 1945, that the pressure to conform became so strong that the majority found it irresistible. Until then, the most that one can safely say is that Japanese left school with an awareness of their duty to the state, expressed in traditionalist phraseology, and that they were encouraged to retain it in adult life. The fact that this sat oddly with the habits and ideas they were acquiring from the West was not yet a deeply felt contradiction.

CHAPTER 13

Fifty Years of Foreign Wars

1894–1945

Japan's foreign relations in the first half of the twentieth century were in many ways conditioned by the nature of the Meiji Restoration. Ever since 1858 a prime objective of national policy had been to keep the West at bay, whether by reform at home or diplomatic action. In the first stage, lasting until 1894, institutional change and the creation of western-style armed forces were seen as a means of restoring the country's independence with respect to tariffs and legal jurisdiction: that is, revising the unequal treaties. The question had first been raised directly by the Iwakura embassy in America, though without success. Thereafter it surfaced from time to time on the diplomatic agenda, but the moment for decision never seemed right, not least because of British opposition. Japanese frustration mounted, exemplified in 1886 by a bomb thrown at the foreign minister's carriage; the Meiji reforms began to raise the country's repute abroad; and a deal was finally struck in London in 1894. Japan agreed to open the interior to foreign trade, while Britain accepted the abolition of consular courts and tariff controls. Other treaty powers followed suit.

Despite a measure of euphoria at this achievement, the change did not immediately bring equality of esteem. Nor did the world become an easier place to live in. Japanese fears and aspirations, which had supported, or even driven, the Meiji policies to this point, therefore retained their force. They were directed now into different channels, however. Japanese soon became convinced that, if treaty revision were not enough to meet their ends, it was time to try something of another kind. Its nature emerged within the next ten years. Using methods that were sometimes military and territorial, sometimes economic, a new generation of leaders began to build for their country a position in East Asia that would, they hoped, provide lasting defence against the West. In the broadest sense, the process had public support. On the one hand it led to empire, both formal and informal. On the other it brought fifty years of intermittent war: against China (1894–5) and Russia (1904–5); within China in the context of the European struggle with Germany (1914–15), then in Siberia after the Bolshevik revolution (1918–22); and finally in a crescendo of expansion, Manchuria (1931) and the rest of China (1937) before spreading to the whole of East and Southeast Asia, as well as much of the Pacific (1941–5). Between 1894 and 1945 there was not a single decade when Japanese troops were not in action overseas.

The last and greatest of these wars, which drew in the United States and several of the European powers, ended in disaster. Outgunned, unable to match American production and technology, Japan was in the end pushed back within her older frontiers. Surrender came in 1945 after atom bombs were dropped on Hiroshima and Nagasaki. For many Japanese this meant that a dream had turned to nightmare. For most it signalled that the Meiji policies of Wealth and Strength had failed. In some respects they were wrong (Chapter 14).

Industry and empire

The weakness and disunity of China and Korea in the last part of the nineteenth century put temptation in the way of Japanese leaders. A few, in the tradition of Hideyoshi, cherished ambitions of hegemony in East Asia. The idea of a developing trade in textiles made the prospect of political influence on the mainland attractive to many more. On the other hand, the more cautious recognised, as Kido and Ōkubo had done in 1873, that for Japan to prosper within the framework of the treaty port system, which was much too well established to be dismantled for her benefit, she would have to be circumspect. To disrupt the pattern of relations in East Asia might give the West a chance to further interests of its own.

All these considerations entered into the decisions of Itō Hirobumi's government concerning the Sino-Japanese War of 1894–5. The conflict grew out of disputes with Korea that went back as far as 1868. For twenty years or more they had been capable of settlement by diplomacy, but in 1894 a Japan grown more self-confident opted for hostilities. An army was landed in Korea. It achieved immediate success, not only against Korean forces, but also against those that China, acting within the framework of the ancient tribute system, sent to aid them. The Japanese navy established control of the seas. In less than a year Korea was occupied, and China sued for peace.

The terms Japan imposed at Shimonoseki in April 1895 were harsh. China was to renounce all claims to suzerainty over Korea; to pay a large indemnity (in bullion); to cede Taiwan (which had never been involved in the fighting); to make over to Japan a lease of the Liaotung peninsula in south Manchuria (the key to the land and sea routes between Korea and Peking); and to promise a commercial treaty, putting Japan on equal footing with the western powers in China's foreign trade. The clause concerning Liaotung proved unsustainable. Within a matter of weeks Russia, backed by Germany and France, demanded that the peninsula be restored to China, on the grounds that its retention by Japan would undermine the region's balance of power. Itō had to swallow his pride. Japan duly relinquished Liaotung.

Much of the indemnity China paid was spent by Japan in the next few years on an armament programme designed to ensure that so public a rebuff could not occur again. The Japanese navy was made more powerful. Six divisions were added to the regular

Japan asserts a degree of independence. A newspaper cartoon
(*Yorozu Chōhō*, 1894) celebrates the year in which the Japanese 'pupil'
achieved two foreign policy successes that were not wholly welcome
to his western 'teacher': treaty revision and an attack on China.

army. Taiwan was developed as a defensive outpost to the south. Economically, too, Japan became stronger. Taiwan had a valuable sugar crop; new privileges in the China trade translated into markets for Japanese goods. Against that, the international environment was becoming more threatening. Within three years of the Shimonoseki treaty, a fresh wave of western imperialism, which had begun in Africa in the previous decade, had spread to China. The powers – Britain and America reluctantly, France, Germany and Russia with appetite – set out to acquire spheres of influence, within which China was forced to grant them certain exclusive rights concerning railways, mining and loans. Germany acquired a dominant position in Shantung. Russia, having taken over the lease of Liaotung in 1898 – insult added to injury in Japanese eyes – secured mining concessions in Manchuria, together with the right to build railways connecting Vladivostock and Liaotung to the Trans-Siberian. As the final blow, when violent outbreaks, led by Boxers, spread from northern China into Manchuria in the summer of 1900, Russian troops moved into the region to protect their country's interests. They showed little disposition to withdraw.

In this company Japan was a weakling still. Her protests were ignored, and she lacked the force to make gains of her own that might serve to balance Russia's. Fortified by an alliance with Britain, signed in January 1902, she began a vigorous diplomatic campaign to reduce or limit Russian advances, but this, too, had little effect. In the winter of 1903–4, therefore, convinced that Russia posed a threat not only to the land route for her trade to China, but also to Korea and hence by extension to Japan's home islands, Tokyo decided on recourse to war. The Trans-Siberian, after all, was still only single-track in places, which would limit the reserves that Russia could bring to bear.

In February 1904 a Japanese army once more landed in Korea. Moving quickly north, it crossed the Yalu River to enter Liaotung and put Port Arthur under siege. The Japanese navy had already blockaded the port, together with Vladivostock. There then followed a year of heavy fighting, spreading as far afield as Mukden, in which substantial casualties were suffered on both sides. Port Arthur fell in January 1905. In May of that year the Russian Baltic fleet, sent halfway round the world to relieve Vladivostock, was met and soundly defeated in the Tsushima Straits. Psychologically, the victory was decisive.

Following American mediation, peace talks were held in Portsmouth, New Hampshire, in August 1905. Once again Japan made the most of her military advantage. Her freedom of action in Korea was recognised; the lease of Liaotung was transferred to her, along with Russian mining rights in the area and the railway that linked Port Arthur to Harbin (the future South Manchurian Railway); the southern half of Sakhalin (Karafuto) was conceded to Japan again, reversing an agreement made in 1875. In this way, not only did Japan acquire a ready-made sphere of influence of her own in China and strengthen her defences to the north, but Korea was made a Japanese protectorate (late 1905), then formally taken over as a colony in 1910.

The Russo-Japanese War coincided with an important stage in Japan's economic development. Since 1895 the country's higher profile in the world, coupled with the armament programme, had led to greater government expenditure on war-related industry. This in turn had required investment in infrastructure. Increased output of iron and steel, a better supply of power from both coal and electricity, more railways and shipping – these headed the list. A need to limit dependence on imports in order to bring the balance of payments under control – the Russian war brought a rapid increase in borrowing overseas – created opportunities in the manufacture of engineering goods. The result was rapid progress in the growth of heavy industry. By 1914 Japan produced 21 million tons of coal a year, a third of the steel she required, nearly 600,000 kilowatts of electric power. She possessed 7,000 miles of railway track, much of it nationalised, six shipyards capable of building vessels of a thousand tons or more, one-and-a-half million tons of merchant shipping. In such a context Manchuria's coal and iron took on an added significance. True, Japan did not become a net importer of coal until about 1930, but she bought

70 per cent of her iron ore abroad as early as 1914. Most of it came from north China (including Manchuria) and Korea.

Taken together, the victory over Russia and industrial development at home changed the emphasis of policy towards the Asian mainland. Defence of a sphere of influence, 'bought with Japanese blood', became axiomatic for the high command and most politicians. This gave the army a stronger voice in the making of decisions. The claims of the export trade to be considered Japan's overriding economic interest overseas were weakened. There were now industrial companies, often undercapitalised by international standards, that needed protection against British and American competition, putting Japan much more in the position of France or Russia or Germany with respect to China. This meant that equality of trading opportunity there – what Britain and America called the Open Door – was no longer quite so automatically the first priority of those who spoke for Japanese business.

Despite this, the Open Door remained official policy for most of the years before 1930. It was championed by Itō Hirobumi until his assassination in 1909. Thereafter the professionals of the Foreign Ministry took up the running, supported by the financiers and large trading companies. Their critics came mostly from the services, especially the Kwantung Army, which as garrison of Liaotung had a vested interest in continued expansion on the mainland. It found backing in firms with investment in Manchuria, not least the South Manchuria Railway Company, a quasi-government concern founded in 1906, which was involved in mining as well as railways.

What might be termed the 'Manchuria party' was as a rule the weaker of the two, but it had influence enough to ensure that Japan regularly made an exception of Manchuria when framing her commitment to the Open Door. More directly, the knowledge that they could look to powerful friends in Tokyo encouraged Japan's more reckless patriots, even some army commanders, when tempted to take action on the mainland on their own initiative. In the winter of 1911–12, when China was busy overthrowing the Manchu dynasty, Japanese army leaders sponsored attempts to organise an independent Manchuria under a Manchu figurehead. They failed because the Japanese cabinet would not back them, but they had set an example that others were to follow in later years.

One could argue that official plans for China in the aftermath of revolution were more dangerous still to the region's tranquillity. They were certainly more far-reaching. When war broke out in Europe in 1914, distracting the attention of the powers, Tokyo seized the opportunity to strengthen Japan's position in East Asia. Having declared war on Germany, ostensibly in accordance with the Anglo-Japanese alliance, the government sent troops to take over the German sphere of influence in Shantung. This done, China was presented with the bill. It took the form of what are called the Twenty-one Demands, spelling out, first, specific items relating to railway rights in Manchuria, over which Japan and China had been in dispute, then the disposal of Germany's former rights in Shantung, which Japan now claimed. To this was to be added the appointment of Japanese 'advisers' in the Chinese capital. Even more ominously, China was required 'not to cede or lease to any other power any harbour or bay or any island along the coast of China'. Along with other yet more controversial items, described as 'highly desirable' but not 'essential', this would have made the country a Japanese protectorate in all but name.

Ignoring international protest, which was muted by the exigencies of the European war, Japan embodied the substance of these demands – leaving aside the 'highly desirable' category – into treaties that China was forced to sign in May 1915. They triggered a wave of Chinese nationalist protest. To buttress the agreements, Tokyo accordingly used the leverage it had secured through its contributions to the war against Germany to win from its allies (even, if ambiguously, the United States) promises of support for its gains at the time when a postwar settlement came to be decided. Efforts were also made to find friends in China. During 1917 and 1918 a number of loans were made to the regime in Peking, supposedly to fund economic development, in reality to bolster the power of politicians who were well disposed towards Japan, while obtaining lucrative contracts for Japanese concerns. The term 'co-prosperity' was employed to describe the relationship. As stated by Nishihara Kamezō, who arranged the loans, Japan's aim was 'to develop the limitless natural resources of China and the industry of Japan by co-ordinating the two, so as to make possible a plan for self-sufficiency under which Japan and China would become a single entity'. Prime Minister Tōjō Hideki was to use similar wording about the Co-prosperity Sphere in the early part of 1942.

Nishihara's initiative failed, largely because the Peking leaders could not deliver their side of the bargain. Other Japanese, who looked towards the more distant north, were no more successful. In the confusion that followed the Bolshevik revolution in Russia, a force of Czech volunteers, unable to continue fighting on the eastern front after Russia's separate peace with Germany, decided to make their way out of Russia along the Trans-Siberian. Their objective was Vladivostock. America, Britain, Canada and France, urged on by Japan, agreed to help the Czechs by sending an expedition to Siberia to secure the last part of their line of retreat. The force to be employed was intended to be modest, but for the Japanese army the opportunity was not one to be missed. It deployed five divisions in 1918, instead of the one that had been promised, identifying their task as being 'to maintain peace in the Far East by occupying various strategic points in Russian territory east of Lake Baikal'. This was a good deal more than saving the Czechs. Local puppet regimes were established under Japanese supervision in the area north of the Amur. Operations were later undertaken as far away as northern Sakhalin.

In the end it all came to nothing. The cost was enormous; the western powers became restive about Japanese actions; no reliable anti-communist government took shape. Meanwhile Bolshevik troops advanced steadily from Omsk. In January 1920 the United States decided to withdraw, soon followed by Britain, Canada and France. Two years later Japan reluctantly did the same. The failure seriously weakened those in Japan who had hoped for a 'forward policy' on the mainland, backed by force. The army even lost public reputation. In the 1920s, it was said, army officers had trouble finding young women willing to marry them.

One result of the débâcle was to put China policy once again into the hands of the Foreign Ministry and its domestic allies. This brought a renewal of the emphasis on trade and the treaty port system, a kind of economic diplomacy for which Shidehara Kijūrō, foreign minister in 1924–7 and 1929–31, was the principal spokesman. He started from a position of strength. The Versailles settlement had given international recognition to Japan's wartime gains in China. As a permanent member of the League of Nations council, she had status as one of the great powers. Even the agreements made at the Washington Conference of 1921–2, which set out to restore as much as possible of the treaty port system in a China by now divided among rival warlords, had not decisively weakened her. Commitment to the Open Door and China's territorial integrity had been reaffirmed, but no attempt was made to reconcile this with the concept of spheres of influence. A four-power pact, designed to replace the Anglo-Japanese alliance, embodied promises by Britain, France, Japan and the United States to act in accordance with these platitudes, but provided no machinery of enforcement; while another treaty limiting naval armaments, for all that it was bitterly opposed by Japan's armed forces, still left her with the strongest navy in the west Pacific.

Given these advantages, Shidehara was able to play a leading role in the affairs of the treaty ports during his terms of office, promoting Japanese trade and resisting any changes in the tariff structure that might damage it. Manchuria was ring-fenced as a Japanese sphere. Nevertheless, the situation inside China was too turbulent for this state of affairs to go unchallenged for very long. Chiang Kai-shek, leading the army of the Kuomintang (Nationalist Party), had already begun the task of uniting the country by force, starting in the south. Since almost all his followers and the majority of their rivals, notably the communists, were implacably hostile to the unequal treaties, his progress towards the north was accompanied by repeated demands for treaty revision. Britain and America were willing to consider it. Shidehara was not, or would do so only within very strict limits.

Manchuria was also a stumbling-block to international co-operation. It was not only a major source of coal and iron for Japan, but also a key strategic holding. In the view of the Army General Staff and the Kwantung Army, if China – including Manchuria – were united under Chiang Kai-shek, this would pose a threat to the whole of Japan's position on the mainland, even put the home islands in jeopardy, much as Russia had done earlier in the century. Events in China south of the Great Wall, in other words, were as much the army's business as the Foreign Ministry's. Some army officers were willing to take action on this assumption.

The result was an attempt in 1928 to force the cabinet's hand. The local warlord in Manchuria, Chang Tso-lin, whose rise was due in part to the patronage of the Kwantung Army, was proving difficult to control. In particular, he began to set himself up in the region round Peking as a rival to Chiang Kai-shek. This was unwelcome to his Japanese army sponsors, who had no wish to see Manchuria dragged into the mire of China's national politics. A plan was therefore made to remove him and find a more amenable ally. In June 1928 a bomb was detonated under the warlord's train as it was approaching Mukden. Chang died within a few hours; but before any further steps could be taken, Tokyo disavowed the plot and took steps to punish the conspirators. Shidehara – out of office at the time of the incident – was brought back to the Foreign Ministry; and the Kwantung Army was left to nurse its wounds, aware that any further action of the kind would need to be better organised.

The struggle for Greater East Asia

Japanese actions in Manchuria after 1928 took place against a very different background of politics at home. Between 1914 and 1918, while Europe was devoting itself to war production, the Japanese economy was enjoying a mushroom growth. Despite high costs and relative inefficiency, heavy industry found ready markets for its armaments, ships and machinery overseas. In the absence of European competition, Japanese consumer goods pushed into new areas. The prosperity this brought did not survive the peace, but it lasted long enough to bring about important changes in society. Commerce and industry became of greater consequence; the political parties they favoured won control of the Diet; party cabinets were formed, pursuing 'liberal' policies. Universal manhood suffrage came in 1925. The army lost several divisions, the navy's budget was cut. Shidehara was left free to engage in economic diplomacy with significant public support.

Outside politics there was a relaxation of social discipline, especially among the young, typified by the popularity of dance halls and a taste for popular entertainment of the western kind. In Europe and America these things were a response to the end of the killing. In Japan they were imported fashion, widely criticised as such by traditionalists. They branded the habits of the age – including most of the parliamentary ones – as a betrayal of the past, a descent to what Confucian moralists had always described as 'luxury'. Such moral condemnation carried over into reactionary politics, reinforced by a fear of socialism, as the postwar slump brought distress to the workers, provoking strikes and 'dangerous thoughts'. To many Japanese in the 1920s, something seemed seriously wrong with the body politic. An increasing number joined 'patriotic societies', in which disgruntled officers from the nation's forces joined hands with civilian visionaries and radicals. In this were the roots of what came to be known as 'ultra-nationalism'.

The temperature was raised to fever pitch by the world economic crisis of 1929 and 1930. As international markets collapsed and governments turned to protectionism to defend what was left of them, Japan suffered more than most. Farmers, deprived of customers for silk, their main cash crop, were reduced to penury, even starvation in some regions. Small businesses, trading in cotton textiles, were brought to ruin by foreign barriers to their exports. Larger firms survived, even grew, but only by putting pressure on their suppliers and their workforce. Inevitably there was unrest. Out of it came demands, sometimes backed by violence, for another 'restoration' to save Japan. This time it was to be a Shōwa Restoration, taking its name from the reign-title of the Meiji emperor's grandson, Hirohito, who had come to the throne in 1926. In the vanguard of the movement were the patriots, organised in private societies, mostly small, and modelling themselves on the samurai activists who had brought down the Tokugawa. In 1932 and 1936 they attacked members of the cabinet and leaders of the country's business establishment, seeking through assassination to persuade the army to seize control.

In this they were disappointed, because the generals proved unwilling in the last resort to dismantle the Meiji state. All the same, they not only created an atmosphere of terror, in which liberals knew their lives to be at risk and political parties were reduced to wary silence, but also changed the terms on which foreign policy was made. Shidehara's claim to have been acting in Japan's best interests by co-operating with the powers for the sake of trade seemed to many to be arrant nonsense in the world as it looked in 1931. The army's insistence on defending and exploiting Manchuria was much more in tune with the times. What is more, since neither the high command nor civilian governments were so ready now to restrain the hotheads, the stage was set for a situation in which military decisions emerged as often as not from below in the next few years: that is, from the 'young officers' of the General Staff – lieutenant colonels, at most – or from the independent actions of overseas commands. It was not until 1937 that Tokyo was in control again, and then not fully.

The first evidence of what this meant in practice came in 1931. As the Kwantung Army grew more and more convinced that the Chinese Nationalists were on their way to uniting China, two of its staff officers, recently appointed from the General Staff, prepared to 'insulate' Manchuria by bringing it more fully under Japanese control. In September 1931, with the collusion of colleagues in the War Ministry and General Staff, but without the authority of the cabinet or the high command, they manufactured an incident on the railway outside Mukden, which provided the pretext for a movement of Japanese troops. Southern Manchuria outside the areas that Japan already controlled was quickly occupied. Despite Tokyo's efforts in the next few weeks to limit the scope of the hostilities, the occupation was steadily pushed north on grounds of 'operational necessity'; and early in 1932 there was even a clash with Chinese forces as far south as Shanghai, followed by a naval bombardment of Nanking.

In only one respect was the central government's authority maintained. Facing criticism in the League of Nations, Tokyo vetoed army plans to make Manchuria a formal Japanese dependency. Nothing daunted, army leaders found an alternative. Pu Yi, the Manchu emperor whom the Chinese had deposed in 1912, was brought out of retirement in Tientsin in March 1932 to be made head of state in a supposedly independent Manchuria, renamed Manchukuo. The Kwantung commander-in-chief was appointed ambassador to it, responsible for defence as well as law and order; Japanese advisers filled all key posts in its administration.

One consequence was Japan's withdrawal from the League of Nations in 1933. Another was a domestic struggle for power, in which the advocates of a Shōwa Restoration were eventually defeated, but at the cost of leaving policy, especially the conduct of foreign affairs, more and more in the hands of the country's military leaders. Of the twelve prime ministers in office between May 1932 and August 1945, four were admirals and four were generals. It is within this context that one has to set the decision to mount a full-scale assault on China in the summer of 1937. A clash with Chinese troops on the outskirts of Peking, not unlike others that preceded it, was this time allowed to escalate, reflecting a confidence within the high command that total victory would be possible. Large reserves were committed; operations were begun against Shanghai and up the Yangtse to Nanking; a naval blockade was declared for the whole of the Chinese coast. Chinese forces suffered a series of defeats, accompanied by heavy bombing of mainland cities and a number of atrocities against the civilian population, most notoriously in Nanking. Despite this, the government of Chiang Kai-shek refused to surrender. Instead, it withdrew to Chungking, whence it continued to fight a defensive campaign in the southwest. Elsewhere guerrilla forces emerged, mostly communist, to challenge what had become a piecemeal Japanese occupation of the country. By 1939 this had spread to most of China's main cities and communication routes. Though never formally declared – the hostilities were known to Japanese as the China Incident – this was war.

Meeting the cost of the campaigns, which imposed a painful burden on Japan's financial and industrial resources, required major reorganisation at home. In both Japan and Korea, steps were taken to ensure greater integration of the government machine. In areas that were in the process of becoming dependencies, puppet regimes were established under military supervision. The economy was more tightly regulated. The National Mobilisation Law of April 1938, though not at once put fully into effect, provided for the direction of manpower and investment into firms of military importance, together with control over wages and prices, and government operation of key industries, if required. In Manchukuo an Industrial Development Company was established in December 1937, designed to expand both the production of industrial raw materials for export to Japan and the provision of transport and power supply in Manchukuo itself. A year later similar companies were formed in north and central China.

This was what the prime minister, Konoe Fumimaro, described in December 1938 as the New Order in East Asia. It was to be a means of bringing together the economies of the region for the sake of common defence against the West. Japan, as the heart of it, would furnish industrial and management skills, financial expertise and political co-ordination. Around Japan would be territories forming an inner core – Korea, Manchuria, North China – providing industrial raw materials and some supporting industries. Beyond this again was a perimeter, comprising most of China, which would be a captive market for Japanese goods, earning foreign currency to pay for vital imports from the rest of the world. Within Japan the political parties were to be combined in a single patriotic structure.

In the event, the New Order failed to deliver all that was required of it. One reason was that the China war dragged on, a constant drain on men and *matériel*. Another was that modern war required a broader spectrum of resources than East Asia on its own could offer. Self-sufficiency therefore proved elusive. Oil was the most important missing ingredient, but the list of desiderata included rubber, tin, tungsten and other rare metals as well. International trade could undoubtedly provide them, but the outbreak of war in Europe in September 1939 made supplies more difficult to get. Western countries, whose needs were much the same, had the advantage of controlling many of the areas of production. Some of these were in Southeast Asia, a largely colonial region. Others were in the Americas, available for the most part through trade with the United States. Since Japanese policies in China were deeply offensive to a sector of American opinion, and the Roosevelt administration was moving towards the support of Britain against Japan's new-found partner, Germany, this trade, too, posed major problems.

Japan's military leadership, therefore, began to consider seriously the plans long urged by some for an 'advance to the south', extending the New Order into Southeast Asia. A Tripartite Pact with Germany and Italy, signed in September 1940, following German victories in the summer campaign of that year, made resistance from the European colonies less likely to be a serious obstacle. The German invasion of Russia in 1941 was thought to remove the danger of any Russian intervention in the north. That left America's intentions as the principal question mark. American economic pressure on Japan was growing: it escalated from an embargo on exports of scrap metal in September 1940 to a ban on oil shipments to Japan in August 1941. Deciding on a response was urgent.

The assessment in Tokyo was that without Indonesian oil the country's stocks would very soon fall too low for any large-scale military action to be conceivable. The Dutch showed no signs of making it available. This being so, an attack on Southeast Asia would have to be made no later than December 1941, if it were to be made at all. Allowing time for the disposition of men and ships, the diplomats therefore had until October to reach a settlement in Washington. After that it must be war, or confession of failure. The decision to be taken was a highly controversial one. There were many men of importance in Japan's political life, including the emperor and some of his advisers, who still held to Shidehara's view of foreign affairs. War with the United States was for them unthinkable. Equally, there were senior naval officers who believed that such a war could not be won. The debate was accordingly difficult and long drawn out. It was not until the talks in Washington were seen to have failed that the die was finally cast.

The Japanese strategy, as it then emerged, was to notify a breakdown of relations, followed at once by an attack on bases from which America and Britain might be able to counter an assault on Southeast Asia. Because of bureaucratic incompetence, however, the timing went awry. The note breaking off relations with the United States – which itself was not crystal clear – was not delivered until after carrier planes had carried out a strike against the US Pacific fleet's main base, Pearl Harbor in Hawaii. This was on the morning of Sunday, 7 December 1941. Other raids took place elsewhere: on Wake, Guam, Midway, Manila and Hong Kong. All were outstandingly successful. A few days later the battlecruiser *Repulse* and the battleship *Prince of Wales*, the most powerful British naval vessels in the region, were sunk by Japanese aircraft to the north of Singapore.

These operations opened the way to a series of Japanese conquests in Southeast Asia. Hong Kong surrendered on Christmas Day. Manila was taken on 2 January 1942 and occupation of the Philippines quickly followed. Japanese troops, moving down the Malay peninsula from Thailand, took Kuala Lumpur on 11 January, and Singapore, Britain's supposedly impregnable naval base, on 15 February. The Dutch in Indonesia surrendered on 9 March, and the greater part of Burma was overrun by the end of April. Japanese control had meanwhile been established in most of the smaller islands of the archipelago and western Pacific.

These victories did not immediately bring the war to an end, as many Japanese would have wished. Heavy land fighting continued: in China; along Burma's frontier with India; in the island approaches to Australia. At sea, though much of America's battle fleet had been sunk or badly damaged at Pearl Harbor, the aircraft carriers had survived. This made it possible to contest the command of the seas to the west and south of Hawaii. Nor, it transpired, was the Co-prosperity Sphere, as it was now to be called, able to bring the desired relief to Japan's hard-pressed economy. Tōjō Hideki, prime minister since October 1941, described it in January 1942 as 'an order of co-existence and co-prosperity based on ethical principles with Japan serving as its nucleus', but none of its component parts was to derive much prosperity from it. The fighting itself had caused a great deal of destruction, not least to key plants like oil installations. Administrative chaos, also a product of war, disrupted local economies and communications. The result was widespread hardship and discontent, made harder to bear by the harshness of Japanese rule in many areas. It was not only in China that guerrilla movements took up arms against the invaders.

Nor did Japan's war industry receive all the raw materials it had been led to expect. There was no effective rail route to the south through China and mainland Southeast Asia, despite attempts to complete it using local labour and prisoners of war. Shipping routes came heavily under attack, first from American submarines, later from aircraft. Three-quarters of the Japanese merchant fleet had been sunk by 1945. The shipbuilding industry lacked the steel to replace it, even the skilled manpower by the end. Similar problems bedevilled aircraft production, despite the priority it was given.

The war, in fact, became a contest to be decided as much by industry and technology as by actual fighting; and although the campaigns in China and in Burma continued, sapping Japanese military strength, the focus shifted to the Pacific, where fighting on the ground was minimal. The American response to early Japanese successes came from two directions, starting in earnest in 1943. In the southwest Pacific, land forces under General Douglas MacArthur pushed up the island chains from Guadalcanal (February 1943) through Morotai to Leyte (December 1944). Luzon was invaded in January 1945, Manila taken in the following month. Meanwhile an 'island-hopping' advance was taking place across the central Pacific under Admiral Chester Nimitz. The technique he used was to bring together land, sea and air forces in overwhelming strength to isolate and seize small island targets, which then became bases for another similar advance. It was applied to Kwajalein in the Marshall Islands at the beginning of 1944, to Saipan in the Marianas in the following summer, then to Guam and the Palau group within a matter of weeks. The two prongs met in the Philippines in 1945. While MacArthur defeated the Japanese army there, Nimitz destroyed most of what was left of the Japanese fleet in two important naval battles.

It was by then quite clear to Japan's inner ring of leadership that the war was lost, though few were willing to admit it. A small group of diplomats and political figures close to the emperor made peace overtures secretly through Russia, but the army high command, hoping for at least a stronger bargaining position, continued to call for resistance to the death. More men, even schoolboys, were called to the colours; suicide units were formed, including pilots – known as *kamikaze* after the 'divine wind' that was said to have scattered the Mongol invading fleet in the thirteenth century – their task to crash antiquated planes, packed with explosives, on enemy ships; volunteers were organised among civilians to try to make sure that any landing on the

Japanese islands would face unsustainable casualties. A declaration by the allied leaders, meeting at Potsdam in July 1945, that Japan must submit to unconditional surrender, followed by military occupation, did not weaken this show of public resolve. The war would have to be ended by military action, it appeared.

Once the forces under MacArthur and Nimitz had joined, they carried out landings on Okinawa in April 1945, the first on actual Japanese soil. The invasion was bitterly contested, a warning of what might be encountered elsewhere. The same had been true at Iwojima in the Bonins a few weeks earlier. Nevertheless, these two events brought all Japan within easy flying range of American bombers, so making possible a massive aerial bombardment, directed at both industry and morale. All Japan's largest cities, except Kyoto, came under attack; damage and casualties were extensive, not least in Tokyo. The next step was to be an invasion of Kyushu. Before it could begin, however, a new weapon, the atom bomb, entirely changed the pattern of events. Dropped first on Hiroshima on 6 August, then on Nagasaki three days later, it caused casualties on a horrifying scale and forced even the imperial council to contemplate surrender. Reinforcing the effect, Russia declared war on Japan on 8 August, moving troops into Manchuria. Even so, the war minister and the service chiefs of staff resisted calls for peace until the emperor personally intervened. His vote left no option.

There were attempts by junior officers to overturn the decision – they set fire to the prime minister's residence and broke into the palace to find and if possible destroy the recording of the emperor's surrender speech, without success – but despite their action, plus several military suicides, an announcement of unconditional surrender was made public on 15 August. In a radio broadcast, received in silence for the most part by shocked and often unbelieving crowds, not all of whom could understand the language that was used, Hirohito broke the news for which wartime propaganda had never prepared his people. The war, he said, had developed 'not necessarily to Japan's advantage'. The country must therefore 'endure the unendurable and suffer what is insufferable'. On 2 September members of an interim cabinet, led by the foreign minister and army chief of staff, signed the instrument of surrender aboard the American flagship in Tokyo Bay.

CHAPTER 14

Postwar Japan

It is tempting to end a history of Japan with the events of 1945. By any standard they were cataclysmic. Yet from the perspective of half a century later they seem to mark a change of direction, not a new beginning. The same emperor continued to reign, using the same reign-title. The Shōwa emperor (Hirohito) did not die until January 1989. The institutions of government, though much reformed, remained almost wholly western in their inspiration. Industry, when it revived, did so under much the same leadership as before the war, building on familiar foundations. Many elements of traditional religion survived – with less official support and in competition with new variants – and the Japanese people remained wedded to a culture that was part western, part Sino-Japanese.

It is nevertheless undeniable that defeat had a major impact on their lives. Political parties, dependent – in theory, at least – on the popular vote, became enormously more influential. So did the business interests that provided them with funds. Industry's success took on a different character from that of the early twentieth century, resting now on the production of high-tech goods for sale to the world's most advanced economies. It also spread affluence more widely through the population at home. In a wider context, external influences on Japan, political, economic and cultural, came much more from America than Europe, contributing to a national *weltanschauung* that was more concerned with trade, the United Nations, the Cold War and the Pacific Rim than empire in Asia. Simultaneously, lifestyles and social attitudes became more and more like those of other industrial countries: less respectful to authority, more consumer-led, temporal-minded, culturally brash by the standards of an older generation.

The main source of this shift of emphasis in the postwar years was American military occupation, lasting from 1945 to 1951. Its first task, determined before surrender, was to disarm Japan and remove the country's wartime leadership. This involved both war crimes trials and an extensive 'purge', banning many thousands of Japanese from posts in government, politics, education and the media. Once this was accomplished, the focus shifted to reform. The scope of reform was founded on the belief that Japanese aggression between 1931 and 1945 had derived from fundamental faults in the body politic – not, as many Japanese asserted, from a temporary aberration, distorting the course that had been set in Meiji – and that these must be corrected in order to make the country welcome as a member of world society. 'Democratisation', in fact, became the head-word for what was being done. It embraced a multiplicity of changes to institutions and the law, enforced, ironically, by an alien military authority.

The first steps were negative ones. The emperor, under pressure from General Douglas MacArthur, Supreme Commander for the Allied Powers (SCAP), denied his own divinity in his New Year rescript for 1946. The greatest of the Shinto shrines, which had been closely linked with the imperial myth, lost their official funding and special status. A ban on 'militaristic and ultra-nationalist' ideology in schools was introduced in October 1945, soon followed by suspension of the course in 'ethics' (*shūshin*). The peerage was abolished, as were the army and navy. The huge business agglomerates (*zaibatsu*), accused of being co-conspirators of those who took Japan into war, as well as obstacles to free business competition in time of peace, were ordered to be broken up into their component parts. An anti-monopoly law was passed in April 1947 to prevent the emergence of comparable successors.

The 'positive' measures, introduced in large part during 1946 and 1947, included the substitution of a more liberal constitution for that of 1889. The preparation of a draft was at first entrusted to the Japanese authorities, but the result was so at odds with American expectations that GHQ took over the work itself. Its version was made public in March 1946, promulgated in the emperor's name in the following November, and came into force in May 1947. The Diet, it stated, was to remain bicameral, but both houses were to be elected by universal adult suffrage: the upper house partly by prefectures, partly by a national constituency, the lower house by multi-member electoral districts. Half the members of the upper house were to stand for election every three years, much like the US Senate. The lower house was elected for a four-year term, but could be dissolved if the government fell, like the British House of Commons. Dissolution was to be the signal for a general election. The lower house had the right of final decision on all key issues, including the budget; the prime minister was elected by it; his cabinet was responsible to the Diet, not the emperor.

Two provisions of the constitution were particularly objectionable to Japanese conservatives. One was its description of the emperor as 'the symbol of the state ... deriving his position from the will of the people'. The other was the statement (Article IX) that 'the Japanese people forever renounce war as a sovereign right of the nation' and would therefore maintain no land, sea or air forces. American governments were to find this clause an embarrassment when they later looked to Japan as a Cold War ally.

Some changes were made in order to reduce the power of the central bureaucracy. A Local Autonomy Law (April 1947) gave some of its functions to prefectural and city administrations, whose governors and mayors were to be elected. The Home Ministry was to be abolished, and police forces put under regional or local control. Responsibility for schools was entrusted to boards of

education, elected locally; the authority of the Ministry of Education with respect to textbooks and curricula was watered down.
Supervision of the judicial system was transferred from the Justice
Ministry to a newly established Supreme Court, which had the
power to rule on the constitutionality of laws. A revised Civil
Code spelt out the constitution's more general references to civil
rights, including the legal and political equality of women.

The declared purpose was to give Japan a form of government
that would be subject to the will of the people, though for several
years American GHQ was to remain the principal guardian of
their liberties. It performed that function long enough, in fact, to
ensure that a different generation of leadership was firmly installed
in power. Once this was done, the pressures grew to bring the
occupation to an end. In Washington, voices were raised to say
that it was now an unnecessary drain on American resources. In
Tokyo, the staff of GHQ considered that they had already done
what they had been instructed to do. Consequently, peace talks
started. In September 1951 a treaty was signed in San Francisco
by all the countries that had been engaged in war with Japan,
except Russia, China and India. It came into force when rati-
fications had been exchanged in 1952. This relieved the United
States of its responsibility for Japanese government, but it left
unresolved the question of American strategic interests in the
region, where Cold War conflict was still a real possibility. To
safeguard these interests, an American-Japanese security pact was
also signed, extending to Japan a promise of nuclear protection in
return for the lease of American bases in the Japanese islands.
Arrangements were included for legal jurisdiction over American
servicemen there, similar to those in Meiji period treaty ports.

Insofar as this made Japan independent, it began a testing time
for 'democracy'. Out of the bewildering array of political parties
that had been formed in the winter of 1945-6, four had by this
time emerged as of greatest consequence. Two were broadly
conservative: the Liberals and the Democrats. The others were of
the left: the Socialists and the Communists, each divided into
'hardline' and 'parliamentary' factions. The Liberals, led by a

former diplomat, Yoshida Shigeru, were at first the strongest. As a principal architect of the peace treaty and the security pact, Yoshida used the American patronage this gave him to chip away at the postwar reforms that conservatives found distasteful. Some measures of decentralisation were rescinded; men who had been 'purged' were brought back into public life; action was taken to remove communists and others of the extreme left wing instead, including a number of trade union leaders. The first moves were also made towards giving Japan – in practice, if not in name – an army and navy again. They began with a quasi-military National Police Reserve, reorganised in 1954 as the Self Defence Force. Its constitutionality was justified, though not to all Japanese by any means, by the claim that it would not be made available for service overseas. It eventually became large, efficient, well equipped, complete with land, sea and air arms; and it won in following years a measure of public acceptance, though never, since the constitution was not revised, the standing of a regular army and navy.

Yoshida's policies encountered a good deal of opposition in Japan, enough to bring his resignation at the end of 1954. Almost all on the left considered his 'reverse course', as the retreat from occupation policies was called, to be wholly unacceptable. They could expect support in this from a considerable body of the general public, who were enjoying their newfound liberties. Against that, socialism was still regarded as dangerous by a majority. This influenced the view that people took of the Cold War, to which Japan was irretrievably committed, it seemed, by the defence agreement with America. As was to be expected in the only country that had suffered nuclear attack, there was a widespread sentiment opposed to any kind of international action that might lead to war. It could readily be exploited by those who took a hostile stance towards the rights and wrongs of American policy. Both Russia and China had active spokesmen on the left. The neutralist bloc, largely Asian, also had political friends.

Yoshida's resignation left the conservatives weaker in the face of this discord. It also alarmed Japan's business interests, which saw the country's prospects of economic recovery endangered by political instability. Business leaders, therefore, acting collectively through management associations, of which the most powerful was Keidanren, proposed a plan to bring together the Liberals and the Democrats to form an all-embracing conservative party, able to check the rise of the Socialists. They offered generous finance to such an organisation. The result was the Liberal Democrat Party (LDP), founded in 1955. It was to provide Japan with cabinets for more than thirty years.

The first serious test of this realignment came in 1960, when the security pact was due for renewal. The revised agreement, presented to the Diet for approval, was denounced as contrary to the peace clause of the constitution. There was disorder in the lower house, large-scale demonstrations on the streets outside, threats of a general strike. Riot police were used on a massive scale to restore order in the capital. The treaty survived, as did the Liberal Democrats (minus their prime minister, who resigned), but the issue remained the most sensitive one in Japanese politics for many years. It was always likely to surface again whenever there was fear that nuclear weapons might be brought to Japan, or a dispute arose about the legal status of American servicemen.

Having survived this crisis, the LDP was able to devote itself to rounding out a structure that would keep it safely in office. This rested on a tripod of power. One leg of it was provided by the upper levels of the central bureaucracy, serving as experts, advisers and executive. Members of it, especially in the early years, were likely to be recruited into the party and the cabinet on retirement (a translation known as *amakudari*, or 'descent from heaven'). The second leg was business, providing money in enormous quantities for party funds, on the understanding that those who used it to get themselves elected would adopt a range of policies designed to favour economic growth. The third was the Liberal Democrat Party itself, providing an electoral and parliamentary machine. It depended not on a broad membership base, but on the careful cultivation in every constituency of persons of influence, able to deliver votes. The system was expensive to run. Money was at the heart not only of electoral success, but also of party unity, since the LDP consisted of a number of rival factions, united only in their hostility to those who challenged them for office. Contributions from the party's central funds helped to reinforce co-operation.

After 1990 there were signs that this successful system was breaking down. Corruption, an almost inevitable result of the way in which the parties were financed, began to undermine public support. The end of the Cold War and the disintegration of Soviet Russia reduced the voters' suspicions of socialism. It also made unity easier on the left. Most disturbing, the 'economic miracle', for which the Liberal Democrats had always claimed the greater part of the credit, appeared to be coming to an end. Faced by a growing rigidity in its business structure, major miscalculations in financial decisions, and fierce competition from Asia's 'tiger' economies, Japan relapsed into a sharp recession that proved resistant to government efforts to bring about recovery. Many blamed the LDP. Some of its factions broke away as splinter parties, making new political alliances. Coalition cabinets were formed, in one of which a largely Liberal Democrat cabinet even had a Socialist prime minister. The situation, it seemed, was reverting to that existing before 1955. It is not yet clear when, or whether, a stable pattern will re-emerge.

Disillusion, prompted by defeat, left a lasting mark on Japanese attitudes, not only in the widespread hostility that existed to nuclear weapons and any hints of national rearmament, but also with respect to economic growth. If the Meiji search for Strength had been discredited, Wealth had not. A belief that it should now become Japan's principal aim underpinned the government's efforts to craft recovery in the early postwar years, then prompted national pride in rising performance figures, as recovery was transformed into prosperity. Industrial achievement was not only a contribution to political stability; it was also a source of international prestige. For both reasons it was held in high regard.

The end of the war left the Japanese economy in ruins. War factories had fallen idle. Those producing for the domestic consumer market had long since been deprived of much of their manpower and materials. Millions were unemployed, their numbers swollen by demobilised servicemen. Farms could not produce enough to feed the population, despite strict rationing, while much of what food there was found its way into urban black markets, or was bartered by farmers in return for household goods to the city-dwellers who crowded the trains to the countryside. Road transport was minimal for lack of vehicles; electric power supplies were frequently interrupted; coal was scarce; the population was hungry, confused, demoralised. Recovery was therefore an immediate priority, not only for Japanese governments, but also for American GHQ, which saw in these conditions a constant threat of unrest.

The chances of achieving it were better than they might have seemed to the superficial observer. There was still a good deal of undamaged industrial plant – the devastation caused by bombing is rarely as complete as it looks in aerial photographs – and skilled labour able to put it to use. There was a corps of efficient managers, most of whom escaped the 'purge'. Bureaucrats, who had learnt the techniques of controlling the allocation of capital and raw materials for the benefit of the munitions industry, were able to apply them to reviving peacetime factories and distribution networks. And crucially, the occupation proved to be a benevolent one. Food was shipped from America (prompting changes in diet and eating habits). American technology was made available to Japanese firms, often in partnership arrangements. Demands from the war-torn countries of Southeast Asia, that they be given Japanese plant by way of reparations, were rejected or ignored.

By the time war broke out between North and South Korea in 1950, recovery had proceeded far enough in Japan to enable her industry to provide a good deal of the equipment, other than arms, needed by the United Nations army that moved into the war zone. This was itself a major stimulus to production, accounting for currency earnings of nearly $600 million in 1951.

The peace treaty then made another stage of development possible by removing most constraints on Japanese export trade. The timing was fortunate. The world economy, it transpired, was on the eve of a period of rapid expansion. Japan, which possessed a growing domestic market, a government ready to make capital available and a population with a high propensity to save (a response to years of hardship), was in a position to profit by it. In 1960 the country's real growth rate was 13.2 per cent. Something like it was maintained for the whole of the succeeding decade.

The Ministry of International Trade and Industry (MITI) played a vital role in this achievement. It did so not only by the use of its familiar methods of control, but also by ensuring that the greatest benefits of growth were channelled to businesses that seemed likely to make best use of them. Some were old-established concerns: both Mitsui and Mitsubishi, whose trading companies had been dissolved in the occupation's early years, were back in large-scale operation by 1955. Others – in steel production, for example – were newly formed cartels, conceived and then approved by MITI. The anti-monopoly law was revised to make them legal.

The most successful companies in the export trade were those engaged in shipbuilding and the manufacture of high-technology items like cameras, electrical consumer goods and automobiles. All these depended on heavy capital investment. A few, especially the makers of automobiles, had long been famous names, often important in war production, but others were of recent origin, exploiting what were in effect new markets both at home and overseas. By contrast, the textile industry languished, except those sectors of it that depended on artificial fibres. Since these were petrochemical products, while most other firms that contributed largely to supply Japan's export markets were large-scale users of energy, the development once again increased Japan's dependence on imported oil, as war had done. Most of it, however, came now from the Middle East; and when Arab oil producers sharply raised their prices in 1973, then again in 1979–80, the 'oil shocks', as they were called, made the first serious dent in Japanese prosperity.

The larger import bill brought a general price rise, driving annual growth rates down to 5 per cent. Though adjustment and recovery came more quickly in Japan than in many countries, growth never in fact regained the annual levels of the 1960s.

At this point a different problem came into prominence. The drive to expand export sales as a contribution to prosperity had already produced a favourable balance of trade before 1973. Thereafter rising oil costs set it back for a time, but after 1980 it began to grow again, as government efforts to reduce the country's oil consumption achieved success. By 1990 the favourable balance reached an annual level of $90 billion. This caused alarm among the country's trading partners, especially the United States and the European Community, who threatened a variety of restrictions to counter what they saw as undesirable exploitation of their open markets. Negotiations on the subject quickly became acrimonious. They were not made easier when Japan began to use the surpluses she earned by trade to finance direct investment overseas, whether by buying bonds and real estate, or by establishing factories under Japanese ownership. The latter, it was clear, were in part intended as a way to bypass any restrictions that might be imposed on imports coming directly from Japan.

One result of higher foreign earnings was to strengthen the yen in the world's financial centres. This proved in the long run to have disadvantages for Japan. By raising the price of export goods, it not only made it easier for local manufacturers to compete with them in places where Japan had hitherto been able to dominate the market – Korea, Taiwan, Hong Kong and Singapore among the earliest, soon followed by China, Thailand and Malaysia – but also gave the industries of those areas a better chance to challenge Japan in other parts of the world. Japanese businessmen, aware that their labour costs, when translated into foreign currencies, were in many cases much too high, took two steps to restore their competitive position. One was to reduce the size of their labour force in Japan. The other, known as 'hollowing out', was to transfer manufacturing to countries where labour, though sufficiently skilled, was cheaper. Japanese products began to be marketed under labels that described them as 'made in Korea', 'made in Singapore', even 'made in Britain'. This involved in many instances a transfer of technology and know-how that was bound to improve the competitiveness of potential rivals.

Despite this, Japan in the 1980s had the world's second strongest industrial economy. Production of steel was greater than that of the United States. So was that of automobiles: some six million units were exported every year. Exports as a whole produced a large and rising trade surplus, much of it used to finance investment overseas. As a result, Japan became a major international creditor for the first time in her modern history. Prosperity, it was predicted, would last well into the final decade of the century.

The prediction was wrong. At the beginning of the 1990s, property prices, which had been raised to unsustainable levels by generous lending policies on the part of financial institutions, suddenly fell. Banks were left with huge outstanding loans, many of them irrecoverable. Credit grew tighter. The government made the situation worse by raising taxes to strengthen revenue. From this point on, Japan moved rapidly into recession. Business confidence declined, unemployment began to rise, consumption fell. In the summer of 1992 the Tokyo stock exchange index stood at less than half its earlier peak.

Government efforts to restore the situation in the next six years were unsuccessful. By 1998 the financial structure was looking more and more fragile, the yen had weakened, cabinets were shaky. The Liberal Democrats suffered an electoral defeat, the prime minister resigned. To all appearances the 'economic miracle' was at an end.

Thirty years of prosperity, starting in the 1960s, brought about far-reaching changes in Japanese life. It carried forward the urbanisation, begun in the Edo period, to the point where three-quarters of Japanese already lived in towns and cities by 1973. Still more worked in them, for every city had its spreading fringe of suburbs and dormitory areas. Even some country-dwellers, nominally farmers, commuted to urban types of employment. Officially, farmers made up 9 per cent of the population by 1980, but they contributed less than 3 per cent to the national product. Underlining the statistics, an urban and suburban belt spread westward along the Pacific coast from Tokyo, stretching more than 300 miles to Osaka, then farther west along the northern shores of the Inland Sea. One can travel all the way by rail and rarely get a glimpse of genuine countryside. Elsewhere the concentration is less dense, but this is because so much of Japan's terrain is mountainous, providing neither industrial nor farming land.

Employees of Japan's largest firms, together with office workers, form a large proportion of the residents in these urban areas. They fall into three categories. At the top is management, characterised by what is known as the 'salaryman' (*sarariman*). He is usually recruited, like his equivalents in the state bureaucracy, from male university graduates (few women have found a place in their ranks, though the number has slowly been increasing). Recruitment and starting salary depend on the reputation of the candidate's university, more than on the academic attainment of the individual; promotion is by seniority, except that the less efficient are diverted to the fringes as they near the top; loyalty to the company, measured by conscientious attendance and long hours, is held to be a primary virtue. Salaries have not as a rule been generous at any level, but other advantages exist to compensate: job security (usually known as 'life employment'), regular bonuses, company housing, health and pension schemes. Wives, whose husbands more often than not are late home from the office, are left to deal with the home and the children's education. They have little to do with the husband's 'business' life.

A little lower in the scale come the members of the company's 'permanent' workforce, though the social distinction is not sharply drawn. Having a less prestigious education than the *sarariman*, they nevertheless enjoy the same expectation of life employment, subject to job changes and retraining, plus a similar range of employee benefits. These are the workers most likely to be unionised. Revision of the labour laws between 1945 and 1947 gave employees the right to organise and strike, as well as guaranteeing a health insurance scheme and accident compensation. By the end of 1948 there were 34,000 separate unions with nearly 7 million members, two-fifths of the industrial workforce; but strikes, coupled with the participation of union leaders in radical politics, attracted the hostility of both conservative cabinets and American military government. The 'red purge' of 1950–51 checked the trend, leaving most trade unions as 'company' unions, concerned almost wholly with wages and working conditions. This has remained true ever since, though the labour movement as a whole has had its ups and downs.

A large part of a company's workforce – as much as half in some cases – is described as 'temporary': that is, does not have a guarantee of life employment. Traditionally it is also paid less well, though differentials have narrowed in recent years. Those who belong to this category of workers can be hired and fired with relative impunity, as the fortunes of the business fluctuate, so their presence constitutes an economic safety valve, increasing job security for the rest; and since they are the ones least likely to be unionised, their disabilities are not as much a cause of turbulence as one might otherwise expect.

Medium and smaller companies, engaged perhaps in subcontracting, or in the distribution and service industries, have remained to a greater extent family owned and differently structured. They tend to have a smaller 'permanent' workforce, to employ more family labour, to offer lower pay. They, too, therefore contribute to economic flexibility, part of a general pattern that has kept formal unemployment remarkably low. It remains low by European standards, even if one takes account of the concealed unemployment to which the system in practice leads.

Since 1990, while Japan has been in recession, not all characteristics of the business world have remained the same. There has been a reduced commitment to lifetime employment at almost all levels. Sometimes salarymen change jobs voluntarily, looking for better opportunities. Sometimes they are subject to compulsory early retirement. More women are being employed, often part time and usually at lower pay than men. This has gone hand in hand with an increase in divorce, perhaps in middle age or later, when the children have left home and wives can think of taking up jobs again. None of this would be particularly surprising in Europe or America. In Japan it suggests that the social habits always thought to be part of the 'economic miracle' are not immutable. As Japanese society continues to evolve, it becomes more and more like that of other capitalist countries.

One thing that has not changed is preoccupation with the 'ladder' of education. In Meiji the state education system was designed to train a skilled and biddable population, some members of which could expect by virtue of ability to make their way upward through the ranks of a powerful bureaucracy. Occupation policy set out to reform both the structure and the ethos, though it was more successful with the former than with the latter. Education became the principal means of recruiting a business élite that was almost as bureaucratic as the state's. Attempts to put greater emphasis on freedom of access, variety and individual attainment, by contrast, fell all too often by the wayside, despite a very great increase in the number of universities and colleges. As a result, education is still seen primarily as the route to success in life, not as a means of self-fulfilment. Entry to one of the best universities, whether state or private, is considered a career advantage second to none. It is most likely to be attainable by those who attend one of the better schools. Since these, like the universities, choose their students by competitive examination, the 'struggle to achieve' is pushed back even into primary education. Parents make savings from the family budget to pay for children as young as five to go to special cramming classes in the evenings and school holidays. University entrance is known as the 'examination hell'.

This underlines the importance of a feature of modern Japanese life that began with the Meiji reforms: the break with hereditary status as the determinant of a person's 'place' in society. Another significant feature, this time looking back to the Edo period, has been a rising standard of living. Those who governed Japan between 1868 and 1945 were more concerned with the nation's strength than with the people's welfare, except in so far as the latter was an element in the former. After defeat, the economy became psychologically more important; and one element underlying this was a widespread desire to secure a better life, itself a form of revulsion against the past. Japanese not only looked for higher incomes. They also sought to spend them in new ways, ways that had more in common with the tastes of Edo townsmen (*chōnin*) than with the traditions of the samurai that had shaped so much of what could 'properly' be done in the 1930s.

The affluence that derived from industrial growth spread to all levels of the population through higher wages, bonuses and profits (Japan is not to any great extent a *rentier* society). Real wages in 1970 were comfortably more than double the prewar norm. One consequence was the ability to buy a range of more expensive foodstuffs, bringing unmistakable increases in the height and weight of the younger generation. The national rugby team, though still smaller as a rule than its opponents, is not now disastrously outweighted. Girls are no longer universally tiny – and they are better dressed, mostly in the western style. Even so, a much smaller proportion of the household budget has been needed in recent years for food and clothing than was true in the nineteenth century. Housing is expensive, especially in the cities, but it still leaves more for the costs of education and entertainment, including television sets and hi-fi, even private cars. Most of the consumer durables are much like those to be found elsewhere. They are, after all, Japanese exports.

In fact, in material things Japanese life is with few exceptions a replica of western life. So it is in much else. People watch imported movies, dubbed in Japanese. They flock to concerts by western classical orchestras and pop groups. They eat western snacks and meals (Japanese food is more expensive). In addition, Japan produces conductors, violinists and ballet dancers of note, who perform throughout the world. Japanese painters of reputation are as likely to be influenced by the French Impressionists as they are by the classical art of the Japanese school.

So far has this development gone that it is doubtful whether one should continue to call the civilisation of Europe and America 'western' when writing of Japan. To most Japanese it is so normal a part of everyday life that they accept it as their own, something they are free to modify if they wish, just as much as Italians or Americans. In other words, there is now a Japanese version of modern culture, just as there are national variants elsewhere.

Tradition has changed in response to the shift of emphasis, but has not been completely overwhelmed. For the most part it is found in isolated pockets, instead of comprising a pervasive element running through society as a whole. Most adjustments tend to be those that will increase the appeal to a popular audience. Kabuki, for example, has become brisker, indulging even more than in the past in showmanship. *Sumō* tournaments have reduced the amount of preliminary ritual before their bouts for the benefit of the television cameras. Woodblock prints have found a market in Christmas cards. *Ikebana* seeks out rare and more colourful flowers; its most 'modern' exhibitions have been known to include bicycle wheels (shorn of their tyres) in the arrangements. Yet in some respects – in the transmission of skills, or the relationship of master and 'disciple' – the traditional arts and sports remain highly conservative. The methods of public presentation have changed much more than social attitudes.

This is not entirely true of language. For a hundred years or more, Japanese has been adjusting to the social needs thrown up by time, as well as to the demands of fashion and technology: simplifying its structure and to a limited degree its writing forms, borrowing words and phrases from a variety of other languages, inventing new expressions of its own. This has made much of classical and medieval literature, both poetry and prose, harder for the present generation to understand. The *Tale of Genji*, for example, is best known in a twentieth-century Japanese 'translation'. Against that, what is now written by novelists, scholars and commentators of every kind can reach a very much wider audience. To this end, form and style have also been greatly modified. It is possible today to buy any number of books, fictional, technical, or educational, published as *manga*, that is, the kind of strip-cartoons that were developed for the less serious pages of the daily papers.

One disadvantage of a language that loses touch with much of the literature of the past is that it cuts off many people from a knowledge of the history and ideas of their country before the present age. Outside the schools the task of explaining them in Japan has fallen more and more to those whose first concern is entertainment in television and film. Their interests are inevitably selective. The life of the samurai is a favoured topic, as it has long been. It appears in productions that range from what used to be called 'B class movies' to the glossier serials of the major TV channels. At a more elevated level, it is the subject of films that gave Kurosawa Akira a world reputation as a director. *Rashōmon* is a tale (much revised) from *Konjaku monogatari* (Chapter 4), *The Seven Samurai* one that is set in the Sengoku wars (Chapter 7), *Ran* a version of the *King Lear* story with the principals converted into Japanese feudal lords. This is fiction, but the historical detail is meticulous. Also historical are many discussions of Japan's response to the West that can be heard on current affairs programmes or read in magazines. Some years ago there was a long documentary film about the Tokyo war crimes trials that drew many customers to cinemas in the cities. Japan can hardly be said to lack a consciousness of the past, albeit an impressionistic one.

Yet the strength and influence of the old religions is difficult to assess. Visit festivals and you will see throngs of visitors, including many family groups. Go to a shrine or temple at other times and most of the few who are there are likely to be elderly (or tourists). True, Buddhism and Shinto have given birth to so-called 'new religions' since 1945, but this might be as much a sign of weakness as of vigour. Zen has acquired a role in management training, Shinto in the siting of factories and office blocks. Lip-service is paid to the value of Confucian ethics by economists and right-wing politicians. Nevertheless, the impression remains that Japan has been overwhelmingly secular in its thought ever since Tokugawa times. A survey in 1983 concluded that less than a third of Japanese admitted to having a personal faith.

The most straightforward explanation of the changes in postwar Japan is that they have simply been another phase of continuing modernisation, a convergence of institutions, attitudes and culture with those of other industrial states. From this point of view, there are parallels with what took place after Japan began to adopt Chinese civilisation in the sixth and seventh centuries. Prince Shōtoku then did not know the extent of what he was setting in train. *Mutatis mutandis*, nor did Commodore Perry in 1853.

GLOSSARY

Ashigaru Foot-soldiers. During the Sengoku period (q.v.), *ashi-garu* emerged as the lowest-ranking members of the feudal class, having status below that of samurai proper. They served as the rank and file of a feudal army, or as clerks, guards and messengers in time of peace.

Asuka period The period extending from the formal arrival of Buddhism in Japan (supposedly AD 552) to the founding of Nara in 710. Art historians use 645 as its terminal date.

Azuchi period The period in the second half of the sixteenth century when Oda Nobunaga was hegemon in Japan, taking its name from his castle on the shores of Lake Biwa. It is commonly combined with the years of Toyotomi Hideyoshi's supremacy, named after his castle on the outskirts of Kyoto, to provide a label, Azuchi-Momoyama, for the last thirty or forty years of the century.

Bakufu The *de facto* central administration of Japan under a Shogun (q.v.). First established in simple form by Minamoto Yoritomo towards the end of the twelfth century, it became more elaborate in later periods, especially under the Tokugawa, when it was staffed by some hundreds of samurai officials. The separate phases of its history are identified either by reference to the place where its headquarters was located (Kamakura Bakufu, Muromachi Bakufu, Edo Bakufu) or, in the case of the last two, by the name of the family holding power as Shogun (Ashikaga Bakufu, Tokugawa Bakufu).

Bushi See under Samurai.

Chōnin Townsmen. The non-samurai inhabitants of feudal towns (merchants, artisans, labourers) in the late medieval and Edo periods.

Daijōkan The Council of State, as established under direct imperial rule, first in Nara and Heian, then briefly in the Meiji period. Its senior minister was the Daijō-daijin (sometimes translated 'Chancellor').

Daimyo A feudal lord of the later medieval and Edo periods, defined as one who held land rated at 10,000 or more *koku* (see *Kokudaka*). Historians describe daimyo of the late fifteenth and sixteenth centuries as Sengoku daimyo, implying that the institution was not then fully developed. Daimyo of the Edo period were divided into *fudai daimyō* (direct vassals of the Tokugawa) and *tozama daimyō* ('outside' daimyo, usually having greater independence and larger lands, but not allowed to hold Bakufu office).

Edo period The period when the Tokugawa ruled Japan as Shogun from their capital, Edo (modern Tokyo); customarily taken to have begun with the battle of Sekigahara in 1600 (though Ieyasu did not become Shogun until 1603) and to have ended with the fall of the Tokugawa in January 1868.

E-maki Picture scrolls, covering a wide range of subjects. Originally introduced from China during Nara, they became a characteristically Japanese art form from the twelfth century onwards.

Era-name (*nengō*) A calendrical system, adopted from China in the seventh century, in which short periods of time are given labels (*nengō*), chosen by the imperial court for their auspicious character. Years are identified by their serial place within them: thus Taika 1 = 645, Taika 2 = 646, and so on until the *nengō* is changed. In early centuries *nengō* were changed whenever events were thought to call for it, but in modern times Japan has followed Chinese practice in making them coincide with imperial reigns. The Meiji period, Taishō period and Shōwa period (q.v.) all had single *nengō*, which have posthumously become the emperor's reign-title. The practice continues.

Fudai daimyō See under Daimyo.

Fukoku-kyōhei 'Enrich the country, strengthen the army'. Originally a Chinese tag, it was modified in Japan during the second half of the nineteenth century to be the slogan under which a commercial-industrial economy was to be established and the country's military establishment reformed on western lines.

Gokenin Housemen; vassals of a feudal lord. In the Edo period, the lowest level of those with full samurai rank (cf. Samurai).

Gōshi Country samurai. Those who in the sixteenth century (after Hideyoshi's Sword Hunt) were allowed to remain in the village and continue to cultivate land, instead of moving to their lord's castle town. They lost status as a result, ranking below those of full samurai standing.

Hatamoto Bannermen. Samurai of superior status to the majority of *gokenin* (q.v.).

Heian period The period when the imperial court still ruled Japan from the emperor's capital of Heian (later known as Kyoto), i.e. from the late eighth to the late twelfth centuries.

Kamakura period The period 1185 to 1333, when the Bakufu controlled Japan from a capital in Kamakura. Cf. Bakufu.

Kami Deities of the Shinto pantheon, usually translated 'gods and goddesses' (without distinction of sex), though not all were anthropomorphic.

Kampaku One of the principal offices used by the Fujiwara to dominate the imperial court after 880. It can be described as regent to an adult emperor. Cf. Sesshō.

Kangō The 'tally' used to identify official Japanese tribute ships in missions to China during the Muromachi period. It consisted of a slip, stamped with the Chinese imperial seal, which bore the two ideographs making up the name Japan. This would be torn in half, one retained in China, the other handed to the Japanese envoy then visiting China. A future envoy would be required to bring the matching half to establish his authenticity.

Kokudaka A form of measurement of land in terms of its annual yield, expressed in units of *koku* (*c*. 5 bushels) of rice. The system came into use in the sixteenth century as a means of assessing land values that was simpler to estimate and more meaningful in feudal terms than money.

Meiji period The reign of the Meiji emperor, properly 1867–1912, but usually taken to start with the overthrow of the Tokugawa in January 1868. Cf. Era-name.

Momoyama period See under Azuchi period.

Muromachi period The years 1336–1573, when the Ashikaga Shogun claimed to exercise authority in Japan from their head-quarters in the Muromachi district of Kyoto.

Namboku period The years 1336–92, when Japan had two rival imperial lines. The northern court, supported by the Ashikaga, was in Kyoto. The southern court, comprising Go-Daigo and his descendants, was in exile in the mountains south of the Nara plain. The latter were eventually recognised as legitimate.

Nara period The years 710–84, when the imperial court was located at Nara (Heijō).

Nengō See Era-name.

Ritsuryō **system** The set of institutions, laid down in legal codes and statutes (*ritsuryō*), by which Japan was governed in the eighth and ninth centuries.

Rōjū Elder. The title of members of the senior Tokugawa council in the Edo period, as well as those holding similar office in some daimyo territories.

Sakoku 'Closed country'. The policy of national seclusion, insti-tuted by Tokugawa Iemitsu between 1633 and 1639, by which Japanese were banned from trading or travelling overseas (though some exceptions were made with respect to Ryukyu and southern Korea). Asian traders were still allowed to come to Japanese ports under strict regulation, but among Europeans only the Dutch were given this privilege. The restrictions ended after 1854, when Commodore Perry concluded an agreement 'opening' Japanese ports.

Samurai Members of the feudal military class, usually, though not necessarily, those who were not lords; more formally described as *bushi*. First became a significant element in Japanese society in the late Heian period (q.v.). In time a number of subdivisions took shape, varying in rank and status: see *Gokenin, Gōshi, Hatamoto*.

Sankin-kōtai 'Alternate attendance'. The system, based on Ashi-kaga precedents, but finalised by the third Tokugawa Shogun, Iemitsu, requiring feudal lords to reside part of the time in the

Shogun's capital. Under the Tokugawa, they were required to spend at least half their time in Edo (in yearly or six-monthly periods, depending on the location of their domains).

Sengoku period The years of civil war from *c.*1460 to 1560; the label derives from Chinese history, where it is usually translated 'Warring States'. The civil wars in Japan continued in fact until 1600, but the last part of the period is more often called Azuchi-Momoyama (q.v.).

Sesshō Regent to an under-age emperor. One of the offices used by the Fujiwara to dominate the imperial court from the late ninth century (cf. Kampaku).

Shōen A private landholding (often misleadingly translated 'manor'). Complex structures of land rights, held under different legal arrangements, which came into existence in the Heian period as a means of escape from the burdens associated with the *ritsuryō* system. Characteristic of Japanese landholding in the medieval period, they were finally broken up by the Sengoku wars.

Shogun Abbreviation of *Sei-i-tai-shōgun*, 'barbarian-subduing generalissimo'. This was originally an imperial title, bestowed on the commanders of forces that were employed against the turbulent frontier tribes of the north, but it was taken by Japan's *de facto* feudal rulers from the late twelfth century to give a supposed legitimacy to their power (cf. Bakufu).

Shōwa period The reign of the Shōwa emperor (Hirohito), 1926–89. Cf. Era-name.

Shuin-sen Red seal ships. Japanese junks (some foreign owned) that were licensed to trade to the ports of south China and Southeast Asia in the late sixteenth and early seventeenth centuries. Permits, each for a single voyage, were first issued under the vermillion seal (*shuin*) by Hideyoshi in 1590. Tokugawa Iemitsu brought the practice to an end in 1635 as part of his policy of 'closing' the country (cf. *Sakoku*).

Shūshin 'Ethics'. The course in Confucian ethics and nationalist ideology, taught in Japanese schools from the Meiji period to 1945.

Sonnō-jōi 'Honour the emperor, repel the barbarian'. The slogan under which mid-nineteenth-century samurai activists set out to rally opposition to the foreign treaties and Tokugawa rule.

Taishō period The reign of the Taishō emperor, 1912–26. Cf. Era-name.

Tozama daimyō See under Daimyo.

Ukiyo 'Floating world'. Term used to describe the life and culture of *chōnin* of the cities of the Edo period, typically the world of actors and courtesans.

Wakō Japanese pirates, in particular those (not all Japanese) who attacked the coasts of China and Korea between the thirteenth and sixteenth centuries.

Yamato The oldest Japanese name for Japan. In historic times, the name of a province extending southward from Nara.

Zaibatsu 'Financial cliques'. More specifically, the large family owned financial-commercial-industrial combines of modern Japan before 1945.

BIBLIOGRAPHY

This list includes no books in Japanese. Although the work of Japanese scholars provides the foundation for almost all modern publications on Japanese history in western languages, this one is not primarily intended for those who can read Japanese, so a few Japanese works are listed in translation, but not otherwise. Section A cites a small number of general works, from which readers can obtain more detail than is given in the text. Most contain useful bibliographies of their own. Section B adds a selection of translations and more specialist studies, chosen for the light they throw on particular periods or aspects of Japanese history. The list as a whole is not intended to be exhaustive or representative.

Section A: General works

The most considerable English-language treatment of Japanese history is *The Cambridge History of Japan* (Cambridge: Cambridge University Press, 1988–). It is eventually to consist of 6 volumes, but vol. 2 has not yet appeared. Among works by individuals, the best is that by George Sansom, *A History of Japan* (3 vols, London: Cresset, 1958, 1961, 1964). The same author's earlier book, *Japan: A short cultural history* (rev. edn, London: Cresset, 1962; first published in 1931), is in some respects out of date, but is still worth reading for its insights on many topics (especially Buddhism, perhaps). Both Sansom's books end with the Edo period. For a general survey of the modern period, see W. G. Beasley, *The Rise of Modern Japan* (London: Weidenfeld and Nicolson, 1990). Ryusaku Tsunoda (ed.), *Sources of Japanese Tradition* (New York: Columbia University Press, 1958; later issued as a paperback in 2 vols) provides a range of translations on a wide variety of subjects, both political and cultural, for the premodern and modern periods.

The following books all examine more limited aspects of Japanese history over long periods of time: Takeo Yazaki, *Social Change and the City in Japan* (Tokyo: Japan Publications, 1968); Joseph M. Kitagawa, *Religion in Japanese History* (New York: Columbia University Press, 1966); Shuichi Kato, *A History of Japanese Literature* (3 vols, London: Macmillan, 1979–83); Donald Keene (ed.), *Anthology of Japanese Literature* (London: Allen and Unwin, 1956); Robert Treat Paine and Alexander Soper, *The Art and Architecture of Japan* (Harmondsworth: Penguin, 1955); Akiyama Terukazu, *Japanese Painting* (Cleveland, Ohio: Skira, 1961); Sugimoto Masayoshi and David L. Swain, *Science and Culture in Traditional Japan, AD 600–1854* (Cambridge, Mass: MIT, 1978).

Section B: *Translations and specialist studies*

(1) ANCIENT PERIOD

The most useful of the early chronicles, translated by W. G. Aston, is *Nihongi: Chronicles of Japan from the earliest times to AD 697* (reprint, London: Allen and Unwin, 1956 [1896]). Also of interest (though not easy to find) is R. Tsunoda and C. C. Goodrich, *Japan in the Chinese Dynastic Histories* (South Pasadena, Calif.: Perkins, 1951). Of J. E. Kidder's works on prehistoric Japan, *Early Japanese Art* (London: Thames and Hudson, 1964) concentrates on the tomb culture. Edwin O. Reischauer, *Ennin's Travels in T'ang China* (New York: Ronald, 1955), gives an account of a Japanese tribute mission to China in the ninth century. On Heian art and society there are two good studies: Rose Hempel, *The Heian Civilization of Japan* (Oxford: Phaidon, 1983), and Ivan Morris, *The World of the Shining Prince: Court life in ancient Japan* (London: Oxford University Press, 1964; Harmondsworth: Penguin, 1969). Helen Craig McCullough has translated a chronicle of the period: *Ōkagami, the Great Mirror: Fujiwara Michinaga (966–1027) and his times* (Princeton, NJ: Princeton University

Press, 1980). The most famous piece of prose literature of Heian, Murasaki Shikibu's novel *The Tale of Genji*, has most recently been translated by Edward Seidensticker (Harmondsworth: Penguin, 1981).

(2) MEDIEVAL PERIOD (C. 1150–1550)

John W. Hall, *Government and Local Power in Japan 500 to 1700* (Princeton, NJ: Princeton University Press, 1966), is an important study of political institutions in the context of feudalism. More colourful in its subject-matter is Paul Varley, *Warriors of Japan as Portrayed in the War Tales* (Honolulu: Hawaii University Press, 1994). Several medieval chronicles have been translated: Delmer M. Brown and Ichiro Ishida, *The Future and the Past: A translation and study of the Gukanshō* (Berkeley, Calif.: California University Press, 1979); Paul Varley, *A Chronicle of Gods and Sovereigns: Jinnō Shōtōki of Kitabatake Chikafusa* (New York: Columbia University Press, 1980); Helen Craig McCullough, *The Taiheiki* (New York: Columbia University Press, 1959). Wang Yi-t'ung, *Official Relations between China and Japan 1368–1549* (Cambridge, Mass: Harvard University Press, 1953), though not very readable, is the best-documented account in English of Ashikaga relations with the mainland. Marion Ury, *Tales of Times Now Past* (Berkeley, Calif.: California University Press, 1979), translates sixty-two tales from *Konjaku monogatari*, providing a representative sample of medieval fiction. On art, Shimizu Yoshiaki (ed.), *Japan: The shaping of daimyo culture 1185–1868* (London: Thames and Hudson, 1989), is the annotated catalogue of a very good exhibition, while Hideo Okudaira, *Emaki: Japanese picture scrolls* (Rutland and Tokyo: Tuttle, 1962), describes a medieval art form that is of immense value to the historian. Both books are lavishly illustrated.

(3) EARLY MODERN PERIOD (C. 1550–1850)

Japanese history from the sixteenth century has an extensive literature in English as well as Japanese, which makes it more difficult to choose books for inclusion here. One theme has been that of the Tokugawa political structure, widely held to be distinctive, if not unique. The chapters on the subject by John W. Hall and Harold Bolitho in vol. 4 of the *Cambridge History* provide the best summary. More controversial has been the question of how far social and economic change in the Edo period paved the way for later modernisation. A recent survey is Chie Nakane and Shinzaburō Ōishi, *Tokugawa Japan: The social and economic antecedents of modern Japan* (Tokyo: Tokyo University Press, 1990). Gilbert Rozman has made a comparison of Chinese and Japanese cities and towns in *Urban Networks in Ch'ing China and Tokugawa Japan* (Princeton, NJ: Princeton University Press, 1973). An older but still useful work is Charles Sheldon, *The Rise of the Merchant Class in Tokugawa Japan 1600–1868* (rev. edn, New York, 1973 [1958]). Ronald Dore has examined the role of education in *Education in Tokugawa Japan* (London: Routledge, 1965). Maruyama Masao considers some of the implications of intellectual history in this context: *Studies in the Intellectual History of Tokugawa Japan*, trans. Mikiso Hane (Princeton, NJ, and Tokyo: Princeton University Press and Tokyo University Press, 1974). Eiko Ikegami has more recently analysed the effect of changing circumstance on the samurai code in *The Taming of the Samurai* (Cambridge, Mass.: Harvard University Press, 1995).

Much of Edo prose fiction is a commentary on contemporary society. See, for example, Howard Hibbett, *The Floating World in Japanese Fiction* (Oxford: Oxford University Press, 1959), which includes some translated material, and G. W. Sargent, *The Japanese Family Storehouse . . . Translated from the 'Nippon Eitai-gura' of Ihara Saikaku* (Cambridge: Cambridge University Press, 1959). Art is very well illustrated in William Watson (ed.), *The Great Japan Exhibition: Art of the Edo period 1600–1868* (London: Royal Academy of Arts, 1981). On the woodblock print, the Edo art form best known in the West, see Sadao Kikuchi, *A Treasury of Japanese Wood Block Prints, Ukiyo-e* (New York: Crown, 1969).

Another major topic is that of Japan's relationship with the outside world before and during the years of national seclusion. George Sansom, *The Western World and Japan* (New York and London: Knopf, 1950), is a perceptive survey of the cultural aspects, in particular. Michael Cooper (ed.), *They Came to Japan: An anthology of European reports on Japan 1543–1640* (London: Thames and Hudson, 1965), offers some fascinating sidelights. George Elison, *Deus Destroyed: The image of Christianity in early modern Japan* (Cambridge, Mass.: Harvard University Press, 1973), examines Japanese anti-Christian sentiment; Ronald P. Toby, *State and Diplomacy in Early Modern Japan* (Princeton, NJ: Princeton University Press, 1984), takes a revisionist look at the nature of seclusion; and Donald Keene, *The Japanese Discovery of Europe 1720–1830* (rev. edn, Stanford, Calif.: Stanford University Press, 1969; first published 1952), is chiefly concerned with 'Dutch studies' in Japan.

(4) THE MODERN PERIOD (FROM C. 1850)

The general works cited in Section A deal quite fully with the main strands of modern political and economic history. They can usefully be supplemented by Oka Yoshitake, *Five Political Leaders of Modern Japan: Itō Hirobumi, Ōkuma Shigenobu, Hara Takashi, Inukai Tsuyoshi, Saionji Kimmochi* (Tokyo: Tokyo University Press, 1986), since such biographies are hard to come by in English. The reforms carried out after 1945 have been reconsidered in some detail in Robert E. Ward and Sakamoto Yoshikazu, *Democratizing Japan: The Allied Occupation* (Honolulu: Hawaii University Press, 1987). An earlier book by Kazuo Kawai, *Japan's American Interlude* (Chicago, Ill.: Chicago University Press, 1960), provides a moderately conservative Japanese viewpoint on the same subject. Readers who have a technical interest in economic questions would do well to seek guidance elsewhere, but W. W. Lockwood, *The Economic Development of Japan: Growth and structural change*

1868–1938 (Princeton, NJ and Oxford: Princeton University Press and Oxford University Press, 1955), is an admirable introduction, jargon-free and non-mathematical. The postwar years have been abandoned to the economists.

Japan's response to the West in the mid-nineteenth century, which has played a key part in modern history, has been widely studied. Marius Jansen, *Sakamoto Ryōma and the Meiji Restoration* (Princeton, NJ: Princeton University Press, 1961), looks in some detail at the samurai activists of the 1860s. W. G. Beasley, *Japan Encounters the Barbarian: Japanese travellers in America and Europe* (New Haven, Conn.: Yale University Press, 1995), is a study of the Japanese who went overseas as diplomats or students, in order to learn about the West (plus some of their predecessors). In *The Autobiography of Fukuzawa Yukichi* (reprint, New York: Columbia University Press, 1966 [1934]), one such traveller gives his own account of his motives and experiences. An historical novel by Shimazaki Tōson, *Yo-ake Mae*, translated by William Naff under the title *Before the Dawn* (Honolulu: Hawaii University Press, 1987), reconstructs local attitudes to the events of the Restoration years in a rural part of Japan.

More analytically, Carol Gluck, *Japan's Modern Myths* (Princeton, NJ: Princeton University Press, 1985), traces some of the later repercussions of the stimulus given in this period to Japanese nationalism, while Robert K. Hall (ed.), *Kokutai no Hongi*, trans. J. O. Gauntlett (Cambridge, Mass.: Harvard University Press, 1949), makes available a major text used for the 'ethics' course in schools in the twentieth century. Herbert Passin, *Society and Education in Japan* (reprint, Tokyo: Kodansha, 1982 [1965]), treats education more widely, starting from the Edo period and including a number of translated documents.

Foreign policy after the Restoration has inevitably come in for a great deal of attention. Ian Nish, *Japanese Foreign Policy 1869–1942* (London: Routledge, 1977), provides an excellent introduction. There are several studies of important aspects of the subject: Marius Jansen, *Japan and China: From war to peace, 1894–1972* (Chicago, Ill.: Rand McNally, 1975); W. G. Beasley, *Japanese*

Imperialism 1894–1945 (Oxford: Clarendon, 1987); Ramon Myers and Mark Peattie, *The Japanese Colonial Empire 1895–1945* (Princeton, NJ: Princeton University Press, 1984); Peter Duus, Ramon Myers and Mark Peattie, *The Japanese Informal Empire in China 1895–1937* (Princeton, NJ: Princeton University Press, 1989). On the Pacific War and its origins there are many books, some of them polemical. John Toland, *The Rising Sun: The rise and fall of the Japanese empire 1936–1945* (London: Cassell, 1971), is one of the more sober. Saburō Ienaga, *Japan's Last War* (Oxford: Blackwell, 1979), exemplifies the viewpoint of the Japanese liberal left, while Joyce Lebra (ed.), *Japan's Greater East Asia Co-Prosperity Sphere in World War II* (Kuala Lumpur: Oxford University Press, 1975) provides some very much needed documentary material.

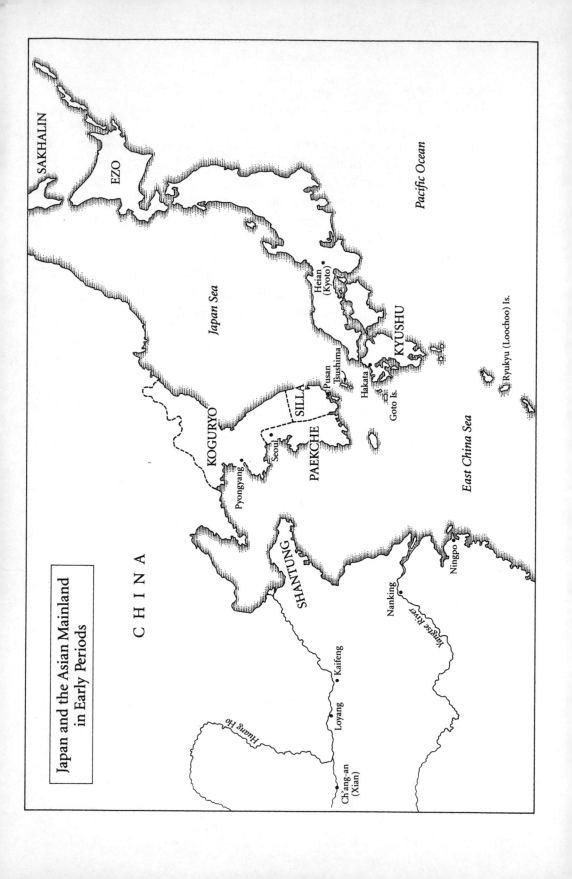

Japan and the Asian Mainland
in Early Periods

CHINA

SAKHALIN

EZO

Pacific Ocean

Japan Sea

Heian
(Kyoto)

KYUSHU

Ryukyu (Loochoo) Is.

KOGURYO

Pusan

Tsushima

Hakata

SILLA

Goto Is.

Seoul

PAEKCHE

Pyongyang

East China Sea

SHANTUNG

Ningpo

Nanking

Yangtse River

Kaifeng

Loyang

Huang Ho

Ch'ang-an
(Xian)

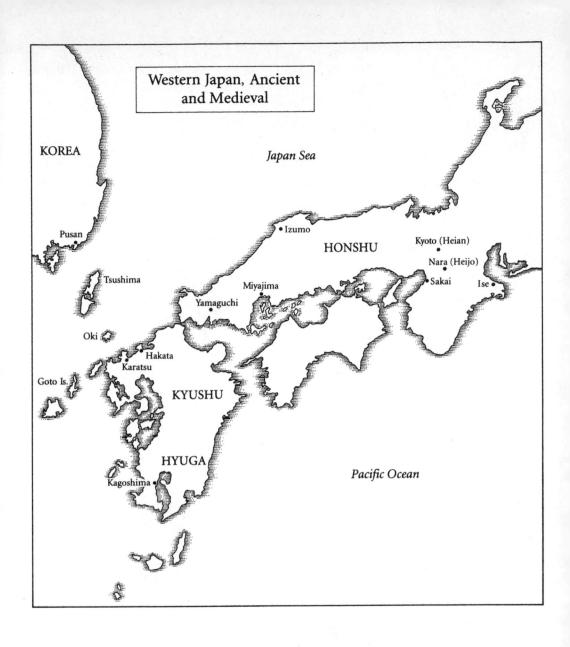

Western Japan, Ancient
and Medieval

KOREA

Japan Sea

Pusan

• Izumo

HONSHU

Kyoto (Heian)

Nara (Heijo)

Tsushima

Miyajima

• Sakai

Ise •

Yamaguchi

Oki •

Hakata

Karatsu

KYUSHU

Goto Is.

HYUGA

Kagoshima •

Pacific Ocean

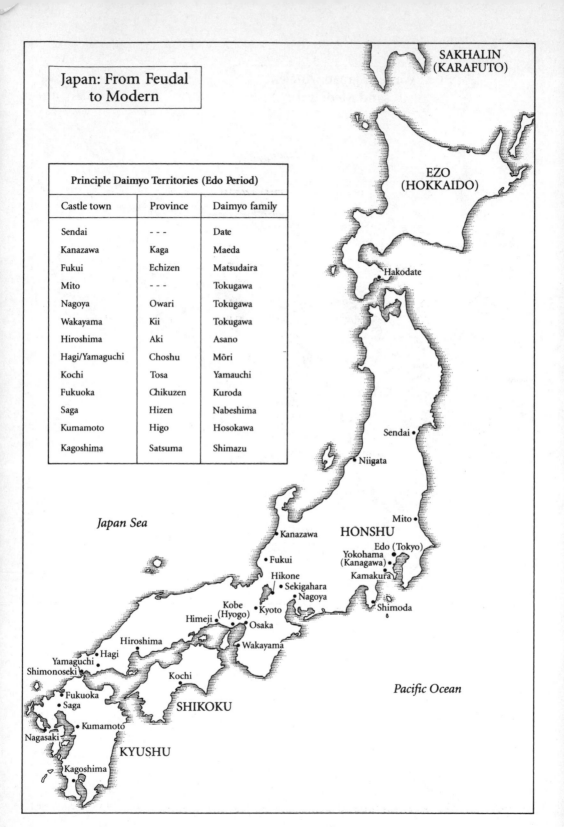

Japan: From Feudal to Modern

Principle Daimyo Territories (Edo Period)

Castle town	Province	Daimyo family
Sendai	- - -	Date
Kanazawa	Kaga	Maeda
Fukui	Echizen	Matsudaira
Mito	- - -	Tokugawa
Nagoya	Owari	Tokugawa
Wakayama	Kii	Tokugawa
Hiroshima	Aki	Asano
Hagi/Yamaguchi	Choshu	Mōri
Kochi	Tosa	Yamauchi
Fukuoka	Chikuzen	Kuroda
Saga	Hizen	Nabeshima
Kumamoto	Higo	Hosokawa
Kagoshima	Satsuma	Shimazu

SAKHALIN (KARAFUTO)

EZO (HOKKAIDO)

Hakodate

Sendai

Niigata

Japan Sea

Mito

HONSHU

Kanazawa

Edo (Tokyo)

Yokohama (Kanagawa)

Fukui

Kamakura

Hikone

Sekigahara

Nagoya

Shimoda

Kobe (Hyogo)

Kyoto

Himeji

Osaka

Hiroshima

Wakayama

Hagi

Yamaguchi

Shimonoseki

Kochi

Pacific Ocean

SHIKOKU

Fukuoka

Saga

Kumamoto

Nagasaki

KYUSHU

Kagoshima

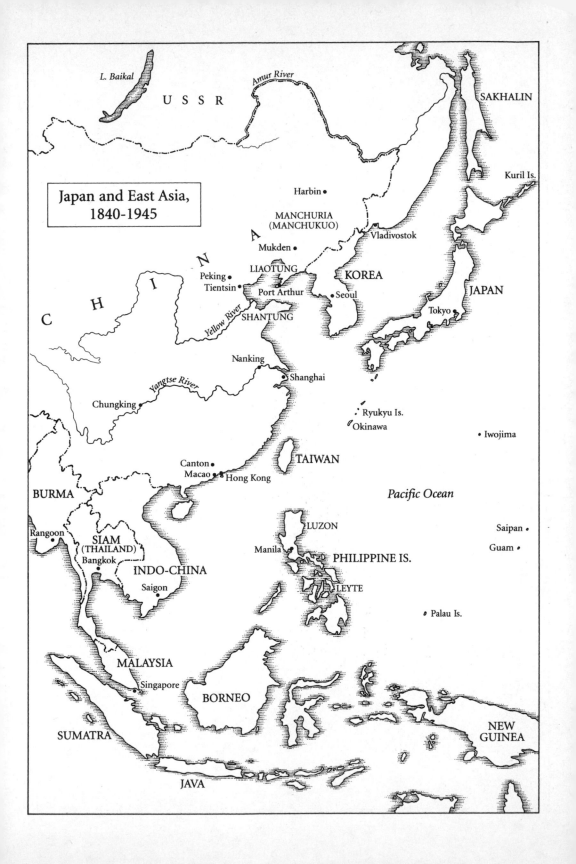

Japan and East Asia,
1840-1945

L. Baikal

U S S R

Amur River

SAKHALIN

Kuril Is.

Harbin

MANCHURIA
(MANCHUKUO)

Vladivostok

Mukden

LIAOTUNG

KOREA

JAPAN

Peking

Tientsin

Port Arthur

Seoul

C H I N A

Tokyo

Yellow River

SHANTUNG

Nanking

Chungking

Yangtse River

Shanghai

Ryukyu Is.

Okinawa

Iwojima

Canton

TAIWAN

Macao

Hong Kong

Pacific Ocean

BURMA

Rangoon

SIAM
(THAILAND)

Bangkok

INDO-CHINA

Saigon

LUZON

Manila

PHILIPPINE IS.

Saipan

Guam

LEYTE

Palau Is.

MALAYSIA

Singapore

BORNEO

NEW
GUINEA

SUMATRA

JAVA

INDEX

Abe Masahiro, 192
agriculture: early, 63, 65–6, 96; Edo period, 152–3, 159, 162–3, 165; modern, 242, 258, 261
Akechi Mitsuhide, 123–4
Akutagawa Ryūnosuke, 74
Alcock, Rutherford, 195, 197
'alternate attendance', *see sankin-kōtai*
Amaterasu, 3–5, 17, 29, 47, 105–6, 178
America, *see* United States
Amida (Amitabha), 47, 70, 75, 100, 101, 104
Amidism, 70–1, 100–1, 172
ancestor worship, 16, 173
Andō Hiroshige, 187
Anglo-Japanese alliance, 234, 237, 239
anti-monopoly law, 153, 259
Antoku, emperor, 80, 81
Arai Hakuseki, 175, 176
architecture: ancient, 31–2, 33–4, 56; feudal, 110–12, 113, 169–70, 183–4; modern, 225
army: 1868–1930, 213, 232, 234–5, 238–9, 241; 1930–45, 243–4, 246–7, 248; political activities of, 218, 236–7, 240, 242–4, 249; after 1945, 252, 255
art: early, 56–9, 75–7; Buddhist influence on, 56–8, 75; medieval, 98–9, 110–15; after 1600, 183–7, 226, 265–6
Asakura Toshikage, 118, 121–2, 123
ashigaru, 118, 121, 155; glossary, 269
Ashikaga house, 79, 89–91, 93, 94, 97, 105, 118; fall of, 116, 117, 122–3
Ashikaga Takauji, 89–90, 93, 94, 106, 108, 118
Ashikaga Yoshiaki, 122–3, 130
Ashikaga Yoshimasa, 99, 112, 115
Ashikaga Yoshimitsu, 91, 94, 99, 103, 109, 111

Ashikaga Yoshinori, 96–7
Asia, policy towards: after 1905, 236–9, 242–6
astronomy, 52–3, 176, 203
Asuka period, 30, 31; glossary, 269
atom bombs, 231, 249
Australia, 247
Azuchi period, 124; castle, 183; glossary, 269

baishin, 154
Bakufu: glossary, 269; *see separately under* Kamakura period, Muromachi period, Edo period
balance of payments, postwar, 260, 261
Ban Dainagon e-kotoba, 77
banking, modern, 223, 224, 261
Bank of Japan, 223
Bashō, *see* Matsuo Bashō
Betavia, 138
be, 14
Benkei, 81
biwa, 49, 60, 107
bodhisattvas, 41, 46, 47, 48, 71, 75
Bolshevik Revolution, 238
bonsai, 99, 115
Britain, relations with: 1840–68, 190–1, 192–3, 197–200, 204–5, 206–7; 1868–1930, 230, 234, 236, 238, 239; 1930–45, 245–6, 247
bronze age, 8
Buddhism: introduction of, 13, 20–1, 41–2, 42–6, 51; and Shinto, 18, 42–8; after mid-Heian, 70–1, 88, 100–4, 172, 267
Buddhist sects, *see* Hossō, Jōdo, Jōdo Shinshū, Kegon, Nichiren, Ritsu, Shingon, Tendai, Zen
bugaku, 59–60
bugyō, 126, 132
Buke Shohatto, 130–1, 132

287